Mometrix TEST PREPARATION

I0889385

CLEP®

Western Civilization II Exam Secrets Study Guide

Dear Future Exam Success Story

First of all, **THANK YOU** for purchasing Mometrix study materials!

Second, congratulations! You are one of the few determined test-takers who are committed to doing whatever it takes to excel on your exam. **You have come to the right place.** We developed these study materials with one goal in mind: to deliver you the information you need in a format that's concise and easy to use.

In addition to optimizing your guide for the content of the test, we've outlined our recommended steps for breaking down the preparation process into small, attainable goals so you can make sure you stay on track.

We've also analyzed the entire test-taking process, identifying the most common pitfalls and showing how you can overcome them and be ready for any curveball the test throws you.

Standardized testing is one of the biggest obstacles on your road to success, which only increases the importance of doing well in the high-pressure, high-stakes environment of test day. Your results on this test could have a significant impact on your future, and this guide provides the information and practical advice to help you achieve your full potential on test day.

Your success is our success

We would love to hear from you! If you would like to share the story of your exam success or if you have any questions or comments in regard to our products, please contact us at **800-673-8175** or **support@mometrix.com**.

Thanks again for your business and we wish you continued success!

Sincerely,
The Mometrix Test Preparation Team

Need more help? Check out our flashcards at:
http://MometrixFlashcards.com/CLEP

Written and edited by the Mometrix Exam Secrets Test Prep Team
Printed in the United States of America

TABLE OF CONTENTS

Introduction

Thank you for purchasing this resource! You have made the choice to prepare yourself for a test that could have a huge impact on your future, and this guide is designed to help you be fully ready for test day. Obviously, it's important to have a solid understanding of the test material, but you also need to be prepared for the unique environment and stressors of the test, so that you can perform to the best of your abilities.

For this purpose, the first section that appears in this guide is the **Secret Keys**. We've devoted countless hours to meticulously researching what works and what doesn't, and we've boiled down our findings to the five most impactful steps you can take to improve your performance on the test. We start at the beginning with study planning and move through the preparation process, all the way to the testing strategies that will help you get the most out of what you know when you're finally sitting in front of the test.

We recommend that you start preparing for your test as far in advance as possible. However, if you've bought this guide as a last-minute study resource and only have a few days before your test, we recommend that you skip over the first two Secret Keys since they address a long-term study plan.

If you struggle with **test anxiety**, we strongly encourage you to check out our recommendations for how you can overcome it. Test anxiety is a formidable foe, but it can be beaten, and we want to make sure you have the tools you need to defeat it.

Secret Key #1 – Plan Big, Study Small

There's a lot riding on your performance. If you want to ace this test, you're going to need to keep your skills sharp and the material fresh in your mind. You need a plan that lets you review everything you need to know while still fitting in your schedule. We'll break this strategy down into three categories.

Information Organization

Start with the information you already have: the official test outline. From this, you can make a complete list of all the concepts you need to cover before the test. Organize these concepts into groups that can be studied together, and create a list of any related vocabulary you need to learn so you can brush up on any difficult terms. You'll want to keep this vocabulary list handy once you actually start studying since you may need to add to it along the way.

Time Management

Once you have your set of study concepts, decide how to spread them out over the time you have left before the test. Break your study plan into small, clear goals so you have a manageable task for each day and know exactly what you're doing. Then just focus on one small step at a time. When you manage your time this way, you don't need to spend hours at a time studying. Studying a small block of content for a short period each day helps you retain information better and avoid stressing over how much you have left to do. You can relax knowing that you have a plan to cover everything in time. In order for this strategy to be effective though, you have to start studying early and stick to your schedule. Avoid the exhaustion and futility that comes from last-minute cramming!

Study Environment

The environment you study in has a big impact on your learning. Studying in a coffee shop, while probably more enjoyable, is not likely to be as fruitful as studying in a quiet room. It's important to keep distractions to a minimum. You're only planning to study for a short block of time, so make the most of it. Don't pause to check your phone or get up to find a snack. It's also important to **avoid multitasking**. Research has consistently shown that multitasking will make your studying dramatically less effective. Your study area should also be comfortable and well-lit so you don't have the distraction of straining your eyes or sitting on an uncomfortable chair.

The time of day you study is also important. You want to be rested and alert. Don't wait until just before bedtime. Study when you'll be most likely to comprehend and remember. Even better, if you know what time of day your test will be, set that time aside for study. That way your brain will be used to working on that subject at that specific time and you'll have a better chance of recalling information.

Finally, it can be helpful to team up with others who are studying for the same test. Your actual studying should be done in as isolated an environment as possible, but the work of organizing the information and setting up the study plan can be divided up. In between study sessions, you can discuss with your teammates the concepts that you're all studying and quiz each other on the details. Just be sure that your teammates are as serious about the test as you are. If you find that your study time is being replaced with social time, you might need to find a new team.

Secret Key #2 – Make Your Studying Count

You're devoting a lot of time and effort to preparing for this test, so you want to be absolutely certain it will pay off. This means doing more than just reading the content and hoping you can remember it on test day. It's important to make every minute of study count. There are two main areas you can focus on to make your studying count.

Retention

It doesn't matter how much time you study if you can't remember the material. You need to make sure you are retaining the concepts. To check your retention of the information you're learning, try recalling it at later times with minimal prompting. Try carrying around flashcards and glance at one or two from time to time or ask a friend who's also studying for the test to quiz you.

To enhance your retention, look for ways to put the information into practice so that you can apply it rather than simply recalling it. If you're using the information in practical ways, it will be much easier to remember. Similarly, it helps to solidify a concept in your mind if you're not only reading it to yourself but also explaining it to someone else. Ask a friend to let you teach them about a concept you're a little shaky on (or speak aloud to an imaginary audience if necessary). As you try to summarize, define, give examples, and answer your friend's questions, you'll understand the concepts better and they will stay with you longer. Finally, step back for a big picture view and ask yourself how each piece of information fits with the whole subject. When you link the different concepts together and see them working together as a whole, it's easier to remember the individual components.

Finally, practice showing your work on any multi-step problems, even if you're just studying. Writing out each step you take to solve a problem will help solidify the process in your mind, and you'll be more likely to remember it during the test.

Modality

Modality simply refers to the means or method by which you study. Choosing a study modality that fits your own individual learning style is crucial. No two people learn best in exactly the same way, so it's important to know your strengths and use them to your advantage.

For example, if you learn best by visualization, focus on visualizing a concept in your mind and draw an image or a diagram. Try color-coding your notes, illustrating them, or creating symbols that will trigger your mind to recall a learned concept. If you learn best by hearing or discussing information, find a study partner who learns the same way or read aloud to yourself. Think about how to put the information in your own words. Imagine that you are giving a lecture on the topic and record yourself so you can listen to it later.

For any learning style, flashcards can be helpful. Organize the information so you can take advantage of spare moments to review. Underline key words or phrases. Use different colors for different categories. Mnemonic devices (such as creating a short list in which every item starts with the same letter) can also help with retention. Find what works best for you and use it to store the information in your mind most effectively and easily.

Secret Key #3 – Practice the Right Way

Your success on test day depends not only on how many hours you put into preparing, but also on whether you prepared the right way. It's good to check along the way to see if your studying is paying off. One of the most effective ways to do this is by taking practice tests to evaluate your progress. Practice tests are useful because they show exactly where you need to improve. Every time you take a practice test, pay special attention to these three groups of questions:

- The questions you got wrong
- The questions you had to guess on, even if you guessed right
- The questions you found difficult or slow to work through

This will show you exactly what your weak areas are, and where you need to devote more study time. Ask yourself why each of these questions gave you trouble. Was it because you didn't understand the material? Was it because you didn't remember the vocabulary? Do you need more repetitions on this type of question to build speed and confidence? Dig into those questions and figure out how you can strengthen your weak areas as you go back to review the material.

Additionally, many practice tests have a section explaining the answer choices. It can be tempting to read the explanation and think that you now have a good understanding of the concept. However, an explanation likely only covers part of the question's broader context. Even if the explanation makes perfect sense, **go back and investigate** every concept related to the question until you're positive you have a thorough understanding.

As you go along, keep in mind that the practice test is just that: practice. Memorizing these questions and answers will not be very helpful on the actual test because it is unlikely to have any of the same exact questions. If you only know the right answers to the sample questions, you won't be prepared for the real thing. **Study the concepts** until you understand them fully, and then you'll be able to answer any question that shows up on the test.

It's important to wait on the practice tests until you're ready. If you take a test on your first day of study, you may be overwhelmed by the amount of material covered and how much you need to learn. Work up to it gradually.

On test day, you'll need to be prepared for answering questions, managing your time, and using the test-taking strategies you've learned. It's a lot to balance, like a mental marathon that will have a big impact on your future. Like training for a marathon, you'll need to start slowly and work your way up. When test day arrives, you'll be ready.

Start with the strategies you've read in the first two Secret Keys—plan your course and study in the way that works best for you. If you have time, consider using multiple study resources to get different approaches to the same concepts. It can be helpful to see difficult concepts from more than one angle. Then find a good source for practice tests. Many times, the test website will suggest potential study resources or provide sample tests.

Practice Test Strategy

If you're able to find at least three practice tests, we recommend this strategy:

Untimed and Open-Book Practice

Take the first test with no time constraints and with your notes and study guide handy. Take your time and focus on applying the strategies you've learned.

Timed and Open-Book Practice

Take the second practice test open-book as well, but set a timer and practice pacing yourself to finish in time.

Timed and Closed-Book Practice

Take any other practice tests as if it were test day. Set a timer and put away your study materials. Sit at a table or desk in a quiet room, imagine yourself at the testing center, and answer questions as quickly and accurately as possible.

Keep repeating timed and closed-book tests on a regular basis until you run out of practice tests or it's time for the actual test. Your mind will be ready for the schedule and stress of test day, and you'll be able to focus on recalling the material you've learned.

Secret Key #4 – Pace Yourself

Once you're fully prepared for the material on the test, your biggest challenge on test day will be managing your time. Just knowing that the clock is ticking can make you panic even if you have plenty of time left. Work on pacing yourself so you can build confidence against the time constraints of the exam. Pacing is a difficult skill to master, especially in a high-pressure environment, so **practice is vital**.

Set time expectations for your pace based on how much time is available. For example, if a section has 60 questions and the time limit is 30 minutes, you know you have to average 30 seconds or less per question in order to answer them all. Although 30 seconds is the hard limit, set 25 seconds per question as your goal, so you reserve extra time to spend on harder questions. When you budget extra time for the harder questions, you no longer have any reason to stress when those questions take longer to answer.

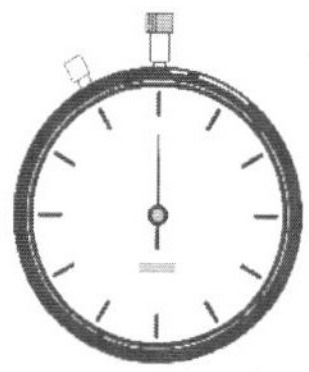

Don't let this time expectation distract you from working through the test at a calm, steady pace, but keep it in mind so you don't spend too much time on any one question. Recognize that taking extra time on one question you don't understand may keep you from answering two that you do understand later in the test. If your time limit for a question is up and you're still not sure of the answer, mark it and move on, and come back to it later if the time and the test format allow. If the testing format doesn't allow you to return to earlier questions, just make an educated guess; then put it out of your mind and move on.

On the easier questions, be careful not to rush. It may seem wise to hurry through them so you have more time for the challenging ones, but it's not worth missing one if you know the concept and just didn't take the time to read the question fully. Work efficiently but make sure you understand the question and have looked at all of the answer choices, since more than one may seem right at first.

Even if you're paying attention to the time, you may find yourself a little behind at some point. You should speed up to get back on track, but do so wisely. Don't panic; just take a few seconds less on each question until you're caught up. Don't guess without thinking, but do look through the answer choices and eliminate any you know are wrong. If you can get down to two choices, it is often worthwhile to guess from those. Once you've chosen an answer, move on and don't dwell on any that you skipped or had to hurry through. If a question was taking too long, chances are it was one of the harder ones, so you weren't as likely to get it right anyway.

On the other hand, if you find yourself getting ahead of schedule, it may be beneficial to slow down a little. The more quickly you work, the more likely you are to make a careless mistake that will affect your score. You've budgeted time for each question, so don't be afraid to spend that time. Practice an efficient but careful pace to get the most out of the time you have.

Secret Key #5 – Have a Plan for Guessing

When you're taking the test, you may find yourself stuck on a question. Some of the answer choices seem better than others, but you don't see the one answer choice that is obviously correct. What do you do?

The scenario described above is very common, yet most test takers have not effectively prepared for it. Developing and practicing a plan for guessing may be one of the single most effective uses of your time as you get ready for the exam.

In developing your plan for guessing, there are three questions to address:

- When should you start the guessing process?
- How should you narrow down the choices?
- Which answer should you choose?

When to Start the Guessing Process

Unless your plan for guessing is to select C every time (which, despite its merits, is not what we recommend), you need to leave yourself enough time to apply your answer elimination strategies. Since you have a limited amount of time for each question, that means that if you're going to give yourself the best shot at guessing correctly, you have to decide quickly whether or not you will guess.

Of course, the best-case scenario is that you don't have to guess at all, so first, see if you can answer the question based on your knowledge of the subject and basic reasoning skills. Focus on the key words in the question and try to jog your memory of related topics. Give yourself a chance to bring the knowledge to mind, but once you realize that you don't have (or you can't access) the knowledge you need to answer the question, it's time to start the guessing process.

It's almost always better to start the guessing process too early than too late. It only takes a few seconds to remember something and answer the question from knowledge. Carefully eliminating wrong answer choices takes longer. Plus, going through the process of eliminating answer choices can actually help jog your memory.

Summary: Start the guessing process as soon as you decide that you can't answer the question based on your knowledge.

How to Narrow Down the Choices

The next chapter in this book (**Test-Taking Strategies**) includes a wide range of strategies for how to approach questions and how to look for answer choices to eliminate. You will definitely want to read those carefully, practice them, and figure out which ones work best for you. Here though, we're going to address a mindset rather than a particular strategy.

Your odds of guessing an answer correctly depend on how many options you are choosing from.

Number of options left	5	4	3	2	1
Odds of guessing correctly	20%	25%	33%	50%	100%

You can see from this chart just how valuable it is to be able to eliminate incorrect answers and make an educated guess, but there are two things that many test takers do that cause them to miss out on the benefits of guessing:

- Accidentally eliminating the correct answer
- Selecting an answer based on an impression

We'll look at the first one here, and the second one in the next section.

To avoid accidentally eliminating the correct answer, we recommend a thought exercise called **the $5 challenge**. In this challenge, you only eliminate an answer choice from contention if you are willing to bet $5 on it being wrong. Why $5? Five dollars is a small but not insignificant amount of money. It's an amount you could afford to lose but wouldn't want to throw away. And while losing $5 once might not hurt too much, doing it twenty times will set you back $100. In the same way, each small decision you make—eliminating a choice here, guessing on a question there—won't by itself impact your score very much, but when you put them all together, they can make a big difference. By holding each answer choice elimination decision to a higher standard, you can reduce the risk of accidentally eliminating the correct answer.

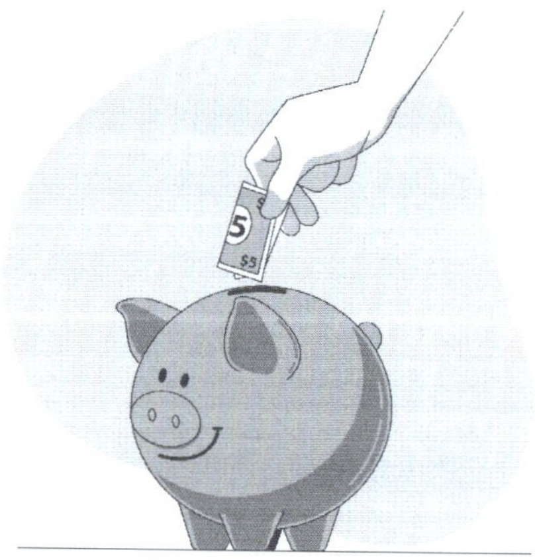

The $5 challenge can also be applied in a positive sense: If you are willing to bet $5 that an answer choice *is* correct, go ahead and mark it as correct.

Summary: Only eliminate an answer choice if you are willing to bet $5 that it is wrong.

Which Answer to Choose

You're taking the test. You've run into a hard question and decided you'll have to guess. You've eliminated all the answer choices you're willing to bet $5 on. Now you have to pick an answer. Why do we even need to talk about this? Why can't you just pick whichever one you feel like when the time comes?

The answer to these questions is that if you don't come into the test with a plan, you'll rely on your impression to select an answer choice, and if you do that, you risk falling into a trap. The test writers know that everyone who takes their test will be guessing on some of the questions, so they intentionally write wrong answer choices to seem plausible. You still have to pick an answer though, and if the wrong answer choices are designed to look right, how can you ever be sure that you're not falling for their trap? The best solution we've found to this dilemma is to take the decision out of your hands entirely. Here is the process we recommend:

Once you've eliminated any choices that you are confident (willing to bet $5) are wrong, select the first remaining choice as your answer.

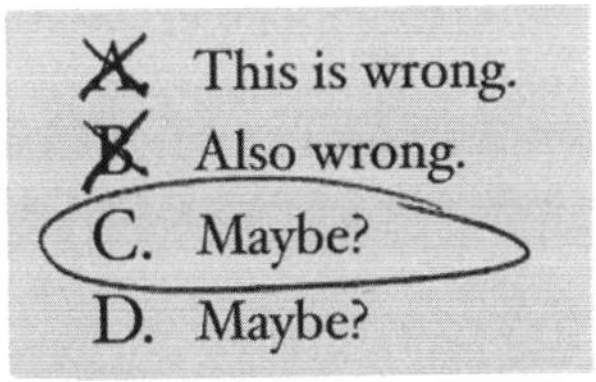

Whether you choose to select the first remaining choice, the second, or the last, the important thing is that you use some preselected standard. Using this approach guarantees that you will not be enticed into selecting an answer choice that looks right, because you are not basing your decision on how the answer choices look.

This is not meant to make you question your knowledge. Instead, it is to help you recognize the difference between your knowledge and your impressions. There's a huge difference between thinking an answer is right because of what you know, and thinking an answer is right because it looks or sounds like it should be right.

Summary: To ensure that your selection is appropriately random, make a predetermined selection from among all answer choices you have not eliminated.

Test-Taking Strategies

This section contains a list of test-taking strategies that you may find helpful as you work through the test. By taking what you know and applying logical thought, you can maximize your chances of answering any question correctly!

It is very important to realize that every question is different and every person is different: no single strategy will work on every question, and no single strategy will work for every person. That's why we've included all of them here, so you can try them out and determine which ones work best for different types of questions and which ones work best for you.

Question Strategies

☑ Read Carefully

Read the question and the answer choices carefully. Don't miss the question because you misread the terms. You have plenty of time to read each question thoroughly and make sure you understand what is being asked. Yet a happy medium must be attained, so don't waste too much time. You must read carefully and efficiently.

☑ Contextual Clues

Look for contextual clues. If the question includes a word you are not familiar with, look at the immediate context for some indication of what the word might mean. Contextual clues can often give you all the information you need to decipher the meaning of an unfamiliar word. Even if you can't determine the meaning, you may be able to narrow down the possibilities enough to make a solid guess at the answer to the question.

☑ Prefixes

If you're having trouble with a word in the question or answer choices, try dissecting it. Take advantage of every clue that the word might include. Prefixes can be a huge help. Usually, they allow you to determine a basic meaning. *Pre-* means before, *post-* means after, *pro-* is positive, *de-* is negative. From prefixes, you can get an idea of the general meaning of the word and try to put it into context.

☑ Hedge Words

Watch out for critical hedge words, such as *likely, may, can, often, almost, mostly, usually, generally, rarely,* and *sometimes.* Question writers insert these hedge phrases to cover every possibility. Often an answer choice will be wrong simply because it leaves no room for exception. Be on guard for answer choices that have definitive words such as *exactly* and *always.*

☑ Switchback Words

Stay alert for *switchbacks.* These are the words and phrases frequently used to alert you to shifts in thought. The most common switchback words are *but, although,* and *however.* Others include *nevertheless, on the other hand, even though, while, in spite of, despite,* and *regardless of.* Switchback words are important to catch because they can change the direction of the question or an answer choice.

✓ FACE VALUE

When in doubt, use common sense. Accept the situation in the problem at face value. Don't read too much into it. These problems will not require you to make wild assumptions. If you have to go beyond creativity and warp time or space in order to have an answer choice fit the question, then you should move on and consider the other answer choices. These are normal problems rooted in reality. The applicable relationship or explanation may not be readily apparent, but it is there for you to figure out. Use your common sense to interpret anything that isn't clear.

Answer Choice Strategies

✓ ANSWER SELECTION

The most thorough way to pick an answer choice is to identify and eliminate wrong answers until only one is left, then confirm it is the correct answer. Sometimes an answer choice may immediately seem right, but be careful. The test writers will usually put more than one reasonable answer choice on each question, so take a second to read all of them and make sure that the other choices are not equally obvious. As long as you have time left, it is better to read every answer choice than to pick the first one that looks right without checking the others.

✓ ANSWER CHOICE FAMILIES

An answer choice family consists of two (in rare cases, three) answer choices that are very similar in construction and cannot all be true at the same time. If you see two answer choices that are direct opposites or parallels, one of them is usually the correct answer. For instance, if one answer choice says that quantity *x* increases and another either says that quantity *x* decreases (opposite) or says that quantity *y* increases (parallel), then those answer choices would fall into the same family. An answer choice that doesn't match the construction of the answer choice family is more likely to be incorrect. Most questions will not have answer choice families, but when they do appear, you should be prepared to recognize them.

✓ ELIMINATE ANSWERS

Eliminate answer choices as soon as you realize they are wrong, but make sure you consider all possibilities. If you are eliminating answer choices and realize that the last one you are left with is also wrong, don't panic. Start over and consider each choice again. There may be something you missed the first time that you will realize on the second pass.

✓ AVOID FACT TRAPS

Don't be distracted by an answer choice that is factually true but doesn't answer the question. You are looking for the choice that answers the question. Stay focused on what the question is asking for so you don't accidentally pick an answer that is true but incorrect. Always go back to the question and make sure the answer choice you've selected actually answers the question and is not merely a true statement.

✓ EXTREME STATEMENTS

In general, you should avoid answers that put forth extreme actions as standard practice or proclaim controversial ideas as established fact. An answer choice that states the "process should be used in certain situations, if..." is much more likely to be correct than one that states the "process should be discontinued completely." The first is a calm rational statement and doesn't even make a definitive, uncompromising stance, using a hedge word *if* to provide wiggle room, whereas the second choice is far more extreme.

⊘ Benchmark

As you read through the answer choices and you come across one that seems to answer the question well, mentally select that answer choice. This is not your final answer, but it's the one that will help you evaluate the other answer choices. The one that you selected is your benchmark or standard for judging each of the other answer choices. Every other answer choice must be compared to your benchmark. That choice is correct until proven otherwise by another answer choice beating it. If you find a better answer, then that one becomes your new benchmark. Once you've decided that no other choice answers the question as well as your benchmark, you have your final answer.

⊘ Predict the Answer

Before you even start looking at the answer choices, it is often best to try to predict the answer. When you come up with the answer on your own, it is easier to avoid distractions and traps because you will know exactly what to look for. The right answer choice is unlikely to be word-for-word what you came up with, but it should be a close match. Even if you are confident that you have the right answer, you should still take the time to read each option before moving on.

General Strategies

⊘ Tough Questions

If you are stumped on a problem or it appears too hard or too difficult, don't waste time. Move on! Remember though, if you can quickly check for obviously incorrect answer choices, your chances of guessing correctly are greatly improved. Before you completely give up, at least try to knock out a couple of possible answers. Eliminate what you can and then guess at the remaining answer choices before moving on.

⊘ Check Your Work

Since you will probably not know every term listed and the answer to every question, it is important that you get credit for the ones that you do know. Don't miss any questions through careless mistakes. If at all possible, try to take a second to look back over your answer selection and make sure you've selected the correct answer choice and haven't made a costly careless mistake (such as marking an answer choice that you didn't mean to mark). This quick double check should more than pay for itself in caught mistakes for the time it costs.

⊘ Pace Yourself

It's easy to be overwhelmed when you're looking at a page full of questions; your mind is confused and full of random thoughts, and the clock is ticking down faster than you would like. Calm down and maintain the pace that you have set for yourself. Especially as you get down to the last few minutes of the test, don't let the small numbers on the clock make you panic. As long as you are on track by monitoring your pace, you are guaranteed to have time for each question.

⊘ Don't Rush

It is very easy to make errors when you are in a hurry. Maintaining a fast pace in answering questions is pointless if it makes you miss questions that you would have gotten right otherwise. Test writers like to include distracting information and wrong answers that seem right. Taking a little extra time to avoid careless mistakes can make all the difference in your test score. Find a pace that allows you to be confident in the answers that you select.

⊘ KEEP MOVING

Panicking will not help you pass the test, so do your best to stay calm and keep moving. Taking deep breaths and going through the answer elimination steps you practiced can help to break through a stress barrier and keep your pace.

Final Notes

The combination of a solid foundation of content knowledge and the confidence that comes from practicing your plan for applying that knowledge is the key to maximizing your performance on test day. As your foundation of content knowledge is built up and strengthened, you'll find that the strategies included in this chapter become more and more effective in helping you quickly sift through the distractions and traps of the test to isolate the correct answer.

Now that you're preparing to move forward into the test content chapters of this book, be sure to keep your goal in mind. As you read, think about how you will be able to apply this information on the test. If you've already seen sample questions for the test and you have an idea of the question format and style, try to come up with questions of your own that you can answer based on what you're reading. This will give you valuable practice applying your knowledge in the same ways you can expect to on test day.

Good luck and good studying!

Absolutism and Constitutionalism, 1648-1715

Treaty of Westphalia

The Treaty of Westphalia (1648) ended the Thirty Years' War that engulfed much of central Europe. In accordance with the provisions of the treaty, Spain granted independence to the Netherlands, the largely Protestant Dutch provinces that had been fighting for independence since the late 1500s. Spain retained control of the primarily Catholic southern provinces, known as the Spanish Netherlands. During the struggle for independence, Dutch leaders had established a republican government that was rather unstable as various people struggled for power. With independence secured, the conflict heated up between those who wanted a strong republican government—these people were called Hollanders because most were from province of Holland—and those who preferred a strong monarchy, led by King William II. Seeking to secure power by force, William led an army against his own citizenry and seemed on the verge of success when he died suddenly from smallpox. With his only heir, William III, a mere infant, the monarchists were left without a strong ruler, and the Hollanders established a republican system.

Glorious Revolution

For many years, England and the Netherlands maintained an ongoing rivalry, and English leaders often conspired with Hollanders to undermine the power of the Dutch monarchy. Ironically, internal dissension in England led to a bloodless revolution by a Dutch monarch. In 1685, English King Charles II died without an heir, leading to the accession of his Catholic brother, James II, to the throne. Parliamentary leaders clashed with James, whom they feared would push for Catholic dominance. Their fears were allayed somewhat by James's Protestant wife, who raised both of their daughters as Protestants. One daughter, Mary, wed Dutch leader William III. When James's first wife died, he married Mary of Modena, a Catholic who soon bore a son. Fearing this heir would usher in a Catholic monarchy, Parliament asked James II to resign and invited Mary and William III to take the English throne. In 1688, William led a Dutch force to England. James fled to France, which resulted in a new monarchy in the bloodless coup known as the Glorious Revolution.

End of the Golden Era

Despite internal strife and frequent conflicts with other nations, the tiny Netherlands experienced its greatest level of economic and political influence for about 100 years after the Twelve Years' Truce of 1609. Most of its power lay in its powerful navy and skilled merchant class that carefully built up trade networks and established shipping monopolies throughout the globe. While many other European nations were focused on gaining lands within Europe, the Dutch recognized the financial future of world trade and acted accordingly. Many of their rivals were slower to take full advantage of trade as a political tool. When they did, the Dutch golden era began to come to an end. Scholars differ as to when this "golden era" officially ended. Some establish it in 1702, when William III died without an heir, ushering in another stadholderless period led by weak officials. Others mark it at 1713, when the Treaty of Utrecht signified English dominance over Dutch interests. Either way, the Dutch nation would never again be as influential as it was during the 1600s.

Dutch Economic and Social Developments in the 1600s

Economically, the Dutch Republic gained most of its wealth from its overseas colonies, along with charges for shipping goods for other countries. It monopolized trade routes to its full advantage.

The enormous wealth brought in by trade allowed for a higher than average standard of living for most Dutch citizens, who tended to be well-educated and highly skilled. Unlike many other European nations, the Netherlands had only a small noble class, left over from the pre-Republic era. Most of the leading citizens were business leaders who had built their own wealth. For that reason, Dutch society was much less rigidly class-based than most of Europe. This was reflected in Dutch religious tolerance. Although Calvinism was the official religion of the Republic and some Reformed Church leaders tried to drive out members of other faiths, the Netherlands was generally one of the most religiously diverse nations in Europe. Many people fleeing religious persecution settled in the provinces, greatly enhancing the culture and economic strength of Dutch society.

EVENTS LEADING TO THE DEATH OF CHARLES I

- In 1628, Parliament presented Charles with the Petition of Right, which limited the powers of the monarchy. Charles responded by dismissing Parliament.
- Charles tried to impose absolute rule in England, a movement that persecuted Puritans and led to war with Scotland.
- In 1640, Charles recalled Parliament in order to approve taxes for his wars. He and Parliament constantly struggled over the power of the monarchy.
- In 1641, Ireland rebelled. Parliament approved sending troops against Ireland, but proposed that it, not the king, command the army. Charles refused.
- In 1642, Charles led troops against the House of Commons, sparking the English Civil War, the first stage of the English Revolution.
- In 1645, Oliver Cromwell's New Model Army defeated Charles's troops; Charles fled to Scotland, where he was arrested and returned to England.
- In 1647, Charles escaped and led his supporters against Cromwell's troops, who crushed them.
- Charles was tried for treason, found guilty, and beheaded in 1649.

LEGAL AND GOVERNMENTAL ISSUES OF THE ENGLISH REVOLUTION

The primary issue raised by the English Revolution was how power should be balanced between the monarchy and the legislature. King Charles was a strong believer in the divine right of kings and absolute monarchy. Members of Parliament believed that they should make the laws and check the power of the monarch. The Petition of Right was the first of several important statements Parliament passed that reflected its strong belief in the sovereignty of citizens. The petition said that the king could not raise taxes without the approval of Parliament, declare martial law, board soldiers in private homes during peacetime, or imprison anyone without bringing formal charges against that person. Charles never fully supported these ideas and openly violated them.

The English Revolution was also fueled by religious conflict. Charles strongly supported the Catholic-influenced Anglican Church and repressed any denomination that challenged Anglicanism. The Puritan Church became a particular target; in fact, many of Charles's strongest opponents in Parliament were Puritans.

DEVELOPMENTS UNDER OLIVER CROMWELL

Oliver Cromwell ushered in a radical new style of government never before witnessed in Europe. When he and his supporters seized control of Parliament in 1653, they refused to seat any supporters of the monarchy. This new revolutionary Parliament, called the Rump Parliament, voted to abolish both the monarchy and the House of Lords. Theirs would be a government ruled by a single legislature. They declared England to be a commonwealth, patterned after the republic of ancient Rome. The Rump Parliament approved the nation's first constitution, the Instrument of Government, which gave the vote only to landowners. Cromwell became the lord protectorate of

Parliament. Despite the absence of a monarch, Cromwell was clearly in charge of the country. His five-year reign, an era called the Protectorate, was a virtual dictatorship in which he frequently used military power to suppress political dissent. Cromwell did support religious freedom, however.

Navigation Act of 1651

The Navigation Act of 1651 was designed to counter Dutch control over ocean trade. Parliament wanted to boost England's economy by expanding trade, but the Dutch shipping monopoly stood in its way. The Navigation Act required that all English import goods be transported by either English ships or ships of the producing country. This law would prevent third-party nations, such as the Netherlands, from controlling sea transports. Dutch anger over the laws led to war between the Netherlands and England that lasted from 1652 to 1654. Fighting resulted in a virtual stalemate, which ultimately proved a victory for England and further boosted Cromwell's reputation as a military leader. The English navy regained its prestige as a fighting power, and English leaders proved they were willing to protect commercial trade with military might if needed.

End of the English Revolution

Although Oliver Cromwell achieved some successes during his reign, many members of Parliament began to resent his dictatorial style and use of the military to suppress opposition. Many began to feel that the government was a republic in name only. As tensions increased, Cromwell dismissed Parliament, seizing rule as a lone dictator. Cromwell's ability to maintain power, however, relied on the loyalty of his army. After he died in 1658, his son, Richard, became lord protector. Unlike his father, Richard could not maintain the army's loyalty. In 1660, Parliament reconvened and joined with military leaders to oust Richard and restore the English monarchy. They invited Charles II, exiled son of the executed King Charles, to return to the throne. The coronation of Charles II in 1660 ended the revolution that had begun with the English Civil War and ushered in the Restoration era.

Louis XIV

Louis XIV and the Divine Right of Kings

The divine right of kings was Louis's belief that God ordained his rule. Because of this divine right, he believed that the monarch should have absolute power over the state and citizenry. Most of the major decisions during his 72-year rule reflected this belief. In addition to building the palace at Versailles as a grand showplace to reflect the prestige of the throne, he adopted the symbol of the Sun to reflect his belief that his power extended as far as the Sun's rays. For this reason, he earned the nicknamed of "the Sun King." To secure his power, Louis always kept a close eye on the nobility, to the extent of requiring some to live at the palace. Nobles gained and maintained power only by currying favor with the king. All government officials reported directly to the king, and few government policies went into effect without his approval.

Domestic Developments in France

Major domestic reforms during the reign of Louis XIV involved religion and economics. Seeking to ensure that France remained a Catholic country, Louis repealed the religious freedoms granted by the Edict of Nantes. Non-Catholics were required to convert or leave the country. As a result, some 200,000 Huguenots immigrated to other nations. In the long run, this loss of a largely middle-class population weakened the nation's economy. At the same time, Louis's main advisor, Jean-Baptiste Colbert, was attempting to strengthen the economy through a series of reforms. He implemented subsidies to support businesses, tariffs on foreign imports, colonization efforts, and public works to improve transportation. He also implemented a massive overhaul of the nation's tax system, which had historically been corrupt. Under the new system, taxation was more equitable across class lines, and collection systems sought to prevent malfeasance.

Affect of France's wars

Louis XIV was very concerned with French security. To protect the nation, he increased the size and strength of the military and sought to expand France's eastern border to the Rhine River. Achieving this goal would ensure that the country was buffered on all sides by natural landforms. His attempts to gain control of eastern lands led to a succession of invasions and wars. These efforts frightened other European nations, leading several to form alliances against France. The Netherlands, England, and Sweden formed one alliance. Austria, Brandenburg, and Spain formed another alliance. These unified efforts prevented France from fully reaching the Rhine, though France did gain some eastern lands. The costly wars strained the public finances of France.

Legacy of Louis XIV

Ruling for 72 years, Louis XIV left a long-lasting imprint on both France and the entire European continent. His theories of absolute monarchy influenced many other rulers who increased their own power and tried to emulate the opulence of Louis's court at Versailles. Louis's efforts to expand the French military built a force that was at one point the largest army in the world. He also supported exploration into North America, which led to French colonization of many areas, the largest of which was Louisiana, claimed by Robert La Salle and named after the monarch. Yet Louis's insistence on fighting what, in the long run, turned out to be futile wars for land weakened France's military and ultimately led to the losses of territories gained early in his reign. The costly wars also weakened the French economy, as did the loss of the Huguenot population. Louis's style of governing depended upon having a strong monarch. When the kings who followed him proved to be weak, the nobles moved to regain their power.

War of Spanish Succession

The War of Spanish Succession was fought over who would control the throne of Spain. Louis XIV's grandson, Philip V, inherited the throne when the last Habsburg king died in 1700. Because of France's wars and military expansion, other European countries united in opposition to Philip's accession. They feared Louis would use his grandson to unify France and Spain in a mighty alliance against the rest of Europe. During the War of Spanish Succession, allied European armies successfully battled French forces. Fighting finally ended with the Treaty of Utrecht (1713). The treaty allowed Philip V to become the Spanish monarch, but it prevented France and Spain from ever being ruled by a unified throne. France also agreed to cede some of its North American lands to Great Britain.

Habsburgs

During the Thirty Years' War, the Habsburgs lost many lands to Germany, leaving them very wary of entering into more wars. For several years, the Hasburg family focused on rebuilding and expanded their holdings beyond pre-war levels. Enemies often seized upon perceived weaknesses to undermine Habsburg power. For example, when Austrian heir Ferdinand IV died in 1654, his brother Leopold was named to take his place. Many people perceived Leopold, who had planned to join the clergy, as a weak and disinterested leader. Though French officials refused to recognize his claim to the throne, they relented after Leopold agreed to limit his own foreign influence. Similarly, the Habsburg rulers faced uprisings throughout the empire that challenged their power. In many cases, the monarchs had to promise to limit their own power in order to restore peace. Through such diplomacy the Habsburgs slowly rebuilt their empire, seemingly weakening their practice of absolute monarchy.

Hohenzollerns

The Hohenzollerns were a Protestant family that rose to power in the northern German territory of Brandenburg in the early 1600s. During the Protestant Reformation, the family seized many

Catholic-owned lands. By 1648, the family controlled Prussia, leading to the establishment of the state of Brandenburg-Prussia. Leader Frederick William, nicknamed the Great Elector because he was a powerful elector for the Holy Roman Emperor, worked to strengthen the Brandenburg-Prussian army, infrastructure, and economy. His son, Frederick I, became state ruler in 1688 and strengthened his power by consolidating the empire as the kingdom of Prussia, with himself as the first monarch. Frederick increased his power and prestige by emulating the court of French King Louis XIV.

Frederick I vs. Frederick William I vs. Frederick II

Frederick William I inherited the Prussian throne from his father, Frederick I. While his father had tried to emulate the grandeur of the French monarchy, Frederick William believed the government needed to focus on practical matters. Under his rule, Prussia developed a militaristic government and social structure. To raise money for defense, Frederick William implemented a highly-controlled tax collection system and expanded Prussian economic activity. He also instituted mandatory education for children. On a personal level, Frederick William could be brutal with people he perceived to be against him and his goals. For example, when his son and heir exhibited more interest in the arts than in military policy, the king threw the prince into prison and then forced him to watch the execution of his best friend. The strategy apparently had the desired effect, as King Frederick II continued the military expansion started by his father. Known as Frederick the Great, the younger king differed from his father in that he relied more on diplomacy and domestic reforms than on brute force.

War of Austrian Succession

What was actually a series of wars began when Holy Roman Emperor Charles VI died in 1740, leaving a power vacuum in Austria. Prussian King Frederick II tried to expand his country's holdings into the Austrian-controlled and resource-rich Silesia. In 1740, the Prussian army invaded and captured Silesia. The conflict soon expanded to include many allies of Prussia and Austria. Bavaria, France, Spain, and Prussia fought against Austria, Great Britain, the Netherlands, and Russia. The fighting was fueled as much by competition between Britain and France as by concerns within Central Europe. By 1748, the Prussian alliance had defeated the Austrian alliance, signaling an end to Austrian dominance in Central Europe. Maria Theresa emerged as the designated successor to the Habsburg dynasty, with her husband taking the Austrian throne.

Diplomatic Revolution

Austria's defeat in the War of Austrian Succession touched off the Diplomatic Revolution, a shift in alliances that rippled throughout Europe. At the Westminster Convention, Great Britain broke its longtime partnership with Austria to support Prussia. France, Great Britain's archenemy, then formed an alliance with Austria and Russia in order to limit Prussian power. Austrian Queen Maria Theresa hoped this alliance would help the Austrians attack and retake Silesia. French officials agreed only after Prussian forces began threatening France's borders. The new series of alliances set the stage for the Seven Years' War and ensured that few European countries would avoid involvement in the conflict.

Seven Years' War

At the most basic level, the Seven Years' War was fought over the issue of French versus British dominance in Europe. Tensions between the European powers remained high in the years following the War of Austrian Succession, but a conflict in North America caused the spark that set off full-scale warfare. In 1756, British and French forces began fighting for control of the Ohio River Valley, launching a war known within the North American colonies as the French and Indian War. Soon Britain, France, and all of their allies were immersed in a European-based war. No clear military victor emerged, as lands exchanged hands numerous times. Finally, after years of fighting that threatened to drag on interminably, new monarchs in Russia and Great Britain took steps to end the conflict diplomatically. The 1763 Treaty of Paris declared Prussia the permanent ruler of Silesia, gave most French lands in North America to the British, and secured British control over key Asian colonies.

Rise of the Romanovs

Russia experienced a period of instability and unrest following the death of Ivan the Terrible in 1584. Without a clear leader, nobles continuously struggled for power, and civil war threatened the future of the country. To promote stability, the national assembly named Michael Romanov, Ivan's distant relative, as czar in 1613. Because of his young age and lack of education, other members of the Romanov family effectively ruled throughout his reign. The family established stable leadership, restored domestic order, and signed crucial peace treaties with enemy nations, including Sweden and Poland. The patterns they established influenced future Romanov rulers—who would reign for 300 years—by promoting a strong czarist system, suppressing dissent, and forming alliances with groups such as the Cossacks and Ukrainians.

Peter the Great

Events during the Reign of Peter the Great

- Ten year-old Peter became czar in 1682, sharing power with brother, Ivan V.
- Peter became full czar in 1689.
- In disguise, Peter toured Europe to learn about western culture.
- Peter began a reform movement to westernize Russia.
- Russia successfully fought a war against Sweden, gaining lands along the Gulf of Finland and access to the Baltic Sea.
- Peter decreed that the czar could name his own successor.
- Peter moved the capital from Moscow to St. Petersburg, designing the new capital to reflect Russian westernization.
- Peter increased the power of the czar and limited the power of the nobility by adopting a meritocracy system; worthy nobles were rewarded with serfs and lands, a practice that propagated the Russian peonage system.
- Peter expanded czarist influence over church practices, fostering resentment among leaders of the Russian Orthodox Church.
- Peter died in 1725.

Peter the Great's Westernization of Russia

Peter wanted Russia to become a great power and to expand its borders. When Peter became czar, the country was largely landlocked and isolated, with no access to western water routes. Russia would not be able to obtain access to such routes without seizing lands and ports held by the Ottoman Empire. Peter believed that in order to defeat the Ottomans, Russia needed to form alliances with western European countries. Ending isolation and adopting aspects of western culture might help achieve this goal. As he learned more about western culture, Peter became convinced that many aspects of western science, technology, and economic advancement would help improve his own country and its standing in the world.

Events during the Reign of Catherine the Great

Peter III married German princess Catherine II in 1745. Catherine was as ambitious and cunning as Peter was lazy (and possibly, alcoholic or mentally ill). When Peter became czar after his mother, Empress Elizabeth, died in 1761, it was quite obvious that he was incapable of ruling effectively. In

1762, with the support of the army and nobility, Catherine deposed Peter. Her supporters murdered him days later. She reigned as empress for 34 years, during which time Russia greatly expanded its landholdings. By the time of Catherine's death in 1796, Russia had expanded its empire by more than 200,000 square miles and had achieved its goal of expanding sea access through the Bosporus Strait. Catherine, a great patron of the arts, enhanced Russian contributions to literature and painting. She was also ruthless to enemies, and was both feared and admired for her strength as a ruler.

Eastward Expansion of Russia

As the power of the Mongol Empire declined, Russians began to move eastward, settling in Siberia and other frontier regions. Though the cold climate of these eastern settlements could be quite harsh and isolating, the wealth of natural resources allowed the growth of a thriving trade industry. After resolving border disputes and establishing trade relations with China, Russian settlers eventually moved all the way to Alaska. Eastward expansion increased contacts with Asian cultures. Isolated from much of western Russian culture, many of these settlements adopted Asian-influenced customs and formed independent societies. Although some smaller native Siberian tribes became extinct due to disease and intermarriage, many others thrived. For the most part, Russia allowed these indigenous eastern peoples to maintain their own customs.

Competition for Empire and Economic Expansion

Affect of Colonization on European Economies

Prior to the Commercial Revolution and Age of Exploration, European economies were based primarily on local agriculture. As nations acquired overseas colonies, they gained natural resources, trade goods, and new markets for manufactured goods. Many economies became dependent upon global trade. Colonies generated enormous wealth for Europeans, which encouraged even more investment abroad and improved standards of living by buttressing local market economies and increasing opportunities for job specialization. The wealth brought in by colonies also supported military expansion and competition between nations, redefining definitions of political and economic power throughout the world.

African and Asian Roles in European Economic Developments

Africa and Asia became focal points for a great deal of European colonial expansion. The Dutch built much of their economic success upon the trade monopolies they built in East Asia in the early 1600s. Unlike other colonization efforts, such as the Spanish in the Americas, the Dutch gained economic clout by avoiding missionary efforts. Seeing how well the business approach of the Dutch had succeeded, other European countries began to follow suit. Profit became the driving force behind many European colonization efforts in Africa and Asia. Trading companies like the British East India Company took charge of organizing and running these profit-centered colonization efforts. The focus on profitability contributed to Europeans' increasing involvement in the African slave trade. Africa and Asia themselves became prizes in the fierce economic competition between the Europeans.

Mercantilism

Mercantilism was an economic theory that linked national power to colonial expansion. Mercantilists argued that nations should measure their wealth in gold and silver. They believed that because the Earth contained a finite amount of gold and silver ore, nations should try to gain and store as much of these precious metals as possible. Mercantilism became the dominant economic philosophy of the colonial era. Mercantilist nations implemented policies designed to obtain stores of silver and gold, monopolize wealth, and defeat rival nations. Mercantilism also impacted how nations treated their colonies. They passed laws that limited colonial economic activities in order to return as much wealth as possible to the mother nation. Some of these laws fostered resentment and anger among colonists, who wanted to retain more profits for themselves.

Global Economic Factors Between Great Britain and France

While all of the major European powers vied for overseas territories, the conflict became particularly fierce as France and Great Britain became stronger. Both were seeking to increase their influence and power as Spain's dominance declined. Their conflict intensified as they fought over colonial lands. By 1750, the British East India Company had effectively shut French traders out of India and the East Indies and was beginning to dominate African trade as well. The rivalry between France and Great Britain came to a head in North America. For many years, the French had controlled lands in most of what is now Canada, while the British had settled along the East Coast. Conflicts arose as British colonists tried to settle in the lands west of the Appalachian Mountains, where some French traders had already established posts and had made strong alliances with local Native American groups. In 1754, French and British colonists engaged in a military skirmish that evolved into the French and Indian War, a war that spread to Europe and became known as the Seven Years' War.

Shift of British Economic Policies in North America

The end of the Seven Years' War resulted in Great Britain's gaining control over most of France's North American lands. Britain was facing huge war debts and needed to raise revenues. Prior to the war, Britain had largely taken a hands-off approach to the North American economy. So long as the colonies were bringing in wealth, British officials did not try to enforce its mercantilist policies too strictly. After 1763, however, Parliament passed a series of new laws designed to increase cash flow from the colonies and decrease colonial trade with other nations. From Parliament's perspective, the colonists, as British citizens, were required to do their part to support the Great Britain's economy. Many colonists resented these laws, which led to conflict that eventually resulted in the American Revolution.

Affect of British Economic Laws on the North American Colonies

- 1764 – Sugar Act: imposed tax on sugar and other imports from non-British colonies; colonists complained
- 1765 – Stamp Act: imposed tax on written documents, signified by a stamp; colonists boycotted British goods, organized Stamp Act Congress
- 1767 – Townshend Revenue Act: imposed taxes on glass, paint, oil, lead, paper, and tea; colonists signed non-importation agreements, which effectively cut off trade for British merchants; protests by colonists led indirectly to the Boston Massacre
- 1773 – The Tea Act: gave the British East India Company a monopoly on tea shipping to the colonies; colonists threw the Boston Tea Party, tossing British tea into the harbor
- 1774 – Intolerable Acts: a series of laws intended to punish colonists for protests, included the closing of Boston Harbor; colonists organized First Continental Congress; tensions ultimately led to outbreak of war in 1775

Peace of Utrecht

The Peace of Utrecht refers to a series of individual treaties that brought an end to French wars for expansion and settled the issue of Spanish succession. The negotiations primarily involved representatives from France, Great Britain, Portugal, Spain, Savoy, and the Dutch Republic. The negotiations were long and arduous, reflecting general distrust among most of the participants. Negotiations began in October 1711 between representatives of Great Britain and France. One major issue involved the monarchy of France and Spain; Britain and its allies insisted that France and Spain agree never to have a unified monarchy. When, in July 1712, Spanish King Phillip V agreed in writing to renounce any link to the French monarchy, Britain and France signed a formal peace agreement to end fighting between them. The following year, the nations signed the first Treaty of Utrecht.

Spain's Status Changed by the Peace of Utrecht

The treaties marked another step in the decline of the once-mighty Spanish Empire. In a series of treaties, Spain was forced to give up several key European holdings, as well relinquish control over major parts of its overseas empire. Spain ceded the lands of Gibraltar and Minorca to Great Britain. Spain also gave Great Britain asiento, an exclusive right to control the slave trade to Spanish colonies. This trade power would prove very valuable to Britain as the overseas slave trade expanded. In renouncing any future common monarchy with France, a waning Spain ceded what might have been its best chance for a permanent alliance with a greater power. Spain would never again be able to recapture its former glory.

AFFECT OF THE PEACE OF UTRECHT ON RISING POLITICAL PARTIES

The two major British political parties, the Tories and the Whigs, rose to power in the late 1600s. Their views had been solidified in the succession battle that preceded the Glorious Revolution. The Tories (meaning "outlaws") were strong Anglican monarchists who accepted a Catholic king. The Whigs (meaning "horse thieves") supported a strong Parliament and opposed having a Catholic king. The Whigs were also strongly anti-French, viewing France as the perfect example of the type of Catholic-dominated absolute monarchy they opposed. For years the Whig-controlled Parliament resisted negotiating peace with France. When the Tories gained control of Parliament in 1710, they led the way in negotiations that culminated in Utrecht. Whig leaders continued to complain about the provisions of the treaties, which would remain a contentious issue between the two British parties.

AFFECT OF TREATIES ON FRANCE

The treaties ended Louis XIV's efforts to expand the continental French Empire. The French gave up continental lands they had acquired during war and formally recognized other countries' claims on disputed lands. France also had to surrender some of its overseas colonial empire, especially key holdings in North America to the British. These lands included the Hudson Bay territory, Newfoundland, Nova Scotia, and St. Kitts. These would all prove to be important locations for the expansion of British trade in North America. The treaties proved to be one of many steps in the decline of New France, which never really evolved into a strong colonial empire compared to British efforts in North America. By preventing any future joint monarchy by France and Spain, the treaties also weakened French efforts to expand its power through royal family ties. Still, France would remain a formidable force in Europe.

CHANGES IN THE BRITISH GOVERNMENT AFTER 1688

After the Glorious Revolution of 1688, Parliament made a radical move to expand the rights of citizens as well as its own power. More and more British leaders began to reject the concept of absolute monarchy, embracing instead the concept of a balance of powers within the British government. As a result, Parliament created the cabinet and the position of the prime minister in order to balance the monarch's executive powers. A broader idea of a balance of power gained acceptance throughout Europe by the early 1700s and provided the blueprint for British diplomats negotiating the Peace of Utrecht.

ACT OF UNION

The Act of Union was the agreement that created Great Britain by uniting England and Scotland into one country. The act was designed to strengthen the British Isles and deflect threats from expanding France. The act abolished Scotland's parliament; instead, Scottish representatives served in the unified British Parliament. Although some people continued to oppose the union (mainly Scottish citizens, who felt they lost more in the unification), it proved a benefit to the isles in the long run. With Scotland and England no longer competing with one another, Great Britain experienced an economic boom that benefited all regions. The union also gave Britain a stronger position of negotiation during and after the Peace of Utrecht.

SOCIAL CHANGES IN GREAT BRITAIN DURING THE RESTORATION

The restoration of the monarchy in Great Britain, marked by the coronation of Charles II, ushered in not only a political shift, but also a new social era known as the Restoration. Charles II, nicknamed the Merry Monarch, celebrated entertainment, the arts, and personal freedom. He quickly moved to lift many of the oppressive moral restrictions that Puritan leaders had placed on British society. He also encouraged tolerance for Catholicism, allowing previously banished bishops to serve in

Parliament. Charles was a strong patron of the arts, as was his successor, James II. Under their sponsorship, British literature flourished, further encouraging literacy and enjoyment of popular reading and theater.

Demographic Trends

Affect of Colonization on Demographic Trends

Exploration and colonization fueled European population growth through increased food supplies. In turn, colonies provided a home for excess European populations. Colonial migration slowly developed over the 1600s, increasingly dramatically in the 1700s. The Americas benefited most from this migration because thousands of British colonists left the tiny British Isles for the North American colonies. Colonization also led to the forced relocation of Africans, mainly to the Americas, as Europeans looked for an inexpensive labor supply for colonial plantations. The Triangular Trade system that developed maintained a constant flow of people and goods among Europe, Africa, and the American colonies.

Affect of European Wars on Demographic Trends

European wars during the early 1600s greatly decreased the populations of some European countries. For example, the Thirty Years' War alone decreased the population of the Holy Roman Empire by as much as one third. Louis XIV's wars of expansion devastated the French population, as did his edicts against non-Catholics, which led to the migration of hundreds of thousands of Protestants, Jews, and Muslims to other parts of Europe or to the colonies. The French wars also contributed to a famine that killed more than a million people between 1693 and 1694. During the 1700s, European Wars continued to affect populations, though the death toll was balanced by rising birthrates and advances in medical science that improved life expectancy. Most major European countries experienced population growth between 1700 and 1800. However, the continent would not experience a population explosion until the post-1815 era of peace.

Social and Economic Shifts in Europe

Although Europe remained a continent bound by class divisions and traditions, colonization offered new opportunities for social mobility to millions of people. The new economies offered a variety of new jobs for both skilled and unskilled laborers. Colonization also offered the opportunity for land ownership to many previously landless individuals. Many moved to the British colonies as indentured servants who later became small farmers once their service ended. Within Europe, the needs of the new economy (which would include industrialization by the end of the century) and population growth fueled the expansion of urbanization. Instead of urban populations that were concentrated primarily in capital cities such as London or Paris, numerous mid-sized cities began to emerge. These smaller cities continued to expand in number and population as industrialization spread.

The Scientific View of the World

ACADEMIC AND GOVERNMENT SPONSORSHIP

The Scientific Revolution was supported by government sponsorship and private academies of learning. Government leaders came to believe that scientific advances could help in the expansion of commercial interests. Some scientific academies grew out of private scientific societies. Both government-sponsored and privately run academies operated along the same lines. They both sought to bring together scientists to share information and expand learning and experimentation. They also sought to promote the use of the scientific method, separating scientific exploration from religion, mythology, and the magical sciences. The first major scientific society organized in Italy, limiting membership to scientists who had already proven themselves serious academics by publishing their research. Similar groups soon formed in France, Germany, and England. Members of these groups closely scrutinized each others' works, lending legitimacy to their endeavors. By 1700, scientific research was a serious and respected enterprise thanks in large part to the academies.

ISAAC NEWTON

Historians generally consider Newton to be the most influential scientist in the history of western civilization. Newton built on the work of Copernicus, Kepler, and Galileo to prove that the solar system was heliocentric rather than geocentric. Unlike previous scientists, Newton was able to explain why planets revolved around the sun. His findings, published in Principia (1687), used a series of experiments to prove the existence of gravity and explain how it works. Newton posited that gravity works according to natural laws. He expanded this concept into a series of laws of motion that could be proven by mathematical calculations, further helping explain how the natural world works. Scientists quickly accepted Newton's theories and successfully applied them to a variety of fields, including mechanics. Moreover, Newton's laws changed the way people viewed the universe. Many people began to conceptualize the world as driven by natural laws rather than by the whim of God or other spiritual forces.

Isaac Newton developed three important laws related to the motion of objects.

- First Law of Motion (also known as the Law of Inertia) — Says that a body at rest will remain at rest unless acted upon by another force.
- Second Law of Motion — Provides the formula $F = ma$ to calculate the force needed to move an object. An object's mass (m) is multiplied by its rate of acceleration (a) to get the amount of force needed (F).
- Third Law of Motion — Says that for every action, there is an equal but opposite reaction. It explains how forces interact with one another.

These three laws explained how the planets moved and also laid the foundation for both mechanical sciences based on mathematics and new inventions involving movement.

ANTONIE VAN LEEUWENHOEK AND WILLIAM HARVEY

In the early 1600s, William Harvey studied the human circulatory system. He accurately described how blood flowed through the veins, arteries, and heart. Prior to Harvey's findings, most people believed that the body contained two separate circulatory systems: one carrying purple blood that flowed through the veins and one carrying red blood that flowed through the arteries. Harvey proved that veins and arteries were part of one system that carried blood to and from the heart. His careful observations of the heart expanded the science community's understanding of how the muscle functioned. Utilizing the microscope, Antonie van Leeuwenhoek studied life forms too small to be observed by the human eye. In the 1670s, he identified bacteria, which he called animalcules. He also isolated sperm and was the first person to accurately describe red blood cells. During the course of his work, Leeuwenhoek he advanced and improved microscopes to increase their power and clarity.

JOSEPH BLACK, ROBERT BOYLE, JOSEPH PRIESTLEY, AND ANTOINE LAVOISIER

- Robert Boyle — Pioneered the modern science of chemistry; in 1662 he proved that temperature and pressure affect the space that a gas occupies; helped develop the air pump
- Joseph Black — Conducted experiments in the 1750s to illustrate how air could be combined with and separated from solids; proved air was not an element itself, but rather made up of several elements
- Joseph Priestley — Discovered the element oxygen in 1774; developed the phlogiston theory to explain how gases are released during burning
- Antoine Lavoisier — Named Priestley's discovery "oxygen;" discovered how oxygen contributed to fire and how steam evaporated into air; developed gravimetric methods that made possible the isolation, analysis, and categorization of elements; conducted experiments that led to creation of the law of conservation of matter: matter can change form, but cannot be created or destroyed

CHEMISTS RADICALLY ALTERED HUMAN INTERPRETATION OF MATTER

Prior to the development of the field of chemistry, alchemy—a blending of chemical science and magic—reigned supreme. While some alchemists contributed useful discoveries about the nature of physical matter, their main focus was on trying to change the substance of matter into something more valuable (such as turning base metals into gold or transforming liquids into magical elixirs). By the 1700s, many scientists were trying to shift the study of matter from alchemy to the more empirical field of chemistry. They applied scientific methods to analyze the essence of matter and how it changes. In doing so, they disproved many theories of traditional thinking. For example, prior to Lavoisier's experiments, most scientists thought that fire and air were elements.

ADVANCES IN MECHANICAL SCIENCES

One of Newton's greatest contributions to the mechanical sciences was the application of high-level mathematics to physics in order to solve complex theoretical puzzles. For example, followers of Newton argued that the Earth was oblate in shape due to centrifugal force at the Equator, while other scientists argued that gravity at the Equator would cause the Earth to be squeezed and pointed at the poles (similar to a modern football). Scientific expeditions to measure the meridian proved the Newtonians correct, strengthening their other theories. Other influential specialists in mechanics included Leonhard Euler, who developed the calculus of variations; Jean Le Rond d'Alembert and Joseph-Louis Lagrange, who advanced a purely mathematical form of mechanics; and Pierre-Simon marquis de Laplace, who codified all advances in mechanics from the time of Newton's Celestial Mechanics (1799).

SCIENTIFIC METHOD VS. PREVIOUS APPROACHES

The scientific method is a process first developed in the natural sciences to guide researchers. It contains the following steps:

1. Ask a question.
2. Conduct research about the topic.
3. Develop a hypothesis, or a predicted answer, to your question.
4. Test the hypothesis through experimentation.

5. Analyze the results to determine if the hypothesis proves true in full or in part or untrue?
6. Report results and recommend further research.

Prior to the development of the scientific method, most research involved a combination of secretive guesswork and divination. This method encouraged a specific approach that could be observed, repeated, and expanded by others. Rather than being shrouded in secrecy, the system encouraged analysis and repetition by others to legitimate findings.

Rene Descartes

Rene Descartes was a French philosopher, mathematician, and scientist during the early 1600s who strongly supported the belief that physical laws governed the universe. An influential proponent of the scientific method, he also expanded the concept beyond the realm of science. In Discourse on Methods (1637), he argued that all knowledge should be based on facts that can be proven through observation and experimentation. His most famous saying ("I think, therefore I am.") was an attempt to prove his own existence based on the fact that he had the ability to perceive of himself. Descartes' philosophy applied logic and reasoning to every facet of life. Although Descartes died in 1650, his writings influenced many scholars in the late 1600s and 1700s, thinkers who applied his theories to a wide range of new ideas about humans and society.

Thomas Hobbes

Thomas Hobbes was an English philosopher strongly influenced by the chaos that had reigned in his country during the English Revolution. In his influential work, Leviathan (1651), he described the human state of nature as one of chaos in which only the strongest survived. He believed that the earliest human societies lived in a state of violent anarchy. At some point, people who wanted to avoid violence and chaos entered into a social contract with a leader who would bring order and protection. In these early social contracts, the ruler had absolute power, while the people retained only the right of self-protection. In Hobbes's interpretation of the social contract, humans acted solely out of self-interest and cared nothing about the rights and needs of others. However, when people entered into a social contract to improve their own lives and chances of survival, everyone in the society would benefit.

John Locke

English philosopher John Locke became the leading opponent of Hobbes's theories. Although Locke accepted the concept of the social contract, he interpreted it very differently. In his seminal work, Two Treatise on Government (1690), he argued that leaders should not have absolute power. Citizens gave up some rights only in exchange for the protection of government. Locke believed that humans had certain natural rights, such as the right to life, political equality, and property ownership, that no leader could take away. In fact, he argued, people entered into the social contract with governments for the purpose of protecting these natural rights. Any ruler who tried to oppress these rights thus nullified the social contract. People living under such an unjust ruler had a right to overthrow the government and replace its leaders.

Reactions to Hobbes and Locke

Many political leaders accepted Hobbes's view of the social contract as justification for absolute monarchy. This social contract became a focal point for political philosophy for years to come. Hobbes's main critics were church leaders who noted that his contract was devoid of divine intervention. In their view, he seemed to be replacing God with government as the key moralizing agent to hold humans' baser instincts in check. Some political philosophers, including John Locke, embraced the notion of the social contract but viewed absolute monarchs as tyrants worthy of overthrow. Many Enlightenment thinkers embraced Locke's ideas and expanded upon them to challenge monarchical power. Some writers pointed out that most people were born into systems and thus did not have an opportunity to enter into a contract willingly. They argued that legitimate government rested on the will of the governed to continue living under a system.

Bernard Le Bovier

Le Bovier, also known by the title sieur de Fontenelle, was a scientist and philosopher whose greatest contribution was in shaping the way people thought about their place in the world. He first gained fame as a writer of popular literature, writing a series of dialogues involving various famous thinkers from the past. He used these dialogues to challenge modern thinking about science, philosophy, and religion. His scientific research supported many Cartesian theories later disproven by Newton. At the time, however, they gained him great respect, leading to his becoming secretary of the French Academy of Science in 1697. In this role he expanded publications about scientific discoveries and scientists, which helped to disseminate new ideas. He also wrote publications that directly contradicted many religiously-influenced ideas of the time. He emphasized the small role of humans within the great expanse of the universe and noted that many fables and legends had historically arisen independently among various cultures and religions, undermining claims to truth by any one group or belief system.

English Bill of Rights

In 1689, Parliament passed the English Bill of Rights, which permanently limited the power of the English monarchy and expanded the power of Parliament and of English citizens. It was the first major step in the development of Britain's limited constitutional monarchy. The provisions of the English Bill of Rights included:

- Protecting citizens' right to petition the government
- Protecting citizens from excessive bail or cruel and unusual punishment
- Granting Parliament the right to approve of the monarchy
- Limiting the monarchy's ability to suspend laws without Parliamentary approval
- Prohibiting the monarchy from levying taxes
- Prohibiting the monarchy from maintaining a standing army during peacetime
- Reaffirming that the monarchy is subject to laws just like average citizens
- Protecting freedom of speech for members of Parliament
- Declaring Parliament free from interference by the monarchy

British Parliamentary Reforms

Although most members of Parliament welcomed a return of the monarchy with the Restoration, they never fully trusted the crown. Many embraced John Locke's arguments in favor of protecting natural rights. To ensure that the country would never again be subject to an absolute monarchy, Parliament passed a series of laws limiting governmental power. The Habeas Corpus Act of 1679 protected citizens from being jailed without being charged with a crime in a timely manner. In 1689, Parliament made some moves towards religious freedom with the Toleration Act, expanding rights for non-Anglican Protestants. However, because support for absolute monarchy ran highest among Catholics, Parliament continued to bar Catholics from holding office. In 1701, the Act of Settlement established that England would never again have a Catholic monarch in order to preserve Parliamentary checks against the monarchy.

Limited Constitutional Monarchy

Limited constitutional monarchy is a system of government in which the monarch serves as head of state, but an elected body such as Parliament really runs the government. The supreme authority is the written constitution, which protects the rights of citizens and limits the powers of all government officials in an effort to prevent them from abusing their positions. The system developed in England following the passage of the Bill of Rights and subsequent laws basically affirmed that Parliament would be the supreme authority in British government. English monarchs both supported and helped expand this system. King William III selected key members of Parliament to serve as his cabinet and run important government departments in his place. The foreign-born kings George I and George II relied heavily on the cabinet. Robert Walpole, the main cabinet advisor to George II, became the country's first prime minister. By the 1740s, Parliament had solidified the role of prime minister and cabinet, which held much more real power than the monarch. This British model of limited constitutional monarchy would eventually become the norm throughout much of Europe.

Affect of Balance of Power Theories on the Peace of Utrecht

The diplomats who negotiated the treaties were strongly influenced by British economist Charles Davenant's publication, Essays on the Balance of Power (1701). Davenant advocated a balance of power based on economic interests. The theory argued that in order for Europe to remain stable, it needed a balance of power among the major nations. If one country became too dominant, it created an imbalance of power that led to political unrest, economic instability, and war. British writer Daniel Defoe further popularized these ideas in The Review, a periodical. By the time peace negotiations began, the main diplomats representing Britain were convinced that the only way to achieve permanent peace was to limit French and Spanish power. Most of the treaties that resulted during the Peace of Utrecht were designed to diffuse power among all the major European countries and discourage dominance by any one nation.

Benedict de Spinoza

Benedict de Spinoza was a Jewish philosopher from the Netherlands whose views contributed to the growth of humanism. Spinoza supported Hobbes's view of the secular social contract, but he felt that it focused too much on violence and mere survival. Spinoza advocated that a just government must also make allowances for intellectual and religious freedom. To that end, it must be secular, rational, and allow for maximum liberty. Spinoza's prime criteria for judging the effectiveness of government was its usefulness for the individual. If a government proved ineffective by limiting the freedom of an individual to the point that the individual was harmed in some way (even if the government protected that individual's existence), then the individual had the right to reject the government. Spinoza's views served as a precursor for the libertarian point of view that government should be as weak as possible.

Edmund Burke

Edmund Burke was a British philosopher and politician who supported the Whig party. Burke's first major writing in political philosophy, A Vindication of Natural Society (1756), was a satirical attack on deists who championed the power of rational government over religion. Burke's purpose was to caution that any type of government, including a democratic one, could become corrupt and oppress the natural rights of citizens. Later, as a member of Parliament, Burke put these principles into practice by fighting to limit the power of the monarchy and eliminate secret factions within the government. He supported a strong role for opposing political parties that would help check the power of elected officials. Burke's views laid the foundations for the conservative view of limited government.

Period of Enlightenment

Age of Enlightenment

During the 1700s, many people began to believe that humans could use reason, logic, and the scientific method to understand human nature and the meaning of "truth." This philosophical movement came to be called "rationalism" or "enlightenment." Central to Enlightenment thought was the application of the scientific method to political theory. Just as scientists observed natural laws governing the physical world, so there were natural laws governing human behavior. These natural laws, Enlightenment thinkers argued, should form the basis of governmental structures and laws. Governments that did not adhere to the laws of human nature would be doomed to failure. Although most Enlightenment thinkers believed that God created nature and the laws that governed it (including human nature), they viewed God as a distant creator who did not intervene directly in daily life. Thus, they tended to be secularists who believed that government and religion should remain separate domains.

Denis Diderot

Denis Diderot belonged to a group of French Enlightenment thinkers called the philosophes ("philosophers"). They not only developed philosophical ideas, but also tried to apply them to modern society, marking a key component of Enlightenment thought. They publicized their views in essays, plays, pamphlets, and newspapers. In 1751, Diderot agreed to edit a collection of all philosophe writings. This effort became the massive 28-volume Encyclopedia. It represented the collective works of all major Enlightenment thinkers between 1751 and 1772. Knowing the collection existed, many philosophes wrote articles specifically for the Encyclopedia. Diderot and several of the contributors faced imprisonment for their efforts, but the Encyclopedia became widely read throughout Europe, promoting and encouraging Enlightenment ideas.

Baron de Montesquieu

Baron de Montesquieu was a philosopher who supported John Locke's theories on the social contract and natural rights. Montesquieu sought to apply Locke's theories to the search for a perfect form of government. In The Spirit of the Laws (1748), he analyzed a variety of human institutions, customs, and laws to determine what systems worked best in preserving natural rights. His conclusion supported the Parliamentary system that had developed in Britain to the best example of the time. This system was the best, he argued, because of its separation of powers between an executive, legislative, and judicial branch that provided checks and balances on power. Montesquieu's concepts of the separation of powers and checks and balances would greatly influence the revolutionary governments in the United States and France.

Voltaire

Voltaire was the pseudonym for French writer Francois-Marie Arouet, who strongly advocated for religious and personal freedom. Like Montesquieu, Voltaire admired the British system of government but was even more highly critical of French authority. Voltaire condemned the oligarchy held by the monarch, nobles, and church officials in his home country. Imprisonment and forced exile only encouraged Voltaire. His writings proved extremely popular, as he often used satire and wit to make his political points. Some of his best known works include The Philosophical Letters (1734) and Candide (1759). One of Voltaire's most famous quotes reflects his support for freedom of speech: "I may disapprove of what you say, but I will defend to the death your right to say it."

Jean-Jacques Rousseau

Adding to the growing debate on the social contract, Jean-Jacques Rousseau took the concept even further than previous writers. While many Enlightenment thinkers focused on the perils of a strong government, most of them accepted the class divisions of their times. They were elites writing about systems designed to benefit their own social and economic class. Rousseau, however, was one of the few who considered the masses of working-class and poor people as part of the citizenry whose rights needed protection. In 1762, he published his two most influential works, Emile and The Social Contract. Rousseau wrote that human nature was essentially good and moral. Such societal institutions as church, school, and government corrupted the goodness of average citizens. If people had full control over their institutions, he argued, they would choose governments and laws that preserved their natural rights. Thus, he concluded that popular sovereignty was the best form of government. Rousseau's concept of rule by a majority of the common people was truly radical for its time.

Mary Wollstonecraft

The Enlightenment was primarily a movement among male writers, as women in Europe still had few rights of any kind. British teacher and writer Mary Wollstonecraft challenged Enlightenment thinkers to expand their concepts of freedom and liberty to include women. In Thoughts on the Education of Daughters (1787), she advocated for better educational systems for girls, who usually received only a limited education intended to train them to be mothers and wives. Her greatest work, A Vindication of the Rights of Woman (1792), expanded these ideas to argue that girls should not only receive an education equal to that provided for boys, but should also be granted the same political rights as men. Although her ideas were largely discounted by male writers of her age, Wollstonecraft's ideas lived on, inspiring future movements to encompass women's rights.

Jonathan Swift

Jonathan Swift was a popular political writer who used satire to criticize authority figures, especially those in England and Ireland. Swift's biting style brought widespread public attention to anti-government theories. His works reflected efforts to bring Enlightenment thought down from the realm of academic theory into real application for political reform. Two of his best-known works are A Modest Proposal (1725) and Gulliver's Travels (1726). A Modest Proposal was a satirical essay that proposed solving Ireland's very real problems of overcrowding and poverty by using babies of poor families as a food source for the rich. The satire attacked class divisions as well as political inaction. The novel Gulliver's Travels tells the story of a man who ventures to four very strange lands. While modern audiences tend to view the story as merely an exciting fantasy, readers of the 1770s recognized its attempts to criticize various forms of government.

Immanuel Kant

Immanuel Kant was a German thinker who attempted to create a new type of ethical reasoning that bridged the gap between two schools of Enlightenment thought: rationalism, which was influenced by Descartes and emphasized reason; and empiricism, which was influenced by Francis Bacon and emphasized experience. Kant proposed a way of applying scientific methods to ethical and political philosophy in such a way that promoted the greatest good for humans. Beginning with A Critique of Pure Reason (1781), Kant published a series of works that discussed the limitations of human understanding. He pointed out, for example, that no scientific study could be purely objective because the scientist's understandings of the findings are shaped by previous knowledge. Kant's theories inspired a host of followers to rethink how humans understood their own condition and place in the world. His work was the culmination of Enlightenment thought that inspired a new philosophical era.

Jeremy Bentham vs. John Locke

Jeremy Bentham was a British political philosopher whose works focused less on ideal forms of government than on how leaders should go about governing once in power. His most influential work was An Introduction to the Principles of Morals and Legislation (1789) which in essence advised leaders to make policies that do the most good for the governed while causing the least amount of harm. Bentham's ideas became known as utilitarianism. In contrast to Locke's views of the ideal social contract, Bentham acknowledged that in order to achieve good for the greatest number of people, the rights of a small minority might sometimes have to be oppressed.

Influence of the Enlightenment on the American Revolution

American colonial leaders were very familiar with Enlightenment thinkers. Benjamin Franklin, who frequently traveled between the colonies and Europe, promoted Enlightenment writings in his popular pamphlets and newspapers. The Enlightenment practice of questioning authority encouraged American political rebellion in the 1760s. Many colonial leaders, for instance, used Locke's concept of the social contract to justify their protests against what they felt were unfair laws. Thomas Paine became one of the most radical of American Enlightenment writers when he proposed in Common Sense (1776) that the colonies should create an entirely new government without a monarch. With the outbreak of the American Revolution, colonists were able to put into practice radical Enlightenment concepts that were merely theories or inspirations for limited reform in Europe.

Jefferson's Place Among Enlightenment Thinkers

Thomas Jefferson was one of colonial America's best-educated leaders. He had carefully studied Enlightenment thought long before armed conflict broke out within the colonies. He tried to emulate many European Enlightenment thinkers through his eclectic interests in science and the arts. Jefferson used his extensive knowledge and skills as a writer to create a new form of practical Enlightenment thought prior to and during the American Revolution. In 1774, he published A Summary View of the Rights of British America, which systematically sought to justify colonial freedom from Parliamentary control using many rational arguments of Enlightenment philosophers. Most scholars credit Jefferson with the Enlightenment influences evident in the Declaration of Independence, of which he was the primary writer.

Influence of the Enlightenment on the Declaration of Independence

The Declaration of Independence, issued on July 4, 1776, sought to explain and justify the American colonists' breaking away from British rule to form a new nation under a new government. Many scholars consider the Declaration of Independence the prime example of Enlightenment thought put into action. The document most clearly reflects the social contract theory of John Locke, mirroring his definition of natural rights with the declaration that "all men are endowed by their Creator with certain unalienable rights, that among these are life, liberty, and the pursuit of happiness." Following Locke's theories, the Declaration of Independence notes that all power of government derives from the consent of the people to be governed. Because the role of government was to protect individual rights, the people had a duty to rebel if the government failed to do so. To the colonists, the British government had failed to fulfill its part of the social contract. Therefore, the American colonists were justified in dissolving that contract and creating a new one, just as Locke had argued.

Articles of Confederation

The Articles of Confederation was the document under which the US government functioned from 1781 to 1789. It was the first experiment in new, non-monarchical government. Reflecting

Enlightenment distrust of federal authority, the Articles provided for a weak central government, with most power reserved for state governments. There was no federal executive and only a one-house legislature in which each state had an equal vote regardless of population. The only powers granted to the federal Congress were declaring war, negotiating peace and treaties with foreign nations, and settling disputes between states. Nine of the states had to agree in order to make decisions, though there was no way for Congress to enforce laws. In the years following the end of the American Revolution in 1783, the Articles proved insufficient for running a unified country. In 1789, the Articles were replaced with the US Constitution, which sought to establish a check and balance system between various branches of the federal government, as well as between federal and state governments.

US Constitutional Government vs. European Constitutional Governments

The most obvious difference was the lack of a monarch. Most European constitutional governments were limited constitutional monarchies, meaning that a king or queen remained as head of state, while a prime minister served as head of an executive branch and a parliament served as the legislative branch. In the US government system, the president served as head of the executive branch, as well as the head of state. The American congress was similar to European parliaments in its creation of an upper and lower house, though the American system took greater steps to avoid recreating a European-style nobility. In most European parliaments, nobles ruled the upper houses of the legislatures. In some limited constitutional monarchies, such as that of Britain, the legislative branch was the most powerful arm of government. The US system of checks and balances sought to ensure that no one branch—executive, legislative, judicial—gained too much power over the other branches.

American Reforms Regarding Religion

Overall, Enlightenment thinkers were highly critical of organized religion. The history of church influence and religious conflict had led many to believe that churches should not be involved with governments. Some nations took steps to allow greater religious freedom, but national governments were still aligned with official state churches. The United States broke from this tradition by refusing to support a state-sponsored church. Although the colonies, like all British entities, had supported the Anglican Church, they had also welcomed a variety of faiths. Many people had settled in the British North American colonies specifically to practice their religious faith without oppression, and they wanted that freedom to continue. Thomas Jefferson was one of the strongest advocates for American religious tolerance. In 1779, he wrote the Virginia Act for Establishing Religious Freedom, which became a model for religious liberty throughout the colonies. The protection of freedom of religion in the First Amendment established the precedent for separation of church and state, achieving a goal long-sought by many Enlightenment philosophers.

Limitations of the Enlightenment Ideals

As Mary Wollstonecraft pointed out, the Enlightenment was a movement by men concerning the political rights of men. More specifically, it was an intellectual movement among wealthy, white, well-educated men, few of whom envisioned their ideas applying to the masses of poor, uneducated, landless men, much less to women or non-whites. Other than Wollstonecraft, Enlightenment thinkers did little to support women's rights or to challenge slavery and class prejudices. Thomas Jefferson reflected many of the contradictions of the Enlightenment. He wrote eloquently and passionately about the need to protect liberty, equality, and religious freedom, yet he was a slave owner who likely fathered children with at least one woman in bondage to him. It would be many years before new generations of reformers expanded Enlightenment concepts of liberty and equality.

ENLIGHTENED DESPOTISM

Enlightened despotism, also called benevolent despotism, was a popular concept among many philosophers. "Despotism" referred to the absolute powers of a monarch. Supporters of enlightened despotism accepted absolute monarchy as a reality unlikely to fade soon. Instead of fighting the existence of the institution, they tried to improve it by encouraging monarchs to use their powers wisely and justly. Many encouraged well-educated monarchs familiar with Enlightenment thought to embrace ideas such as freedom of speech and religious tolerance. They argued that enlightened despotism was a justifiable form of government under the social contract, so long as the monarch in power protected the people and treated them fairly.

JEAN-JACQUES ROUSSEAU AND THE ENLIGHTENED DESPOTISM

In many ways, Rousseau's ideas on popular sovereignty were a direct assault on the theories of enlightened despotism. Rousseau argued that citizens could not trust any form of government that they did not directly choose. This was a direct attack on the traditions of inherited monarchy. Although shocking for its time, other thinkers slowly began to embrace Rousseau's views. They pointed out how history proved the fallibility of enlightened despotism. While some monarchs had been just and benevolent, others who followed them were unjust and oppressive. Under a traditional monarchy, there was little people could do to check the powers of an absolute monarch; thus, the entire institution should be suspect. Others came to believe that there was truly no such thing as an enlightened despot, since the power held by one person inevitably corrupted them and undermined civil liberties.

AMERICAN REVOLUTION AND THE ENLIGHTENED DESPOTISM

The American Revolution embraced Rousseau's views and challenged whether monarchy was necessary at all. Thomas Paine's forceful arguments against monarchy inspired colonial leaders to create a new type of government. After the success of the American Revolution, anti-monarchist movements increased in Europe. At the same time, supporters of monarchy embraced the concept of enlightened despotism even more. They pressured monarchs to protect their crowns by taking good care of the citizenry, who now were more likely to demand that their leaders uphold the social contract. It became harder for monarchs to exert oppressive powers without experiencing protests. The age of the tyrannical despot was coming to an end.

EUROPEAN ENLIGHTENED DESPOTS

Historians agree that several monarchs reflected ideal qualities of enlightened despots. Although some of these rulers could be ruthless towards their enemies, each was familiar with Enlightenment thought and tried to improve their countries and the lives of many citizens. Their attempts may have helped prevent anti-monarchical revolutions such as those experienced in the British colonies and in France. The enlightened despots of the 1700s included:

- Frederick the Great of Prussia
- Catherine the Great of Russia
- Maria Theresa of Austria
- Joseph II, Holy Roman Emperor
- Leopold II, Holy Roman Emperor

VULNERABILITY OF THE KINGDOM OF POLAND

By the late 1700s, the Kingdom of Poland was beset by numerous domestic conflicts. Although Poland occupied a large expanse of land, its government was weak and inefficient. Arguments among nobles prevented the legislature from taking any major actions or even agreeing on supporting new monarchs. The land was rife with religious and ethnic strife, as Catholic Poles oppressed people of other faiths and ethnicities. Oftentimes oppressed groups turned to neighboring nations for help. For example, ethnic Russians living in Poland would ask for the Russian government to intervene on their behalf during conflicts. Similarly, leaders from Austria and Prussia were often asked to intervene. With each intervention, these powers gained more influence over Poland.

Other Nations Wanted to Control Polish Lands

Poland occupied a key location in Europe. By 1771, the kingdom controlled a huge tract of land linking eastern and central Europe, including much of the southern shoreline of the Baltic Sea. It also bordered the Ottoman Empire, which had important trade links to the Middle East, on the south. Poland also included several major rivers vital to trade and transportation. Yet the Polish government was so ineffective that it often failed to take full advantage of its position for the benefit of the nation. Ethnic strife weakened nationalist loyalties among the citizens; many ethnic Austrians, Prussians, and Russians living in Poland supported a return to control by their own ethnic brethren. Poland's neighbors sensed an opportunity to gain valuable lands and reunite members of their traditional ethnic groups.

Partition of Poland

- 1768 — Russia went to war against the Ottoman Turks, winning territories near the Danube River. Austria, feeling threatened by these victories, prepared for possible war against Russia. Prussian leader Frederick the Great intervened, suggesting that Russia and Austria protect themselves by taking lands from weak neighbor Poland.
- 1772 — Russia, Austria, and Prussia signed the First Partition of Poland, with each nation gaining Polish lands. Polish officials agreed rather than risk war with their more powerful neighbors.
- 1791 — Polish reformers, hoping to strengthen the government, adopted a new constitution. Opponents of the constitution sought Russian intervention. Both Russia and Prussia sent troops to overthrow the new Polish government.
- 1793 — Russia and Prussia signed the Second Partition of Poland, each gaining more lands. Polish officials agreed under duress.
- 1794 — Polish leaders attempted an uprising against the Second Partition. Russian and Prussian forces quickly suppressed the protest.
- 1795 — Russia, Prussia, and Austria signed the Third Partition of Poland, dissolving the kingdom of Poland and dividing all remaining Polish lands between them.

Limitations of Enlightenment Ideals

In many ways, the Kingdom of Poland should have been an ideal example of Enlightenment thought, with its weak federal structure and elected monarch. In reality, however, the weak government proved to be Poland's undoing. The Sejm was rarely able to reach consensus on any issue or to enforce its policies. The government was dominated by self-interested nobles who fought more than they led. Ethnic and religious strife undermined Enlightenment pronouncements about equality. In the end, Polish citizens came to distrust the government's ability to protect them. Many embraced the stability offered by stronger neighboring countries. Although the Constitution of 1791 attempted to correct many of the weaknesses of the Polish government, it was too little, too late. Poland was far too fractured to defend itself against greater forces. The Polish experience proved the need for Enlightenment ideas to be rooted in pragmatic goals, such as defense and stability.

Poland's Reflection of Enlightenment Ideals

Many leaders in Poland embraced Enlightenment ideas. In fact, some leaders were already aligned with the style of government practiced in the kingdom. Unlike absolute monarchies of Western Europe, the national legislature of the Polish kingdom, called the Sejm, elected the monarch. Compared to other European countries, Poland's national government was weak by design. The Sejm required a consensus in order to enact any policies, a practice intended to discourage tyranny by the majority and encourage compromise. The Constitution of 1791, inspired by the Enlightenment-influenced US Constitution, attempted to realign the Polish government into an ideal limited constitutional monarchy, with greater emphasis on popular sovereignty and representation.

Partitions on the Polish People

The demise of the Kingdom of Poland was a huge blow to many ethnic Poles. Nevertheless, the experience in many ways only served to strengthen the nationalism of the Polish people. For generations after the Partitions, ethnic Poles resisted assimilation into the Russian, Prussia, or Austrian cultures that controlled their lands. Throughout the 1800s, Poles staged numerous unsuccessful uprisings, which were usually met with armed resistance. Oppression merely begat greater nationalist zeal, as Poles born long after the Third Partition continued to struggle for the creation of a new Polish nation, a goal that would not be achieved until after World War I.

Revolution and Napoleonic Europe

Three Estates under the Old Regime

The Old Regime refers to France before the revolution that began in 1789. Prior to that time, French society was rigidly divided into three classes, or estates.

- The First Estate, made up of Catholic clergy, represented about one percent of the population. The Church held great economic wealth and political power in France, even though it paid no taxes. Corruption was common among many high-level Church officials.
- The Second Estate, made up of the nobility, represented about two percent of the population. Most nobles lived in luxury on large estates that reflected medieval manors more than post-Renaissance economies. They paid few taxes and lived off the service of peasants.
- The Third Estate, made up of working citizens, represented 97 percent of the population. France depended on the labor of the Third Estate, but its members had little political power. While the Third Estate did include professionals and skilled laborers, poor peasants made up the majority of the French population.

Social unrest in France during the late 1700s

The First and Second Estates controlled most of the property in France, charging members of the Third Estate rent for housing and dues to farm the land. During the late 1700s, resentment towards this system began to grow. Medical advances helped improve people's life expectancy, but such advances also increased family sizes, making it harder for poor families to survive. Then, in order to increase profits, nobles and clergymen began increasing rents and dues, while the government increased taxes. The resulting inflation made it more difficult for common people to purchase any goods. Increasingly, members of the Third Estate began to resent the tax-free status of the first two estates. Members of the bourgeoisie, the upper tier of the Third Estate made up of merchants, manufacturers, and professionals, began to demand greater political power. Inspired by the Enlightenment, many bourgeoisie leaders began advocating for protection of their natural rights and liberties.

Louis XV

Louis XV became king in 1715, at the age of five. During his childhood, important nobles ran the government, most of whom tried to increase their own power and wealth. Even upon reaching adulthood, Louis remained a passive king, more concerned with entertaining at the court than addressing the needs of the people. Although France did experience a long period of peace during his reign, domestic instability increased. The country was burdened by debts from the wars of Louis XIV, leading to higher taxes and public debt. While the Third Estate strained under the huge tax burden, the king spent lavishly at the palace. He blatantly ignored the long-term ramifications of his actions, declaring that he intended to enjoy life and let future generations deal with the fallout. By the time he died and grandson Louis XVI came to power in 1774, public distrust of the French government was growing.

Louis XVI's marriage to Marie-Antoinette

Marie-Antoinette was the daughter of powerful Austrian queen Maria Theresa. In 1770, Prince Louis married Marie-Antoinette in order to strengthen France's ties with Austria. As king, Louis XVI was more pragmatic than his grandfather had been, but largely powerless against the strong first two estates. Many people resented his marriage to a foreigner, fearing that Marie-Antoinette was merely a pawn for Austrian dominance over their country. The queen did not help matters by her lavish spending and seeming disregard for the sufferings of the poor. Her famous remark, "Let them eat cake!" was said to have been a response to the peasants' bread famine. During the crises of the early French Revolution, Marie often seemed more decisive than her husband, leading many citizens to fear that she was really in control of the country. This perception only fueled further anger, making her the most hated woman in France.

Events Leading to Revolution in France

France's debts continued to increase due to lavish spending by the upper classes and aid given to the American Revolutionaries. Louis XVI called for a meeting of the Estates General, a body of representatives from all three classes, to approve new taxes. Traditionally, each estate met separately and received one vote. This policy contributed to class divisions, as the upper two estates usually voted together against the Third Estate. When the Estates General convened on May 4, 1789, representatives of the Third Estate refused to follow tradition. Noting that they represented the vast majority of people, they declared themselves the National Assembly and prepared to write a new constitution. Though Louis agreed, he secretly began organizing troops to suppress the Assembly. The peasants acted first, forming an angry mob that stormed Bastille prison on July 14. Marquis de Lafayette organized a revolutionary army called the National Guard, and the Assembly adopted a new French flag of red, white, and blue.

Declaration of the Rights of Man

The National Assembly adopted the Declaration of the Rights of Man and of the Citizen in August 1789. Its provisions included:

- Affirmation that all men are born equal and remain equal before the law
- Protection of freedom of speech, of the press, and of religion
- Protection of the right of citizens to participate in government
- Affirmation that all men have an equal right to hold office
- Protection of the right to a fair trial

The document specifically applied only to men. A group of female revolutionaries led by Olympe de Gouges presented the assembly with the Declaration of the Rights of Women and Citizenesses, extending these rights to females. The National Assembly rejected their document, believing, as did most leaders of the time, that equal rights applied only to white male citizens.

Reforms of the National Assembly

1789 and 1791

- Reorganization of the government's administrative structure into 83 equal districts, or departments
- Election of all local officials
- Seizure of lands owned by the Catholic Church
- Public sale of former Church lands to pay down foreign debts
- Passage of the Civil Constitution of the Clergy (1790), which allowed citizens to elect their own clergy rather than accept appointments from high Church officials
- Government payment of salaries for local clergy and bishops, to be paid out of money received from the sale of seized Church lands
- Constitution of 1791: Divided government into three branches—executive, legislative, and judicial; limited powers of the monarch—no power to make or reject laws without legislative approval

1792 and 1795

The National Convention arose when the Legislative Assembly disbanded in 1792 to organize a more purely republican form of government. The Convention wrote a new constitution that formally abolished the monarchy and established the French Republic. The Convention also established the Committee of Public Safety and the Revolutionary Tribunal. The Convention instituted a draft to engage all young men in military service, a departure from the tradition of reserving military service for the nobility. In the new, more egalitarian army, all young French men served and were eligible to become officers based on merit. The Convention government expanded educational opportunities for children, abolished slavery in French colonies, promoted religious tolerance, and adopted the metric system. It also created a new calendar that began with the revolution.

Problems Caused by the French Constitution of 1791

The French Constitution radically sought to remake the French government. In addition to limiting the powers of the monarch, it dissolved the National Assembly and replaced it with the Legislative Assembly. Problems began almost immediately. The constitution hardened the resolve of monarchists and Catholic leaders, who plotted to undermine the revolution. The executive branch was too weak to enforce laws. The legislature soon dissolved into three factions that fought constantly. These three factions included:

- Conservatives, who supported the monarchy and wanted no further reforms; they tended to congregate on the right wing of the assembly hall.
- Radicals, who wanted further reforms leading to the abolition of the monarchy; they tended to congregate on the left wing of the assembly hall.
- Moderates, who were constantly torn between the other two and tended to sit in the center of the hall.

The modern terms right or rightwing (for supporters of conservative policies) and left or leftwing (for supporters of radical policy changes) evolved from the National Assembly.

Girondins vs. Jacobins

Both the Girondins and Jacobins were French groups who favored creating a republic and abolishing the monarchy. The Girodins, named after the department of the Gironde in southwestern France, wanted to prevent Parisians from dominating any national republican government. Notable Girondins included Jacques-Pierre Brissot and Pierre-Victurnien Vergniaud. The Girondins were most influential in late 1791 and early 1792, pushing anti-émigré reforms and advocating for foreign wars. The Jacobins, named for the Dominican convent where they originally met, wanted Parisians to control the republican government for the benefit of all citizens. Their leaders included Georges-Jacques Danton, Maximilien Robespierre, and Jean-Paul Marat. Over time, the Jacobins pushed for more radical reforms and clashed with the more moderate Girondins.

Main Motto of the French Revolution

Although revolutionaries incorporated many different slogans and mottos during the French Revolution, the one that most endured was "Liberty, Equality, Fraternity." The Enlightenment concepts of liberty and equality were central to the revolution and included in the Declaration of the Rights of Man. The third part of the motto, "fraternity," refers to the kinship and loyalty that all French citizens should feel towards their country. By including "fraternity," revolutionary leaders encouraged a sense of patriotism and stressed that revolution was not treason against France, but rather the ultimate example of doing what was good for the citizenry as a whole. The motto has endured as a symbol of the best notions of the French Revolution.

Committee of Public Safety

The National Convention formed the Committee of Public Safety in 1793 to protect the republic from foreign and domestic enemies. Its duties included enforcing the draft in order to maintain a strong army. It also sought to weaken the growing counterrevolutionary movement, which was made up mainly of strong monarchists and Catholics who opposed the extreme changes brought by revolutionary leaders. As supporters of the counterrevolution clashed with the army, France stood on the brink of civil war. Wanting to squelch the opposition, the Committee set up a secret court called the Revolutionary Tribunal to try enemies of the republic. The tribunal became a tool in the struggle between political factions within the revolutionary government. The dominant Jacobins used the tribunal to suppress dissent from the less-radical Girondins, for example. While the Committee's secrecy and violence instilled terror in some people, it hardened the resolve of active counterrevolutionaries.

Reign of Terror

The Reign of Terror officially began in September 1793, though political violence had been increasing for months prior. The murder of Jacobin leader Jean-Paul Marat by Girondin Charlotte Corday in July heightened tensions. After Corday's execution, Committee of Public Safety leader Maximilien de Robespierre declared that more needed to be done to abolish all enemies of the revolution. Over the next several months virtually any person who questioned Jacobin methods was tried and executed, including Marie-Antoinette and Olympe de Gouges. Soon the Jacobin leaders turned against one another. By the spring of 1794, when France's borders seemed secure against foreign enemies, Robespierre's ally, George Danton, began calling for a decrease in political violence. In response, Robespierre charged Danton and his followers with disloyalty and executed them. In July 1794, other members of the National Convention arrested and executed Robespierre, ending the Reign of Terror. Rather than abolish dissent, the Reign led many French citizens to question the republic and call for a return of the monarchy.

Reforms of the Constitution of 1795

The Constitution of 1795 sought to restore order and stabilize France's economy. It restructured the federal government to consist of:

The Legislative Branch (Corps Législatif):

- Council of 500: 500-member lower house that proposed laws
- Council of Ancients: 250-member upper house that approved or rejected laws proposed by the lower house; members had to be over age 40; selected members of the executive branch

The Executive Branch:

- The Directory: five-member committee of leaders selected by the upper house of the legislature; appointed leaders of all other government departments
- The constitution also reversed some revolutionary reforms. It abolished universal manhood suffrage, for example, allowing only to property owning white males to vote and effectively restoring leadership by the nobility.

The Directory

The Directory was the general name applied to the government that ruled France from 1795 to 1799 (named after the executive branch). It tried to suppress calls for a return of the monarchy by restoring order and ending the Reign of Terror's use of violence as a political tool. Under the Directory, the country did achieve a higher level of stability. The French army continued to win several major victories against foreign enemies, easing fears of invasion. The economy also improved, although many peasants still suffered. The Directory expanded the centralized educational system to improve literacy among upper classes. Overall, however, the Directory government proved to be weak and corrupt. The Directors often fought among themselves and used their positions to gain wealth. Bribery rather than merit became the main pathway to political appointments. While less violent that the Reign of Terror and less elite than the Old Regime, the Directory marked a shift back from republican ideals into oligarchy.

Role of Émigrés During the French Revolution

The émigrés were French nobles who fled the country when the revolution began. Most sought exile in Germany, Great Britain, or Switzerland. These men constantly worked to undermine the revolutionary government. Their main goal was to restore the absolute power of the monarchy. After the Constitution of 1791 was passed, the émigrés plotted with Louis XVI to overthrow the constitutional government and restore the Old Regime. Some émigrés were involved in Louis's attempted escape from France. In an effort to suppress their activities, the revolutionary leaders ordered all émigrés to return to France by January 1792 or be considered traitors subject to death. The government confiscated the property of émigrés who did not return by the deadline. During France's foreign wars, many émigrés fought against their own countrymen. Those who were captured were usually executed. The émigrés inspired both counterrevolutionary views and Jacobin paranoia.

France Declaration of War on Austria

For many years, French leaders had feared Austrian efforts to gain influence in, if not control over, French territories. These concerns had fueled resentment against Louis XVI's wife Marie-Antoinette, sister of Austrian Emperor Leopold II. After the creation of the French Constitution of 1791, Leopold issued the Declaration of Pillnitz, calling for a return of monarchical rule in France. The declaration urged other European monarchs to join forces in supporting Louis XVI and opposing the French Revolution. Many people in France considered this statement to be a call to war. Fearing that Austria would invade France in order to restore the monarchy, leaders of the Legislative Assembly prepared for battle. Some French leaders believed that success on the battlefield would increase respect for the revolutionary government. Thus, in April 1792, France declared war on Austria.

Prussia's Influence of Events During the French Revolution

Prussia became a haven for many émigrés during the revolution. Prussia's king, Frederick William II, sided with his fellow monarch, Louis XVI. Frederick William cosponsored the Declaration of Pillnitz, calling for a return of French monarchical rule. Although French leaders hoped to go to war only against Austria in 1792, Prussia joined forces with the Austrians, and a combined Austrian-Prussian army invaded France. The French forces successfully repelled the invaders. Prussian defeats only added to problems the country was facing under the weak leadership of Frederick William. By 1795, French forces had penetrated far enough into Prussian lands to force Frederick William into signing a peace treaty. As a result, France gained significant lands west of the Rhine River.

Events That Led Up to the Dissolution of the French Monarchy

Initially, Louis XVI and Marie-Antoinette isolated themselves in the palace at Versailles along with some noble supporters. When revolutionaries learned of a banquet the nobles had thrown to honor the monarchs and denounce the National Assembly, they stormed the palace and forced the royal family to return to Paris. When the royal family was caught trying to flee the country in 1791, public sentiment against the monarchy grew even stronger, and support for creating an American-style republic increased. Anti-monarchy sentiments grew as the king and queen plotted with foreign powers against their own countrymen, leading the Legislative Assembly to dissolve the monarchy in August 1792. Armed revolutionaries soon arrested the royal family. The National Convention tried Louis for treason and executed him on January 21, 1793. Marie-Antoinette followed him to the guillotine a few months later.

Foreign Reactions to the French Revolution

Most European governments expressed concern over the French Revolution, which threatened the stability of monarchies throughout the continent. Austria, Prussia, and Sardinia were the first to act with armed resistance to the revolution, though many other governments sympathized with the sentiments expressed in the Declaration of Pillnitz. At first, many US leaders supported the French Revolution, which initially seemed to reflect many of the same ideals and goals of the American Revolution. In addition, the French had lent support for the American cause and expected the same in return. Although the fledgling US government was not in a position to lend military aid to France, several prominent Americans offered financial and moral support. These sentiments began to change, however, as tactics of the French Revolution became increasingly violent. The execution of Louis XVI shocked people throughout the world and contributed to the anti-French alliance among Austria, Prussia, Spain, the United Provinces, and Great Britain. The Reign of Terror further decreased support for the revolution, especially within the United States.

French Army During the Revolutionary Era

Despite the constant domestic and political upheaval of the revolutionary era, the French army increased in power, strength, and success throughout the 1790s. This success was due in large part to the wide-scale draft that enabled France to quickly assemble one of Europe's largest armies. The egalitarian structure of the new army permitted even peasants to rise in rank based on merit, thus allowing the army to become one of the few arms of the French government that truly lived up to the revolutionary ideals of equality. The system encouraged soldiers to perform well, as did the patriotic zeal encouraged by military leaders. As this strong military force pushed back invading forces, it successfully built a buffer zone of protection around the borders of France. French officials also used dissent against other nations to their advantage; for example they encouraged Italian rebellions against Austrian rule. Were it not for its military strength, France might not have survived this turbulent era.

Napoleon Bonaparte

Napoleon Bonaparte (referred to as "Napoleon") achieved success through the French military. Born in Corsica in 1769, he began training for army life at a young age by attending French military schools in preparation for becoming an officer. During the early revolutionary era, he participated in numerous battles, but his reputation really began to grow after he helped suppress a rebellion in 1795 that threatened the creation of the Directory. As a reward for his actions, he received greater responsibility and a promotion. In 1796, the Directors named him commander of the flagging French forces in Italy. Napoleon quickly improved the troops, leading to several key victories. His efforts were largely responsible for Sardinia's peace agreement with France and the Austrian cession of Italy in 1797. Napoleon was a master at promoting his victories. As such, the French public embraced him as a hero. Fearing his popularity, the Directors reassigned him to Egypt. Although his success there was mixed, he convinced the public that he had achieved great victory.

Emergence of Napoleon as Leader France

France was facing new threats by 1799. The corrupt and ineffective Directory had led to wide-scale domestic dissent. Many citizens wanted to replace the government again, possibly even with a return to monarchy. Abroad, French troops were beginning to suffer defeats in the wake of a new offensive by Great Britain, Austria, and Russia. Surrounded by threatening forces, several admirers of Napoleon began to advocate for a coup that would place him and his army in control of the government. Without such a move, many feared, the Bourbon monarchy might return to power. The group launched the coup in November 1799, surrounding the legislature with armed troops. The Directory was dissolved and replaced with a new government led by Napoleon.

French Government Between 1799 and 1804

Napoleon declared that he intended to retain a republican form of government, but that the executive branch should be stronger than the legislative branch. Napoleon argued that a strong executive branch was necessary to maintain order and stability. The government was called the Consulate, after the executive branch. The executives consisted of three consuls, but First Consul Napoleon primarily controlled the group. The constitution gave him virtually unlimited dictatorial powers. He ruled over the army and navy, appointed all officials, and proposed all new laws. The legislature retained only veto power over these proposed laws. Although voters were supposed to choose members of the legislature, the First Consul had the power to remove and appoint representatives as they saw fit. The French citizenry approved the new constitution and Consulate in February 1800.

Achievements of the Consulate Era

The Consulate constitution reaffirmed many principles of the revolution. Although the constitution renewed many laws against émigrés, Napoleon tried to reunite the citizenry by granting amnesty to most émigrés in 1802. That same year, he negotiated peace agreements with Britain, Austria, and Russia. Napoleon also tried to restore peace between the French government and Roman Catholic leaders. Napoleon and representatives of Pope Pius VII signed the Concordat of 1801, which attempted to balance church and state power. The Concordat established religious freedom in France, while acknowledging that most French citizens were Catholic. Church officials agreed to let the French government keep Church property seized during the revolution, and Napoleon retained the right to appoint French bishops. Local parishes and seminaries were to be free from government interference. Domestically, Napoleon reorganized the French legal system into the Napoleonic Code; created the Bank of France to help regulate the economy; and expanded education by establishing and strengthening public high schools, universities, and trade schools.

France Becomes an Empire Under Napoleon

By 1804, Napoleon seemed to have fulfilled his promise of bringing peace and stability to France. Many of his supporters believed this stability would continue only if Napoleon became leader for life. Their efforts received a boost after officials uncovered a British-financed plot to assassinate Napoleon. He quickly arrested the known conspirators and increased measure to strengthen his rule. As part of this move, Napoleon declared France an empire with himself as emperor on May 28, 1804. To secure his position, he asked Pope Pius VII to crown him. In a symbolic gesture of his own power, Napoleon removed the crown from the pope's hand and placed it on his own head. He reinstituted many of the symbols and traditions of Old Regime courts, including hereditary monarchy. He also increased his dictatorial authority, tightly controlling the press and limiting dissent of any kind.

Expansion of the French Empire

1804 and 1812

Emperor Napoleon made clear his intention to expand the borders of the French Empire. In reaction to this threat, Great Britain declared war on France. The British were soon joined by Austria, Russia, and Sweden. Spain, France's old ally, initially sided with Napoleon. French forces gained ground against Austria and Russia, successfully expanding the empire eastward. However, the British navy prevented French and Spanish fleets from successfully invading the British Isles. Napoleon responded by ordering the Continental Blockade, cutting off trade to the British Isles. When Portugal refused to support the blockade, France invaded the Iberian Peninsula, conquering both Portugal and Spain. Outraged Spaniards launched a revolt that was supported by the British. The French continued to have more success in the east, forcing most French enemies to sign peace agreements. By 1812, France controlled most of continental Europe, either directly or through alliances.

Campaign against Russia

Although Russia signed a peace agreement with France in 1807, Czar Alexander I never fully trusted Napoleon. As the French Empire expanded, Alexander feared France would again invade Russia. Also, the Russian economy was being harmed by the Continental Blockade. In 1812, Russia reopened trade with Great Britain. Angered by this move, Napoleon organized the 600,000 man Grand Army to invade Russia. As the French forces marched eastward, the Russians followed a strategy of slowly retreating and destroying anything along the way that could be of use to the French ("scorched earth policy"). When the French invaded Moscow in the autumn of 1812, the Russians destroyed the city, preventing French troops from seeking shelter and supplies during the coming winter. Facing starvation and bitter cold, the French retreated, but they experienced a long, slow winter trek under constant attack from the Russians. Two-thirds of the Grand Army was lost by the time the group returned to Prussia. The Russians then launched an invasion of the French Empire.

End of Napoleon's reign

The Grand Army disaster revealed the weaknesses of French alliances. Austria, Prussia, and Great Britain quickly joined Russia's attack on the empire. By October 1813, Napoleon's forces were defeated at Saxony, forcing his retreat to France. That same year, Spanish rebels overthrew the French on the Iberian Peninsula. In March 1814, France's enemies invaded Paris, forcing Napoleon to relinquish power and retire to the Italian island of Elba. Bourbon king Louis XVIII became king of France, but Napoleon's supporters helped him escape from Elba and gather an army against the king. Napoleon's forces seized Paris in March 1815, forcing King Louis into exile. Napoleon's old enemies, Great Britain, Prussia, and the Netherlands, sent troops into France to stop the coup. They met Napoleon's forces at Waterloo. The French army was soundly defeated, and Napoleon stepped down once more, spawning the expression "he met his Waterloo" to signal a complete and final defeat. Napoleon was imprisoned on the South Atlantic island of St. Helena, where he died in 1821.

Congress of Vienna

The Congress of Vienna was a series of meetings by major European powers to restore peace and stability throughout Europe and to suppress future anti-monarchical revolutions. The meetings began in September 1814, soon after Napoleon's initial defeat, and lasted until June 1815, shortly before Waterloo. Most European powers were represented, although the main delegates were from Great Britain, Austria, Prussia, Russia, and post-Napoleonic France. Delegates hoped to resolve many long-standing territorial disputes and lessen the likelihood of future wars. In the end, they produced the most comprehensive European treaty ever written.

Principles Guiding the Congress of Vienna

Early on in the process, delegates to the Congress of Vienna devised three major principles to guide all decisions that followed. These principles included:

- Restoring territories claimed by France to the nations that had controlled the lands prior to Napoleonic rule.
- Restoring the balance of power in Europe and instilling safeguards to insure that no single nation came to dominate the continent again.
- Restoring all former ruling families to their rightful thrones (Napoleon had replaced many monarchs with members of his own family), acknowledging the principle of legitimacy in hereditary rule.

Outcomes of the Congress of Vienna

- The Netherlands gained the Austrian Netherlands.
- Spain gained the Netherlands' northern Italian states.
- Sweden gained Norway (a possession of French ally Denmark).
- Prussia regained lands along the Rhine River as well as in Poland.
- Great Britain gained French colonies in the West Indies and Mediterranean Sea.
- Russia gained lands in Poland.
- Bourbon monarchies were restored in France, Spain, and the Kingdom of the Two Sicilies.
- Habsburg monarchs retained control over most Italian states.
- France agreed to pay indemnities for war damages.
- Austria, Great Britain, Prussia, and Russia formed the Quadruple Alliance (later the Quintuple Alliance when France joined in 1818) to meet regularly and resolve issues.
- Several nations, led by Russia, Austria and Prussia, signed the Holy Alliance, promising to support Christian principles.
- Most nations joined the Concert of Europe to ensure that the continent retained a balance of power.

The Industrial Revolution

Agricultural Revolution and Industrial Revolution

Agricultural Revolution — Dramatic change in agricultural techniques. Revolutions have occurred periodically since ancient times, most recently beginning in Great Britain prior to the Industrial Revolution. The Agricultural Revolution was marked by a reallocation of land, smaller plot sizes, increased use of technology and scientific management.

Industrial Revolution — Rise in manufacturing that began in Great Britain during the 1700s and soon spread throughout the western world. A second, more American-based wave of expansion took place in the late 1800s that is sometimes called the Second Industrial Revolution. The revolutions introduced new technology, factory-based economies, and consumerism. Great Britain's vast resources in labor, coal, and iron became vital to this new economic model, which eventually replaced agrarian economies in most of the western world.

Technological Advances and Innovations of the Agricultural Revolution

- Seed drill — Invented by Jethro Tull to decrease the amount of seed wasted in hand-scattering system; the seed drill allowed for planting seeds in straight rows.
- Horse-drawn hoe — Invented by Jethro Tull to dig up weeds between rows and break up soil before planting.
- Replaceable blade iron plow — Invented by Jethro Wood; the plow had interchangeable parts so that farmers could easily replace broken blades instead of having to buy an entirely new plow cast in one piece.
- Crop rotation — Popularized by Charles "Turnip" Townshend; based on the observation that soil in fields planted with the same crops year after year wears out quickly; Townshend advocated planting different crops in one field each year to replenish the soil; fields using crop rotation produced higher yields in the long-run than ones that did not utilize the rotation system.

Development of the Textile Industry

In the early 1700s, some companies began organizing cloth making workers in factories under one roof. Their methods of production were traditional and very slow. As a result, several inventors began looking for ways to improve textile production. They began by trying to mechanize the loom system. In 1733, John Kay invented the flying shuttle to move thread across the loom at a faster rate than by hand. In 1770, James Hargreaves invented the spinning jenny, a machine that spun wool into cloth using multiple spinning wheels. At the same time, Richard Arkwright perfected the water frame for carding and combing wool before the spinning process. Companies gradually began replacing waterwheels with steam power for greater efficiency. As production became cheaper and more efficient, prices dropped and demand increased. Textile factories began hiring more workers, especially young women, and even housed them in company dorms. The textile industry became the model for other industries of the time.

Development of Steam Powered Machines

The desire for steam-powered machines arose out of the limitations of water power because the machines needed to be located near a flowing body of water. In 1698, Thomas Savery patented a machine that used steam power to pump water from mines. In 1712, Thomas Newcomen produced a steam engine inspired by Avery's invention. Newcomen's invention, however, was somewhat inefficient and never became widely popular. In 1769, James Watt patented a better version of the steam engine that enabled businesses to harness power for manufacturing. Watt went into business with Matthew Boulton to establish the first steam-powered factories. Soon, steam power was adapted for transportation, improving shipping by boat and railway.

BESSEMER PROCESS

With the increases in manufacturing came a rise in demand for iron, the main material for machines. Iron tended to be very unstable, however, as traditional methods made it hard to remove all impurities from pig iron, which often exploded under steam pressure. Inventors had already developed methods for obtaining steel, a stronger iron alloy, but these methods tended to be very expensive. The Bessemer process, patented in 1856 by Henry Bessemer but developed simultaneously by William Kelly, improved the method for obtaining steel. The process concentrated a blast of air into the pig iron to remove impurities and strengthen the final product—steel. The Bessemer process was cheap and efficient, resulting in a boom in the steel, and subsequently coal (for burning), industries.

NATURAL RESOURCES

Although industrialization created a new economy based on manufacturing, natural resources were key to the revolution. Rivers provided sources for waterpower and inland transportation. Coal became one of the major fuel sources of the revolution. Later, oil became a popular fuel as well. Iron was necessary for the creation of tools and machinery. Other natural resources such as cotton, wool, rubber, and wood were also used extensively in production. The need for natural resources gave rise to secondary industries, such as mining, that fueled the factory-based economies

ELI WHITNEY

An American, Whitney was one of the most important inventors of the early Industrial Revolution. His first major invention was an improved cotton gin, developed in 1793. Whitney's machine allowed for the easy removal of small seeds from green-seed cotton, which grew well in the southern United States but had proven difficult to process because of its stubborn seeds. Whitney's machine was a boon to the southern cotton economy and the textile industry. Whitney also perfected a system of creating interchangeable parts for machines, which allowed for the replacement of broken parts instead of the more costly replacement of an entire item if one section broke. He first applied interchangeable parts to musket production, but the concept soon spread to all types of manufacturing industries, making the mass-production of goods possible.

GEOGRAPHIC SPREAD

The Industrial Revolution began in Great Britain, an area that had an abundance of natural resources, capital, and labor in the mid-1700s. Its rich supply of coal and iron ore fueled production, as did its abundant rivers and easily-accessible harbors for trade. Sensing its own advantage, the British government tried to maintain a monopoly on industrial technology by limiting the sharing of information with other countries. For this reason, the geographic spread of industrialization remained limited until the early 1800s. As some rebels smuggled technology out of Britain, information began to spread. Belgium became the first continental European country to transition to an industrial economy. The United States, boosted by Eli Whitney's inventions, began its transition earlier than most European nations. France finally began to industrialize by the mid-1800s, followed by Germany and a few other nations by the late 1800s. Still, many European economies remained heavily agricultural well into the 20th century.

CAPITALISM

Capitalism refers to an economic system in which individuals or corporations, as opposed to government officials, control the factors of production and privately own their own land and businesses. It is based on the presence of capital, or money, for investment. Under the capitalist system, individuals or businesses use profits from their earnings to invest in additional business ventures that will hopefully produce greater profits to be further reinvested. Capitalism on a small scale had been around for centuries, primarily in the form of commercial capitalism carried out by small merchants. The Industrial Revolution witnessed the development of industrial capitalism, in which investment was on a much larger scale. Capitalism allowed for large-scale investment in new business ventures by numerous individuals, thereby expanding economies.

Causes of the Agricultural Revolution

Europe experienced an Agricultural Revolution in the 1700s due to the enclosure movement. This movement began in the 1500s and 1600s as landowners began fencing off tracts of farmland. Previously, farmers had shared unfenced common grounds for grazing lands. Under the new system, many small farmers became tenants of the landowners, who rented out plots of the subdivided land. The movement encouraged innovation, however, as small farmers tried to better utilize their plots of land in order to produce more with less. They experimented with new types of farming technology, as well as new farming techniques. The field of scientific management developed to apply scientific methods to crop management, improving the overall quality of agricultural production. In the end, the Agricultural Revolution achieved the goal of allowing greater production using less land and fewer natural resources.

Causes of the Industrial Revolution

Increased crop production, along with other factors, led to a huge population boom in Europe during the late 1700s. As farm sizes decreased, many people moved to cities to find work. As a result, there existed a huge source of available labor. Many landowners who were renting out land had capital to invest in new ventures. Opportunity and availability of the factors of production combined with innovation, which allowed for investment in new industries. Great Britain, which had been affected first and most directly by the enclosure movement, originated the era of industrialization, which slowly spread to the United States and other parts of Europe.

Transportation Revolution

The needs of the Industrial Revolution soon gave way to a revolution in transportation. Businesses needed to be able to obtain resources and to ship their manufactured goods to markets. To meet this need, private investors and some governments began to improve roads by paving them with cobblestones and other materials. Some improved water travel by building canals. As river transportation became more important, methods of shipping improved. One of the most important advances was the development of the steamboat, perfected by Robert Fulton's Clermont in 1808. The steamboat vastly improved travel times by water. By the 1830s, steamboats were being used to transport goods across the oceans, expanding global trade. Rail transportation soon followed. By the end of the century, various inventors were experimenting with automobile and flight technology.

Communication Revolution

Just as the Industrial Revolution needed reliable transportation, so it also required good communication. Several inventors began to work on systems that could send messages over long distances. In the 1830,s American Samuel Morse combined Alessandro Volta's battery and André Ampre's magnet to create the telegraph, which he used to send messages via a series of dots and dashes (Morse Code). The use of the Morse telegraph quickly spread during the 1840s. By the 1870s, American Alexander Graham Bell had developed the telephone. In the 1890s, Italian Guglielmo Marconi invented wireless communication, which would eventually allow for radio and television transmission. All of these forms of communication vastly improved the sharing of information throughout the world.

Factory System

The factory system offered a convenient way to organize workers under the new industrialized system. First introduced in the textile industry, the factory system soon spread to most businesses. Rather than having one worker produce an item from start to finish, the factory system housed a group of workers who only carried out one part of the process. Such specialization allowed workers to carry out the same task over and over, while others performed their own specialized tasks on other pieces. This system allowed for the output of large numbers of items, all identical in shape and form. For factory owners, this system saved costs as well as time.

Effect of Wage System on Workers

Prior to the Industrial Revolution, most workers who produced goods were skilled artisans or craftsmen paid by the finished product. For example, before the introduction of factories, most textile workers were women who sewed items at home and were paid by companies based on the number of items they produced, regardless of how long it took to complete the task. The wage system introduced the concept of being paid for one's time rather than for one's output. Since each worker contributed only to part of the task of producing a good, they all created the same output; therefore, the only difference was the number of hours each contributed to production. The wage system also offered more flexibility to owners, who had to factor in wages among fixed costs such as natural resources. If the price of other factors of production went up, factory owners could adjust costs by cutting employees' wages.

Effect of the Industrial Revolution on Female Workers

Despite some degree of exploitation, factories offered unprecedented opportunities for female workers. The factory system originated within the textile industry, which previously relied on the piecework of women taught how to sew from an early age. As an outgrowth of this experience, textile factories were open to hiring young women. Factory owners also realized quickly that they could hire women to work for much lower wages than men. Society generally viewed women's work as "supplemental" to the income of male household members; therefore, their wages did not need to be as high. Eventually, many factories encouraged families to send unmarried daughters to both live and work in the factory communities, where they were housed and offered some educational opportunities not available to many at the time. Eventually some of these women trained in factory work went on to become leaders in unions and the women's rights movements.

Child Labor in the Industrial Age

Just as female labor was less expensive than male labor, child labor was cheaper than adult labor. During an era when many children received little to no formal schooling and farm children usually worked from an early age, most adults accepted the idea of having children working in factories. Their small hands and bodies proved quite nimble and, in some cases, better suited to machine work than those of adults. However, many child workers were exploited, forced to work long hours in dangerous conditions and beaten for errors or infractions. Concerns about the abuse of children in factories led to the oversight of child labor by the British government when Parliament passed the Factory Acts of 1802 and 1833. Still, child labor continued to be the norm in many industrialized countries throughout the 1800s.

Post-Industrial Rise of the Middle Class

The Industrial Revolution gave rise to a new middle class comprised of professionals and managers whose work supported the manufacturing industries. Some served as managers within factories.

Others, such as bankers, lawyers, engineers, and scientists, lent their expertise to new industries. Even the medical profession expanded as scientific research improved medical knowledge. At a time when Europe was still primarily ruled by rigid class divisions, the emergence of the middle class offered an avenue for moving up in class through one's education and financial success. The middle class was even more prominent in the United States, where class divisions were not as rigid by tradition. As the middle class grew, its members began to distinguish themselves from the working classes largely by lifestyle. They lived in larger, nicer homes, had more material possessions, hired domestic servants, and ensured that their children received an education. The middle class promoted the concept that merit, rather than birth alone, could determine a person's success in life.

Adam Smith

Scottish economist Adam Smith is considered the founder of classical economics. He built his theories upon a group of Enlightenment theorists called Physiocrats, men who argued that natural laws should govern economics. In his seminal work, The Wealth of Nations (1776), Smith argued that two natural laws should govern business. The first was the law of supply and demand, which said that prices and supply should reflect demand for goods. The second natural law was the law of competition. Smith argued that in order to compete with one another, rival businesses needed to cut prices. In order make the most profit, however, cutting prices required keeping costs low. The winner in an economic competition would be the most efficient manufacturer. Smith also advocated for free enterprise, arguing that economies worked best when they were free from government interference. Competition among self-interested private owners would produce the greatest good for all. Smith's theories, published just as the Industrial Revolution was beginning, influenced many business practices of the era.

Effects of Modern Economic Theories on Government Policies

Many business leaders embraced Adam Smith's theories and demanded less governmental control over economic practices. This "hands-off" approach by government in economic affairs became known as "*laissez-faire*," after a French term for "let do." Governments increasingly scaled back their involvement in economic regulations, even tariffs, letting private businesses run their course. At first, those paths allowed the exploitation of workers by business owners who were trying to increase profits through low wages and poor working conditions. Many business owners looked to economists such as Thomas Malthus and David Ricardo for support. Both men argued that poverty was a permanent reality of the human condition that could never be alleviated. Some industrialists took these theories as justification for worker exploitation in the absence of regulation.

Contribution of Charles Dickens, Thomas Carlyle, and John Ruskin

All three writers exposed the exploitation that accompanied industrialization in Great Britain. Charles Dickens was one of Britain's most important popular writers of the 1800s. His novels, including Oliver Twist (1838) and David Copperfield (1850), attacked greed and abuse in industrialized Britain, exposing the exploitation of children and other low

Jeremy Bentham and John Stuart Mill

Bentham rejected Smith's idea that individuals acting in self-interest would lead to the greatest common good. Bentham promoted the theory of utilitarianism, arguing that policies were good if they led to the greatest happiness for the greatest number of people. To that end, Bentham called for reform in the justice systems and the development of education so that citizens would be better able to decide what policies would bring the greatest good for the majority. John Stuart Mill rejected the theories of Malthus and Ricardo that accepted poverty as inevitable. Mill believed that all people had a right to be happy and free from poverty. To that end, he promoted education and the expansion of democracy, even to women. The theories of Bentham and Mill inspired many reformers of the 1800s.

British Labor Reform Laws

1802 — Factory Act: prohibited factory employment of children under age 9; limited workday of children between 9 and 13 to eight hours per day, six days per week; teenagers up to age 18 could work no more than 12 hours per day; law proved weak because it contained no enforcement power.

1833 — Factory Act: reiterated laws of 1802; included enforcement measurements by authorizing inspection of factories to ensure that owners were obeying child labor laws.

1847 — Ten Hours Act: set a 10-hour workday for children under 18 and for all women; many factories extended 10-hour day to all workers, but enforcement remained lax and exploitation was common.

British Labor Unions

Although Parliament made some gains in passing laws to improve working conditions, enforcement was very weak and abuses were common. In the face of exploitation and without traditional guilds to help, workers began to organize into what were originally called workers' associations. Later, the associations became known as unions. Workers pooled their money through dues to be shared in case they went on strike to protest conditions or wages. Union representatives who spoke for all workers brought grievances to management, and the two sides tried to work out a compromise through collective bargaining. If the collective bargaining process did not bring about a satisfactory outcome, workers might decide to strike. In Great Britain, labor unions remained limited until the late 1800s, when they began to grow quickly in both influence and stature.

Limited Success of British Labor Strikes

Early labor unions faced fierce opposition from business owners, who had a great deal of influence over Parliament. Confronted with political pressure, Parliament passed the Combination Acts of 1799 and 1800, effectively outlawing unions and allowing for the imprisonment of any workers who demanded higher wages, shorter hours, or better working conditions. Parliament repealed the Combination Acts in 1825 but still outlawed labor strikes. Many unions waged strikes anyway, oftentimes only to have the strikes broken up by government troops. Not until Parliament made labor strikes legal in the 1870s did the practice gain real power. Without government troops to end strikes, factory owners took union complaints more seriously. Unions began to gain many successes through collective bargaining and eventually became important political powers themselves.

Political and Cultural Developments, 1815-1848

BELIEFS OF BRITISH CONSERVATISM

Conservatives, also called "Tories" because most of the movement's original followers came from the Tory Party, promoted traditional rule by elites, private ownership of property and businesses, and strong defense systems. In 1830, John Wilson Croker coined the name "conservatives" to describe the movement. After the Reform Act of 1832 extended voting rights to the middle class, the conservative movement gained supporters. With liberals in control of Parliament throughout much of the mid-1800s, conservatives served as the primary opponents of reform, usually without much success. They believed Great Britain was changing too much, too fast. Their beliefs survived and influenced the creation of the Conservative Party.

EVOLUTION OF THE CONSERVATIVE PARTY IN GREAT BRITAIN

After the passage of the Reform Act of 1832, many followers of conservative philosophies began forming "conservative associations" to express their views and organize resistance against reforms. Conservative Prime Minister Robert Peel began to refer to the Tory Party as the Conservative Party in 1834, though both names continued to be used for many years. The Conservatives maintained a strong voice of opposition in Parliament until disagreements over the protectionist Corn Laws split the party in 1846. The Conservative Party remained politically weak until Prime Minister Benjamin Disraeli reorganized and reenergized the party in 1868. Disraeli convinced the Conservatives to embrace some reforms that balanced human rights issues, such as extreme poverty, while still maintaining traditional values of legalism and strong defense. In this way, the Conservatives moved slightly to the center and attracted new middle-class supporters.

BRITISH LIBERALISM

British liberalism grew out of Enlightenment views of equality. It sought to protect individual rights and civil liberties through a series of reforms that challenged traditional British political practices. Liberals wanted to greatly expand democracy by granting the right to vote to the middle class and non-landowners. They also strongly opposed slavery, which was still widely practiced in the British colonies at the time, and led the abolitionist movement. Liberals also called for reforms to balance income inequality and bring about greater social equality in a country still strongly bound by traditional class divisions. Liberals relied upon momentum from the Enlightenment to win supporters.

POLITICAL REFORMS ACHIEVED BY BRITISH LIBERALS

- 1829 — Catholic Emancipation Act: allowed Catholics to serve in Parliament after acknowledging Britain's Protestant monarchy.
- 1832 — Reform Act: reallocated seats in the House of Commons to better balance representation of less-densely populated rural areas with more populated urban regions; expanded voting rights of the middle class by lowering the amount of property needed to vote.
- 1833 — Factory Act: implemented limits on working hours and conditions for women and children; outlined measures for the enforcement of regulations.
- 1833 — Slavery Abolition Act: abolished slavery in Great Britain and most of its colonies.

- 1833 — Approved government funding for voluntary schools run by charities and religious organizations; provided first step towards some type of public education.
- 1846 — Repealed protectionist Corn Laws; lowered prices of corn goods for common citizens.

FORMATION OF THE LIBERAL PARTY OF GREAT BRITAIN

The Liberal Party emerged first as a reformist branch of the Whig Party, which often allied itself with Radicals on issues. John Russell first referred to the reformers as the Liberal Party in 1839. Many historians mark 1846 as the real emergence of the Liberal Party, when Russell became prime minister. However, the Liberal Party was not officially recognized as a political entity until Prime Minister William Gladstone organized the group in 1868. Under Gladstone, the party succeeded in bringing about a national education system, the legalization of union activities, judicial reform, expansion of the vote to the working class, and the secret ballot. Liberals also tried to democratize the military by abolishing the practice of purchasing commissions.

CHARTIST MOVEMENT

The Chartist movement marked an attempt by a group of radicals to give greater political voice to the working classes. Some of its most influential leaders included William Lovett, James Bronterre O'Brien, and Feargus O'Connor. The group first officially organized as the Workingmen's Association in 1836. The nickname "Chartists" comes from the People's Charter that they wrote in 1838 to outline their reform goals. These goals included:

- universal manhood suffrage
- equal electoral districts
- vote by ballot
- annually elected Parliaments
- salaries for members of Parliament
- abolition of the property qualifications for membership in Parliament

The movement received a huge boost from the economic depression of 1837-38, but declined by the early 1840s. Economic improvement, Parliament reforms, and infighting among Chartist leaders prevented the movement from developing into a wide-scale political revolution. Eventually, however, Parliament came to adopt the Chartist goals.

AFFECT OF LIBERAL REFORMS ON BRITISH COLONIES

Facing colonial unrest and rising calls for American-style revolutions, British reformers sought compromises to keep colonies part of the British empire while allowing them greater self-rule.

- By the early 1800s, many Canadians were calling for independence. After several failed experiments that tried to balance Canada's French and British cultures, the nation was organized as the Dominion of Canada. Each Canadian province also had its own legislative government, while the Dominion Parliament operated independently of London's Parliament. The Canadian model became a blueprint for the British Commonwealth.
- Australia, originally used as a British penal colony, had evolved into a lawless outpost by the early 1800s. In the 1830s, Great Britain, seeking to restore order to the area, began establishing independent colonial governments across the continent, which eventually united as the self-governing Commonwealth of Australia.

- British officials also sought Australia's resource-rich neighbor New Zealand. Rather than take the land by force, British officials signed an 1840 treaty with the native Maori people that established New Zealand as another self-governing colony in the British Commonwealth.

PHILOSOPHIES AND TACTICS OF NATIONALIST AND REACTIONARY MOVEMENTS

Following the Napoleonic era and the Congress of Vienna, reactionaries who wanted to undo democratic reforms of the late 1700s arose in many countries. They rejected Enlightenment ideas as dangerous and wanted to return to the traditions of absolute monarchy. One of leading reactionaries was Prince Metternich of Austria, whose influence was so great that some historians refer to the era following Napoleon as the Age of Metternich. He and his allies strongly opposed liberal reformers, such as those in Great Britain, who wanted to spread Enlightenment ideas throughout Europe. Such ideas were very popular among nationalist groups calling for self-rule. The reactionaries tried to limit liberal influence by suppressing the press and public speech. Metternich also established investigative commissions to monitor and suppress liberal and nationalist groups and then convinced most member nations of the Concert of Europe to follow suit. Rather than end nationalist movements, however, such oppressive tactics merely drove nationalist leaders underground where, convinced them that compromise with reactionaries was impossible, they plotted violent revolution.

GEO-POLITICAL DEVELOPMENTS AND THE RISE OF NATIONALIST MOVEMENTS

The Congress of Vienna and the establishment of the Concert of Europe appeared to have restored traditional rule to Europe. However, the growth of the United States and reforms within Great Britain encouraged many nationalists groups to believe that independence was possible. British officials walked a fine line, encouraging the spread of liberal ideas while trying not to interfere in the domestic issues of other countries. Great Britain did take a stand for religious freedom by withdrawing from the Holy Alliance in 1823. The early 1820s also saw a failed revolt by the Two Sicilies. When Greece revolted against the Ottoman Empire in 1821, Metternich convinced the reactionaries to stay out of the conflict. The Greek revolutionaries received widespread popular support in Europe, with many nationalists and liberals unofficially coming to their aid. After several years of fighting, diplomats from Great Britain, France, and Russia intervened to convince the Ottomans to grant Greece its independence in 1829. This success gave hope to underground nationalist movements throughout Europe.

SOCIALISM

Socialism grew out of the Industrial Revolution as a reaction to the unequal distribution of wealth that had developed between factory owners and common workers. Socialists believed that economic equality was a natural right, as was political equality. Some reformers came to believe that laissez-faire capitalism was not in the best interest of society, since it seemed to promote a disparate economic system. These reformers advocated socialism, an economic system that would do away with profit motive and competition by having the government own the means of production, such as capital and equipment used to produce goods. The government would redistribute profits from production for the good of all in society. In doing so, the system would do away with wealth-based class divisions.

ROBERT OWEN

Robert Owen was the best-known of the utopian socialists, reformers who tried to create model socialist communities in which all residents shared everything in common, without class divisions. Owen and other utopian socialists were inspired by the ideal community described by Thomas More in Utopia (1519). In 1814, Owen entered into a business partnership with utilitarian Jeremy

Bentham. They tried to implement socialist ideals in their business by redistributing profits back to workers through schools for their children, free housing, and low-cost food and clothing. Owen also encouraged union membership and "villages of cooperation" to provide aid to the unemployed. In 1825, Owen came to the United States to establish utopian societies, the most famous of which was New Harmony, Indiana. Although Owen's utopian village model was not widely copied, his ideas influenced socialists and labor reformers throughout the 1800s.

KARL MARX

Although Karl Marx was involved with the socialist movement in Germany, he differed with many leaders of the movement. In addition to viewing utopian socialism as unrealistic, he thought that other socialist reformers were not willing to go far enough in challenging the system. He also believed that all great changes in history developed from revolutions against economic conditions, conflicts he called "class struggles." Marx believed that the capitalist age was leading to a new revolution between the owners of the means of production ("bourgeoisie") and the workers ("proletariat"). The bourgeoisie gained the majority of wealth from the labor of the proletariat. As the income gap between the bourgeoisie and proletariat increased, workers would eventually revolt and overthrow capitalism in order to create a classless society in which everyone would contribute what they could and receive only what they needed: "From each according to his abilities, to each according to his needs." His ideas, published in The Communist Manifesto (1848) (co-authored by Friedrich Engels), shaped all socialist movements that followed.

SOCIALISM VS. COMMUNISM

Socialism refers to the basic theory of a government's owning the means of production in order to ensure that profits and wealth are redistributed for the benefit of all citizens. Socialism may take place on various levels, including local control (such as in utopian villages) or limited federal ownership of certain businesses (such as fuel or other vital natural resources), which allows for some degree of private ownership. Communism, sometimes called "authoritarian socialism," involves a system in which there is no private ownership and the government completely controls all means of production and all economic planning. Based on Marx's predictions in The Communist Manifesto, most Marxists believed that communism would be established after violent revolution by the proletariat. They anticipated that after workers overthrew capitalist society, they would then have to establish a "dictatorship of the proletariat" until all people came to accept the benefits of "pure communism," or the perfect classless society.

POLITICAL GOALS OF DEMOCRATIC SOCIALISM

Democratic socialists believed in the ideas of the classless society but thought that change could come about gradually and democratically rather than through violent and sudden revolution. They wanted to educate the public about the advantages of socialism so that voters would elect socialist leaders. These leaders would slowly shift the economy from capitalist to socialist by buying the means of production and fairly reimbursing owners for the materials. Unlike authoritarian socialism (communism), democratic socialism allows individuals to own private property and gives citizens the opportunity for a voice in setting economic policy through the election of public officials. Democratic socialism became the preferred model of socialism in western Europe.

EVENTS IN FRANCE THAT DEVELOPED INTO REVOLUTION

The Congress of Vienna restored Bourbon rule by naming Louis XVIII king of France. The pragmatic Louis knew that many French citizens still opposed the old monarchy. Fearing new radical revolts, Louis tried to support of the changes and reforms of the French Revolution. In addition to accepting a constitution that limited monarchical powers, he tried to balance conservative and liberal factions within France. When Louis died in 1824, his brother, Charles, ascended to the throne. Unlike Louis,

Charles was an outspoken advocate for the return to absolute monarchy. He tried to abolish many reforms that had been passed after 1789. He also tried to increase taxes on common people in order to reimburse nobles for lands that had been seized and sold to peasants after the French Revolution. Charles's actions outraged both liberals and radicals, who joined forces to protest. Their protests became a full-scale revolt in July 1830. Within days, the revolutionaries had seized control of Paris. Charles abdicated the throne and fled to England.

Dissent in France Inspired Revolutions

Despite efforts by Prince Metternich and other absolute monarchists to suppress liberalism and nationalism, such ideas secretly thrived. Just as the French Revolution had inspired reforms, French resistance to a return of absolute monarchy inspired opposition movements. (Metternich once said, "When France sneezes, Europe catches cold.") Two of the most significant revolts developed in Belgium and Poland. The Congress of Vienna had united the Austrian Netherlands (with a majority population of ethnic Belgians) and the kingdom of Holland under Dutch rule. The Belgians resented control by the Dutch. After the successful French uprising in 1830, Belgians rose up and demanded independence. Polish citizens tried to do the same. Although Poland had ceased to exist after the various partitions split its lands between Austria, Prussia, and Russia, the Polish people longed to reestablish their own nation. Inspired by French citizens, Poles in Russia rose up and demanded independence.

Effects of the Revolutions of 1830

In France, the revolution resulted in the election of a new king, Bourbon liberal Louis Philippe. His appointment marked a compromise between revolutionaries and traditionalists in that the monarch required the approval of Parliament in order to lead. Louis Philippe referred to his position as "citizen king," reflecting a new concept of democratically-approved monarchy. The Belgian revolution resulted in the separation of Belgium from Holland to become an independent country in 1831. The Polish revolution failed miserably. Crushed by the Russian military, many Poles immigrated to western Europe and the United States.

Limits of Liberalism Revealed by the Revolutions of 1830

Although considered a liberal, Louis Philippe failed to fulfill most liberal goals. Many of his policies strengthened the political and economic power of the upper classes. He refused to allow workers to organize labor unions. He also supported high tariffs that benefited industrialists but harmed peasants and workers due to the high prices that followed. The Polish rebels hoped that liberals from other nations would come to their aid, but none did. Overall, the limited success of the 1830 revolutions set the stage for the revolutions that would develop in the 1840s.

Influence of Political Theories on the Outbreak of Multiple European Revolutions

The revolutions of 1848 marked the culmination of years of discontent fueled by new political and economic theories. Economic recessions and income inequality gave rise to growing dissent among workers, many of whom embraced socialist theories. Utopian socialists gained many followers with their ideas about creating a perfect classless society. Even among the middle classes, discontent was mounting in countries where the nobility still ruled. Many industrialists and others gaining wealth from the new economy wanted to expand their political influence. Support for popular democracy and universal manhood suffrage spread. In states still run by absolute monarchs, the people increased calls for constitutional government. In many ways, 1848 marked a new wave of post-Enlightenment revolutions.

Initial Outbreak of Revolution in 1848

By 1848, the French citizenry was vocally disgruntled over corruption in Louis Philippe's government and by economic recession. In February of that year, Louis Philippe issued a decree limiting free speech in an effort to suppress criticism. The citizens responded by rioting in Paris, where they were joined by French troops. Louis Philippe resigned and fled to England. Proclaiming a Second Republic, reformers established a new government that was inspired by socialism. The republican government took an active role in combating the recession by establishing "national workshops" to provide jobs for the unemployed. The government also called for a new constitution and a new National Assembly to be elected through universal manhood suffrage. The new National Assembly, dominated by conservatives, voted to end the national workshops, sparking more riots that ended with the arrest, execution, or banishment of all socialists from France.

Spread of Revolutions of 1848

The initial revolution in France that ended with the Second Republic inspired other rebellions throughout Europe. Many of the protests followed similar patterns in which university students initially led calls for reform and then joined forces with workers to riot. In Austria, riots challenged not only the form of government, but also the heavy-handed leadership of Prince Metternich, who was forced to resign. Inspired by this seeming success, Italian nationalists tried to replace their monarchs with constitutional governments. The rebels succeeded at first, but eventually Austrian forces restored Hapsburg control in the north, while French forces restored Vatican control in Rome. Prussia and the German states also rebelled against Hapsburg rule. Prussian king Frederick William IV agreed to a constitutional monarchy. Members of the German national assembly tried to unite their states, but they could never agree on a new government. Their revolution fell apart after Frederick William IV refused an offer to lead the German states, dissolved the Prussian assembly, and reneged on his promise of constitutional monarchy.

Short-Term and Long-Term Effects of the Revolutions of 1848

Short-term:

- Establishment of the Second French Republic
- Resignation of Austrian Prince Metternich
- Exposure of the need for continued reforms in Austria, Italy, and Prussia
- Large-scale German emigration to the United States to avoid persecution following failed revolutions

Long-term:

- Creation of a new French empire
- Weakening of support for a return to absolute monarchy
- Eventual spread of political and economic reforms
- Eventual unification of German states
- Eventual unification of Italian states
- Spread of power among labor unions
- Expansion of universal manhood suffrage

Politics and Diplomacy in the Age of Nationalism, 1850-1914

Italian Nationalist Movements

Collectively, the Italian nationalist movements are known as the risorgimento ("resurgence"). Although they shared the same goals of unification and liberal reform, most Italian nationalists had to work independently through secret societies due to government oppression. The most influential secret nationalist group was the Carbonari, led by Giuseppe Mazzini. In 1831, Mazzini began openly calling for Italians to join forces in a Young Italy movement. His goal was to unite all of the Italian states in a republic that was ruled by "neither pope nor king." Mazzini was one of the major leaders of the 1848 revolution. When nationalists ousted the pope in Rome, Mazzini and two other leaders took control of establishing a Roman republican government. Though the inability of the movement to maintain their gains revealed weaknesses in the rebellion, it did not end support for unification.

Shifting of the Tactics of the Italian Nationalists

Despite the fact that the 1848 revolution failed to unify Italy permanently, the revolution actually increased support for unification. Nationalists began to rethink their strategy to focus on diplomatic negotiations rather than violent and sudden overthrow. Many nationalists looked to Sardinia for inspiration. By 1849, Sardinia was the only Italian state ruled by a constitutional monarchy under King Victor Emmanuel II. Many liberal reformers in Sardinia's parliament hoped to unite all Italian states under their existing government through slow acquisition. While Victor Emmanuel was not a huge supporter of liberal reforms, he did support this unification strategy, as it would increase his own power. Suddenly, Sardinia became the most important of the Italian states.

Italian Unification

Camillo Benso di Cavour

Camillo Benso di Cavour was chief minister of Sardinia. Under the state's parliamentary government, he held more real power than the king. Cavour used his power to modernize Sardinia and move in the direction of Italian unification. Cavour strengthened the Sardinian army, limited the church's role in government, and modernized the economy by establishing banks, building factories, expanding railroads, and increasing trade. He expanded diplomatic ties by allying with France and Great Britain in the Crimean War and helped negotiate the peace treaty that ended the war. In 1858, Cavour met with French Emperor Napoleon III to form an alliance against Austria, which controlled many Italian states at the time. Cavour planned to draw Austria into war, at which time French forces would aid Sardinia. He hoped that once war began, nationalists in the Austrian-controlled Italian states would revolt. All went according to plan, until Prussia threatened to join Austria, forcing France to withdraw. Although Sardinia was required to sign a peace agreement with Austria, the rebellions in the northern Italian states continued.

Giuseppe Garibaldi

After war with Austria failed to result in unification, Cavour switched tactics and turned to rebels in the kingdom of the Two Sicilies (made up of the southern half of the Italian Peninsula and the island of Sicily). Nationalist Giuseppe Garibaldi led the movement in Sicily. Backed by Cavour, Garibaldi began organizing an army called the "Expedition of the Thousand," which took control of Sicily in 1860 and then attacked the mainland, captured Naples, and began to advance northward. As Garibaldi captured territory and gained popular support, Cavour began to fear that the Sicilians would create their own unified government that would replace Sardinian power. Cavour organized his own army to halt Garibaldi's advance. Finally, all parties negotiated an end to fighting. Over the next several years, the Italian states held plebiscites that approved joining a unified Italian constitutional monarchy under Victor Emmanuel II.

German Unification

Prussia

Prussia was a leading member of the German Confederation created by the Congress of Vienna. Prussia and Austria vied for influence over the German states. As German nationalism increased, many Germans sided more with Prussian than Austrian leadership. The population of Prussia was almost entirely Germanic, while the population of Austria was much more diverse and less united around nationalist sentiments. Nationalist movements in the Austrian-controlled Italian states and the Balkans diverted much of the Austrian leaders' attention south and eastward. As a result, Prussia focused its efforts on Germany, indicating support for eventual unification.

Zollverein

For several years following the Congress of Vienna, the German economy was negatively impacted by high tariffs between the states. Landowners known as the Junkers joined forces with merchants and manufacturers to advocate free trade between the states. Their efforts eventually resulted in the formation of a customs union called the Zollverein in 1834. By 1854, all German states except for Austria had joined the Zollverein, which set economic policies for all members. Under Zollverein influence, German manufacturing and trade increased. The success of the group led to increased support for a unified political system in addition to a unified economic system.

Otto von Bismark

Although the revolution of 1848 failed to create a unified Germanic state, support for unification ran high. Austria continued to be the major impediment to unification. After William I became king of Prussia in 1861, he appointed Otto von Bismark head of his cabinet. Bismark came to dominate the Prussian government with an ambitious plan to strengthen the army and unify the German states. When the Prussian parliament refused to approve taxes for military expansion, Bismark ignored the constitution and implemented tax increases and collections on his own. Although opponents organized protests, many nationalists supported Bismark's goals. He hoped to gain enough military successes to silence his domestic opponents and create a unified country.

Major Wars Instigated by Bismark

- Danish War — When Denmark tried to annex the heavily Germanic duchy of Schleswig, Prussia and Austria joined forces to defeat the Danes in 1864. Afterward, Austrian officials argued for Schleswig and its neighboring duchy, Holstein, to become one German state. Prussia refused and took control of Schleswig, while Austria gained Holstein.
- Seven Weeks' War — Bismark began preparing his army for war against Austria, while convincing France to remain neutral and forging an alliance with Italy. In 1866, Bismark goaded Austria into declaring war over control of Schleswig and Holstein. Prussia quickly defeated Austria. The old German Confederation was dissolved, and a new North German Confederation, dominated by Prussia, was formed.
- Franco-Prussian War — Fearing threats to their eastern border, French officials tried to prevent southern German states from joining the new German Confederation. To end French influence, Bismark manipulated France into declaring war in 1870. Prussia won decisively, forcing the resignation of Napoleon III and occupying much of France.

Austria-Hungary

Hungarian uprisings of 1848

Hungary was one of the largest regions within Austria, but many Hungarians resented Austrian rule. Most Hungarians were descended from the Magyars, a nomadic tribe that had fled Russia and Romania in the 900s. Culturally and linguistically, the Hungarians were very different from other Austrians. During the early 1800s, a nationalist movement arose among the Hungarians. In 1848, nationalist leader Lajos Kossuth led a revolt for Hungarian independence that initially gained success. In 1849, the Hungarian Diet elected Kossuth as "responsible governor president." Austria, joined by Russian forces that feared the spread of revolution into its lands, soon put down the revolution, and Kossuth fled to Turkey. Still, Hungarian nationalists continued to press for independence.

Dual Monarchy

Following the Seven Weeks' War, a weakened Austria acceded to Hungarian calls for independence by forming the Dual Monarchy, better known as Austria-Hungary. Leaders hoped the move would weaken support for complete Hungarian independence while granting greater sovereignty to the region. Under this arrangement, Austria and Hungary had separate parliaments but shared a common monarch (Francis Joseph I), as well as common ministries that controlled war, finances, and foreign affairs for all of Austria-Hungary. Thus the two sides benefited from a common military and diplomatic corps. They also benefited from an economic balance between their strengths and weaknesses. The primarily agricultural Hungary exchanged goods and resources with the heavily industrial Austria.

Domestic challenges Austria-Hungary

The Dual Monarchy did little to suppress nationalist movements among the diverse peoples who lived within Austria-Hungary, such as Czechs, Slovaks, Serbs, Croats, Romanians, Poles, Slovenes, and Ukrainians, all of whom wanted some form of independence and saw little benefits from the new organization. Although the Dual Monarchy had helped ease some calls for complete Hungarian independence, the Hungarians and Austrians continued to be divided by culture and language, leading to resentment. Many Hungarians believed that the Austrians considered themselves a superior people (and many Austrian leaders did). Over time, many Hungarians also came to feel that Austria was gaining greater economic benefits from the arrangement.

Russian Empire vs. the major powers of western Europe

Russia was by far the largest European country in terms of territory and population, with extensive natural resources. Politically, it was the major dominant power of eastern Europe. However, despite its size and influence, Russia lagged far behind the rest of Europe economically. While western Europe was reaping the benefits of the Industrial Revolution, Russia remained a backward agricultural nation dependent upon serf labor. Many of its natural resources remained untapped because they were trapped beneath layers of ice that covered much of the country. These ice flows also locked up Russian ports during the winter months, limiting the country's ability to trade year-round. Russia's large size and diverse population meant that the central government had much less control over local governments than did western European governments. Many Russians lived in relative isolation from one another and the rest of the world. For this reason, liberal reforms gained little influence over the Russian government, which remained dominated by the powerful czar.

Russification program

By the 1830s, some well-educated Russian intellectuals were beginning to embrace western liberal ideas. At the same time, nationalist movements were gaining ground among Russian minorities, especially Poles and Finns. To counteract these trends, Czar Nicholas I began the Russification program to force all citizens of the empire to accept Russian culture. He imposed laws requiring people within Russian-controlled lands to speak Russian, join the Orthodox Church, and follow Russian traditions. Other languages, faiths, and ethnic customs were outlawed. Russification angered many nationalists and increased resentment against the centralized government.

Russia's Main Foreign Policy Goals

Throughout much of the early 1800s, Russian foreign policy was designed to achieve two main goals:

1. To increase Russian influence among Slavic peoples in the Balkans region to help gain access to westward trade routes through the region. To this end, the Russian government promoted Pan-Slavism, a movement to unite all Slavic-speaking peoples under Russian leadership. Ironically, Russia pursued this foreign policy even while domestically trying to suppress Slavic culture through Russification.
2. To expand Russian trade and influence to the east and south. To this end, Russia took advantage of weaknesses in Asia to gain control of lands north of Manchuria. Southward, Russia conquered some lands held by the Ottoman Empire, but defeat in the Crimean War halted this advance.

Reforms of Czar Alexander II

Although Alexander II supported czar autocracy, he wanted to modernize his country. His major reforms included:

- The Emancipation Edict: This law freed all serfs from bondage, effectively freeing the Russian economy from dependence upon agricultural peasant labor; factory owners now had access to low-wage workers; the government bought land from many nobles and resold tracts to farmers, creating a small farming class. Although many former peasants still lived in poverty under the new system, they had a little more freedom and contributed to a vast improvement of the Russian economy.
- Reorganization of local governments: This allowed for the election of local leaders, called zemstvos, for rural districts and councils for provinces and counties; peasants were given the right to vote, although the system still gave more weight to the votes of nobles.
- Restructuring of criminal and civil courts after western models, including limiting powers of the secret police.
- Expansion of education.
- Reduction of required military service from 25 to 6 years, freeing more labor for other pursuits.

Radicalism in Russia

Alexander's reforms faced criticism from many factions. Nobles worried that their power was endangered. Liberals felt that the reforms did not go far enough and hoped for continued reforms. Several radical groups emerged, demanding greater, faster change. The most radical were the nihilists (meaning "nothing"), who believed true change could come about only by overthrowing the entire existing structure and starting a new government from scratch. One radical group that called themselves the Populists arose in the 1870s and encouraged its largely upper-class members to live among peasants in order to understand their suffering. The Populists wanted to seize all noble lands and redistribute them to peasants. Some Populists formed a terrorist organization called the People's Will to plot a violent overthrow of the government. After several failed attempts, they finally succeeded in murdering Alexander II in 1881.

Government's Response to Radicalism

The murder of Alexander II led to a backlash against reform. The next two czars, Alexander III and Nicholas II, blamed liberalism for Alexander's death and vowed to stamp out its influence. They reversed many of Alexander II's reforms and instead tightened government control over the press, church, and education. They expanded the powers of the secret police and increased Russification programs. Linking Jews to radical groups, they encouraged anti-Semitic riots called pogroms that resulted in the death, arrest, or exile of many Russian Jews. Government repression succeeded temporarily in reversing modernization, but it also met with surprisingly resilient resistance. Former peasants who were now wage-workers refused to return to serfdom. Many joined socialist groups that slowly worked for change.

Louis Napoleon

The Second French Republic called for universal manhood suffrage and the election of a president who would be allowed to serve only one four-year term. Most revolutionaries expected a republican leader to be elected president, but instead the citizenry elected Napoleon Bonaparte's nephew, Louis Napoleon. Louis built popular support among soldiers, Catholics, and those nostalgic for Bonaparte's leadership. However, Louis really wanted to restore his uncle's empire. He tried and failed to get the National Assembly to amend the constitution to allow him to serve more than one term. In 1851, Louis staged a coup, arresting 70 opposition members of the assembly. To avoid civil war, he called for a plebiscite to support or reject his rule. By promising to restore order, he won overwhelmingly. Louis instituted a new constitution that established a Second French Empire. He became Emperor Napoleon III. While the emperor tried to modernize the economy, he also suppressed individual rights, creating more of a dictatorship than a democracy.

Crimean War

The Crimean War began as a dispute between Russia and the Ottoman Empire but soon spread to western Europe. To improve his power and status across Europe, Napoleon III strengthened ties with Great Britain and the Ottomans. Conflict erupted between Russia and the Ottoman Empire when Russia claimed authority over parts of the Ottoman-controlled Palestine that housed many Orthodox Christians. France and Great Britain promised to support its Ottoman allies. All three powers declared war on Russia in 1854, sparking the Crimean War (so-called because most fighting took place on Russia's Crimean Peninsula). The war lasted two years and resulted in large numbers of casualties on all sides. The war exposed Russia's need to modernize its military, as the western forces had gained advantages from industrialization. Though Russia finally lost the war, it ceded little territory. Napoleon III gained influence and prestige. Among the most significant outcomes of the war were advances in medicine as field hospitals treated the wounded. (Nurse Florence Nightingale came to fame during this war.)

Developments in France under the Third Republic

Disputes with the French government prevented the adoption of a new constitution until 1875. The Third Republic established a two-house legislature made up of an indirectly elected Senate and a directly elected Chamber of Deputies. The legislature elected the president, who served one seven-year term. The republican government lasted for more than 70 years, but it was often limited in its effectiveness by infighting. Two major reforms of the late 1800s involved legalizing labor unions and establishing free public education for all children under age 13. Meanwhile, radicals and anarchists began to undermine the government, emboldened by several scandals during the 1890s. The failed Panama Canal project weakened the French economy. The unjust treason conviction of Jewish soldier Alfred Dreyfus in 1894 also divided the country. Although the republican government survived, it could never fully unify the country.

International Working Men's Association

The International Working Men's Association, also called the First International, was a socialist labor organization founded by Karl Marx and his followers in 1864. Marx wanted to use the organization to unite workers and bring about the proletariat revolution that he felt was necessary to defeat capitalism. Marx's disorganized group eventually disbanded. After his death in 1889, however, his followers formed a Second International Working Men's Association. As with the first group, the Second International failed to thrive due to infighting between moderate and radical socialists who could never agree on tactics to bring about their ultimate goal of worker revolution.

SDP in Germany

Although socialist leader Karl Marx was German, his country was relatively late to industrialize. Under Bismark, the nation quickly caught up and surpassed many of its western rivals. Bismark encouraged the formation of cartels, or groups of companies, to regulate prices and tightly control the market. Many workers, however, complained that the cartels held down wages. Socialists encouraged government control over industry to improve wages and working conditions. In 1869, socialist leaders banded together to form the Social Democrat Party, which quickly gained popularity among workers. By 1877, the SDP held 12 positions in the Reichstag, the legislative assembly. The upper house, called the Bundesrat, was dominated by nobles who blocked socialist reforms even as the SDP gained popularity.

Bismark's Response to Socialism

Bismark greatly feared the rise of socialism as a threat to his own power and that of the kaiser. As members of the Social Democratic Party gained seats in the legislature, Bismark looked for opportunities to weaken the party. After two different people tried to assassinate the kaiser in 1878, Bismark accused the Social Democrats of being behind the plots (even though he knew they had no involvement). Using the crises as justification, Bismark and the Bundesrat dissolved the SDP-heavy Reichstag, called for new elections, banned socialist meetings, and censored socialist writings. Despite these efforts, voters reelected SDP leaders. Finally, seeing how well the socialists were swaying workers, Bismark changed tactics and issued a series of reforms to appease workers and limit the appeal of socialism. He implemented employer-paid insurance for worker illness or accidents, holiday pay, pension plans, and limitations on work hours. The reforms succeeded in weakening the appeal of socialism and inspired other governments to issue their own similar reforms.

Affect of Franco-Prussian War on Napoleon III's Reign

Napoleon III feared the unification of the German states under Prussian rule, as it might threaten France's borders. As Otto von Bismark began working toward that goal, Napoleon III tried to prepare for the possibility of war. His failed efforts to expand the draft revealed weakening support for his leadership. But Napoleon allowed Bismark to trick him into declaring war. The ill-prepared French forces were overwhelmed by the superior Prussian forces. Trying to exhibit leadership, Napoleon III took control over the French army himself. When he was captured by Prussian forces, the French National Assembly took advantage of his absence to dissolve the Second Empire and establish the Third Republic. Fighting continued until Paris fell in January 1871, but Napoleon III's reign was over.

Rebellion of Parisians against the French Government

The Treaty of Frankfurt, which formally ended the Franco-Prussian War, issued harsh punishments against France for causing the war. The treaty required France to surrender control of Alsace and parts of Lorraine and to pay huge reparations to Germany. The treaty widened a political rift in

France, as most republicans wanted to reject the treaty, but many monarchists wanted to accept it to ensure peace. Most French citizens wanted peace, so they elected a National Assembly that supported the treaty. The strongly republican Parisians, who had borne the brunt of the fighting, refused to accept the treaty. In March 1871, a group of radical republican Parisians tried to establish a new city government called the Commune. The Parisians advocated the end of centralized French government and Catholic influence over the state. The French government responded by sending troops into the city. More than 20,000 Parisians were killed before troops defeated the Communards.

German Empire

The Prussian victory against France cleared the way for unification. On January 18, 1871, representatives of the allied German states met at Versailles to declare the formation of the German Empire. It would include all of the former German states except Austria. Prussian King William I became the first German Emperor, or kaiser, with Otto von Bismark as chancellor (equivalent to prime minister). The constitution organized Germany as a federation made up of 25 states. Each state had its own government in charge of education, local law enforcement, and local taxation. The federal government was in charge of national defense, foreign affairs, and interstate and international commerce. The kaiser appointed the chancellor and led the military in times of war; he also had the right to declare defensive wars on his own and offensive wars with legislative approval. The two-house legislature consisted of the Bundesrat, an upper council made up of 58 appointed members, and the Reichstag, a lower assembly made up of 400 members elected by universal manhood suffrage.

German Constitution and Prussian Domination of Germany

Prussia had been the leading force among the German states for some time and led the way in unification efforts. The constitution assured that this influence would continue. Austria, Prussia's main rival, was not even included in the German Confederation. Berlin, Prussia's former capital, became the capital city for all of Germany. The king of Prussia became the kaiser of the new Germany. The constitution gave Prussia the most delegates in the Bundesrat, appointed by local Prussian leaders. As the state with the greatest population, Prussia also earned the most seats in the popularly-elected Reichstag. For all practical purposes, the new Germany was an extension of Prussian power.

Kulturkampf

Bismark grew increasingly frustrated by resistance to his policies from non-Prussian legislators, especially members of the Centre Party. Because many members of the Centre Party were also Catholic, the Protestant Bismark began to associate the Catholic Church with disloyalty. Arguing that Catholic loyalty to the pope undermined patriotism towards the state, Bismark instituted Kulturkampf ("cultural struggle") to weaken Catholic influence. Bismark expelled all Jesuits from Germany, forbade clergy from taking public political stances on issues, required Catholic clergy to attend German schools, and confiscated church property. He even broke diplomatic ties with the Vatican. The Kulturkampf led to outrage, and many non-Catholics joined forces in protest. The Centre Party actually gained seats in the legislature. By 1887, Bismark had repealed the Kulturkampf policies, re-established diplomatic ties with the Vatican, and forged an alliance with the Centre Party against the socialists.

Resignation of Otto von Bismark

Kaiser William had effectively ceded power to Chancellor Bismark. When William died in 1888, followed shortly after by his son, his grandson, William II, became kaiser. William II was only 29 and held very strong views about the monarchy. He believed that the kaiser, not the chancellor, should run the German government. Specifically, he believed that Bismark held too much power and had divided the country with many of his policies. As William II began increasing his own power and decreasing that of the chancellor, Bismark's resentment grew. After socialists gained more legislative seats in the elections of 1890, Bismark proposed convening the Bundesrat to write a new constitution. William opposed this plan. Using a tactic that had worked with William I, Bismark threatened to resign, expecting the kaiser to refuse. Instead, William II gladly accepted Bismark's resignation. Under William II, Germany grew into a true parliamentary democracy, its military and economy expanded, and it came to rival Great Britain as the leading power of Europe.

Economy, Culture, and Imperialism, 1850-1914

DEMOGRAPHIC CHANGES

DEMOGRAPHIC CHANGES IN HOUSING AND WORK PATTERNS

The Industrial Revolution led to major demographic and workforce shifts during the 1800s. The greatest change was the rise in urbanization, as people flocked from farms to cities in search of factory-related work. Cities based upon the new industrial economy grew at a faster rate than older, traditional urban areas. In 1800, no cities in Western Civilization had reached a population of 1 million. By 1900, several had, including Berlin, London, New York, and Paris. By the late 1800s, the geographic expansion of cities, coupled with an increasing middle class, gave rise to residential areas outside of central cities, which became known as suburbs. Public transportation allowed many people to own homes in the suburbs and commute to work, a trend that would increase in the 1900s. Meanwhile, most city-dwellers in the 1800s lived in rented apartments.

CHANGES IN LITERACY RATES

Literacy rates increased dramatically in the 1800s due to the needs of industry. Even though many children went to work in factories at a young age, industrialists supported programs to promote literacy among workers. The new economy required the ability to read instructions, often including complicated engineering or scientific information. Industrialists believed that a well-educated workforce promoted economic advancement. Also, the ideals of equality fostered by the American and French revolutions extended into education. Not only did some leaders argue that basic education was a right that governments should provide, but they also argued that democracy required educated citizens who could cast informed votes. As literacy rates rose, so too did popular publishing, and paperback novels and newspapers flourished.

DEMOGRAPHIC CHANGES IN FAMILY LIFE

Prior to the Industrial Revolution, all family members contributed economically to the household. Work was centered on the home. As the income of middle-class families increased, a gender division of labor developed. Husbands left the household to earn money while wives stayed home to tend to domestic matters, developing a "cult of domesticity." New inventions made this work easier so that middle-class mothers could focus more attention on childrearing. Ironically, as middle-class families with means to support many children increased, birth rates among the middle class decreased, as women learned more about family planning. Many families chose to focus more resources on fewer children. Lower income families still tended to have more children, and poor mothers tended to work outside the home more often than those of the middle and upper classes, which only widened the gap between demographic and social classes.

DEMOGRAPHIC CHANGES IN RATES OF DISEASE

The rapid increase in urban populations led to crowded conditions in most cities, which initially had no sewer or plumbing systems. The build-up of human waste, garbage, and pollutants from unregulated factories led to increases in disease. The crowded conditions also meant that communicable diseases spread much faster and often with deadlier results than ever before. Rates of such diseases as cholera and typhus increased throughout much of the century. After 1870, many cities finally began to install plumbing and sewage systems, establishing sanitation departments to dispose of garbage, and improving architecture to better regulate indoor temperatures. Advances in medicine also enabled doctors to treat communicable diseases more effectively, slowing the rates at which they spread. By 1900, the rates of many diseases were still much higher than they had been in 1800, but they were slowly coming down from their peaks in the mid-1800s.

Affect of Industrialization on the Global Economy

Industrialization spurred imperialism, expanded global trade, and increased competition between nations. Because industrialized nations competed with one another, they did not want to purchase the raw materials needed for their new economies from their rivals. Such a situation would make them both indebted to and dependent upon the competitors. Instead, nations increasingly looked for new areas of colonization that contained resources necessary to support industry. Nations also looked to new markets in non-industrialized Asia, Africa, and Latin America as sources for marketing their products. Increasingly, industrial leaders came to believe that they could shape the global markets by changing people's buying habits. Under the guise of "civilizing" other cultures, industrialists encouraged native peoples to buy western-made goods. Increasingly the global economy became linked to global politics. During the long period of relative peace between European nations, economic power and third-party conflicts became the primary means of competition between nations vying for global power.

Affect of the Rise of Stock Markets and Corporations on Global Economies

Prior to industrialization, most businesses were very small, owned and managed by one or two individuals. As industrialization increased, factory owners needed capital to expand production. In order to raise this capital, they often reorganized into corporations that were owned by stock holders and run by expert managers. Corporations allowed for massive expansion of businesses, with a focus on profits for stockholders. With profit as the primary motive, many corporations expanded operations into other nations in order to find the cheapest resources and labor or wider markets in which to sell goods. Stockholders could also buy stocks in corporations centered in other nations, thus globalizing individual interests in companies. In some nations, corporations organized into powerful cartels that controlled every aspect of one industry and often wielded significant political influence.

Advances in Transportation

In the late 1800s, numerous inventors from various countries were working simultaneously to develop faster modes of personal travel than the traditional horse and buggy. Some tried steam-powered carriages, followed by electric ones, with limited commercial success. The gasoline-powered automobile, generally credited to Germans Karl Benz and Gottlieb Daimler in the 1880s, revolutionized transportation. Manufacturers in other countries quickly rushed to copy Benz's model, sparking international competition among automakers, who each tried to improve on the product. Still, automobiles largely remained expensive toys for the wealthy until American business leader Henry Ford began mass-producing relatively low-cost cars on assembly lines. The Model T, introduced in 1908, ushered in the age of the auto for common people. By the end of the 1800s, some inventors were experimenting with travel by air, an idea that many people believed totally impossible until Orville and Wilbur Wright successfully flew the first powered airplane in 1903. Airplane technology advanced slowly until the advent of World War I.

Advances in Urban Infrastructure

Initially, many cities affected by the Industrial Revolution experienced rapid population growth with little change to basic infrastructure, a situation that quickly led to problems. By the mid-1800s, many governments began to implement urban design changes to better accommodate the modern population. Wide boulevards and paved streets replaced narrow dirt roads. Modern tenements replaced multi-family housing structures that had been in use since the medieval era. Steel allowed for the construction of stronger, taller buildings. Trolleys improved public transportation. Gas lights, and then electric lights, allowed for greater mobility at night in safer environments. The construction of sewage systems brought some about of the most significant changes by dramatically reducing the spread of disease. By the end of the century, many cities were setting aside large areas of land for public parks and playgrounds as another way to improve people's quality of life.

Advances in Communication and Entertainment Technology

In 1873, German scientist Heinrich Rudolph Hertz theorized the existence of electromagnetic waves. Simultaneously, British scientist James Clerk Maxwell conducted mathematical studies of electricity and magnetism. Italian scientist Guglielmo Marconi used these studies to develop the "wireless telegraph," which utilized radio waves. Unlike Alexander Graham Bell's telephone, patented in America in 1876, Marconi's device did not require wires. As such, it allowed for the transmission of messages over longer land distances, as well as across oceans. Marconi sent the first radio message across the Atlantic in 1901, ushering in a new era in communications technology that extended into the entertainment sector as radio use became more widespread. American inventor Thomas Edison patented several devices that advanced entertainment technology. The phonograph he invented in 1877 quickly became a home entertainment device and spawned a recording industry later made popular by radio. Edison then sought to combine recorded sound with photography to create motion pictures. In the 1890s, his lab produced the Kinetoscope, which launched the modern movie industry.

Advances in Medical Sciences

- 1850s – Austrian scientist Gregor Mendel discovered key secrets about how genes work; his theories became the foundation for the field of genetics.
- 1863 – Louis Pasteur developed pasteurization, a process for killing bacteria in liquids through heat; the process made drinks and food much safer to consume.
- 1865 – British surgeon Joseph Lister developed antisepsis, the use of chemicals to kill disease-causing germs during surgery; this technique greatly decreased rates of infection among wounded and surgical patients.
- 1880s – Louis Pasteur developed vaccines for anthrax and rabies.
- 1880s – German doctor Robert Koch discovered the bacteria that caused tuberculosis and cholera; Koch's work became the basis for the field of bacteriology, improved sanitation by increasing awareness of how germs spread disease, and promoted better personal hygiene.

Inventions That Affected Daily Life

During the late 1800s, the United States experienced an expansion of industry, science, and invention, a time often referred to as the Second Industrial Revolution. Many of the products made during this time quickly spread throughout the United States and Europe. Some major inventions that affected daily life included:

- 1851 – I.M. Singer's sewing machine; allowed for easier home production of cloth goods
- 1867 – Christopher Sholes's typewriter; enabled easier and faster printing of both commercial and personal communication
- 1879 – Thomas Edison's light bulb; allowed for the safe use of artificial light
- 1880 – James Bonsack's cigarette rolling machine; provided for the mass production of low-cost cigarettes, resulting in a dramatic rise in cigarette smoking throughout the western world
- 1888 – George Eastman's Kodak camera; the first camera simple and small enough to be used by amateur photographers

- 1908 – James Murray Spangler's Hoover vacuum cleaner; made cleaning easier and faster
- 1909 – Leo H. Bakeland's Bakelite plastic; enabled the creation of inexpensive storage containers

Impact of Darwinism

In 1831, naturalist Charles Darwin set off on the HMS Beagle to collect information about animal species. This research formed the basis for his 1859 book On the Origin of Species by Means of Natural Selection, which described his theory of evolution. Observing differences in species and considering Thomas Malthus's theory that plants and animals produce more offspring than the food supply can sustain, Darwin argued that over time species evolve in ways designed to improve their chances of survival. He called this process "natural selection," in which the "fittest," or best-adapted creatures, survive over weaker species. Darwin's theories changed the field of biology and led to controversy, as some individuals adapted his theories to form the concept of social Darwinism, the belief that only the strongest people could survive in modern society. Some followers of social Darwinism interpreted it to mean that the "fittest" of society had a moral obligation to provide for the needs of those less capable of achieving success. Others used it to justify racist policies.

Development in Physics

Physics, the science of matter and energy, emerged as a distinct field from chemistry in the late 1800s after Russian Dmitry Mendeleyev developed the periodic table of elements in 1869. Major advances in physics included:

- 1895 — German physicist Wilhelm Röntgen discovered a powerful form of radiation that he harnessed to invent the X-ray machine.
- 1897 — J.J. Thomson, a British physicist, discovered the electron and developed the theory that subatomic particles are the building materials for all substances in the universe.
- 1890s — French scientists Pierre and Marie Curie experimented with what Marie would come to call "radioactivity," a process by which some elements break down and release energy independently.
- 1900 — Max Planck, a German scientist, developed what would come to be known as quantum theory.
- 1905 — German physicist Albert Einstein developed his special theory of relativity as well as the equation $E = mc^2$ to explain the relationship between energy and mass.
- 1911 — British scientist Ernest Rutherford developed a model of the atom that included the nucleus and protons.

Developments in the Social Sciences

The social sciences, or branches of science that focus mainly on the study of people, evolved in the late 1800s. The social sciences included traditional disciplines such as economics, political science, and history, as well as newer fields such as anthropology, archaeology, psychology, and sociology. Some major developments included:

Anthropology

- 1871 — E.B. Taylor of Great Britain set the standards for the field when he published Primitive Culture, which applied the German concept kultur to beliefs and customs of a society.
- 1890 — James George Frazer of Great Britain published The Golden Bough, which compared and contrasted cultures of different societies, now a standard practice in anthropology.

Sociology

- French philosopher Auguste Comte essentially invented the field of sociology by establishing a scientific method for studying social systems.

Psychology

- 1898 — Russian Ivan Pavlov began his studies of conditional reflexes in humans.
- 1890s — Austrian Sigmund Freud began his studies that would establish the framework for modern psychoanalysis.

Romantic Movement

Romanticism was an artistic movement that included literature, music, and the visual arts. It provided idealized imagery that appealed to emotions more than reason. Major contributors/works included:

Literature

- British poets William Wordsworth, John Keats, and Lord Byron
- Scottish author Sir Walter Scott, Ivanhoe
- German playwright Johann Wolfgang von Goethe, Faust
- Americans James Fenimore Cooper, Last of the Mohicans, and Washington Irving, "The Legend of Sleepy Hollow"
- French historical novelists Alexandre Dumas, The Three Musketeers, and Victor Hugo, The Hunchback of Notre Dame

Music

- Germans Ludwig van Beethoven, Johannes Brahms, Franz Schubert, and Richard Wagner
- Polish-born Frédéric Chopin
- Hungarian Franz Liszt
- Russian Pyotr Ilich Tchaikovsky
- Italian Giuseppe Verdi

Visual Arts

- French Eugéne Delacroix
- British John Constable and J.M.W. Turner

Realism

Some artists felt constrained by the idealized vision of the world presented by the Romantics. These artists sought to present more realistic reflections of life. Some realists, later known as naturalists, intentionally tried to portray unpleasant aspects of life. In the United States, some realists specialized in reflecting life in particular regions, earning them the name "regionalists." Some examples of realists included:

- Gustave Flaubert, France, Madame Bovary
- George Eliot (a.k.a. Mary Ann Evans), Great Britain, Middlemarch
- Mark Twain, United States, The Adventures of Huckleberry Finn
- Emile Zola, France, Germinal
- Charles Dickens, Great Britain, David Copperfield
- Leo Tolstoy, Russia, War and Peace
- Henrik Ibsen, Norway, A Doll's House

Impressionists and Post-Impressionists

Inspired by such realist painters such Gustave Courbet and Honoré Daumier, a group of French painters called the impressionists emerged during the 1860s. Impressionists focused on the study of color and light to create vivid images of people and places. Claude Monet and Pierre-Auguste Renoir were two of the most influential impressionists. By the end of the century, the impressionist movement had spread to other western nations. Another group of artists, called the post-impressionists, took the impressionists' focus on light and color one step further by focusing on form more than realistic depictions of life. French painter Paul Cézanne spawned the movement, which soon came to include other painters such as Paul Gauguin, Henri-Émile-Benoît Matisse, and Vincent van Gogh. Sculptor Auguste Rodin applied post-impressionist theories to his forms as well.

Developments in Popular Entertainment

As more people moved to cities and earned wages, new venues for popular entertainment grew. Some, such as concert halls and art museums, offered opportunities for exposure to high culture that had previously been unavailable to rural residents. Initially, many private and religious organizations promoted such endeavors to educate and uplift urban-dwellers. As city planning movements expanded, local governments began to sponsor free public art entertainment. Entrepreneurs created other venues to earn money as well as to entertain. Music halls that provided dance floors and/or performers such as singers, professional dancers, and comedy acts, became very popular. Amusement parks sprang up in some locations, and organized sports became popular. Many of the earliest professional teams were sponsored by companies to increase camaraderie, improve health, and offer competitive outlets for workers. Many non-athletes became fans of the teams, creating new industries in spectator sports as entertainment. Throughout Europe and the United States, entertainment was becoming much more of a public and shared activity.

Goals of European Imperialism

Several factors influenced the rise of European imperialism in the 1800s, but generally they fall under economic, political, or cultural motives. As with earlier periods of expansion, the desire to gain natural resources and new markets spurred expansion. In the 1800s, the needs of industry drove imperialism for economic benefit. During the 1800s, economic competition, rather than direct war, became the focus of conflicts and power struggles between nations. Many leaders considered the economic success of their country to be a matter of national pride. They fought to expand their spheres of influence to gain political advantages over their rivals. Motives for cultural imperialism grew out of the social Darwinist belief that naturally superior people had a moral obligation to improve the lives of "inferior" people. Rudyard Kipling's poem "The White Man's Burden" best expressed this belief. British imperialists in particular used the argument of "civilizing" so-called primitive peoples to justify British expansion, so much so that it was once said "the sun never sets on the British Empire."

French and British Expansion into North Africa

The Industrial Revolution turned resource-rich Africa into a prized land for fueling factory-based economies. The Ottoman Empire that controlled North Africa was so weak that most of this area was virtually independent and vulnerable to European rivals. France began its move into North Africa by occupying Algiers in 1830. In 1854, Egyptian leaders partnered with a French company to build the Suez Canal, connecting the Mediterranean and Red Seas. Facing economic problems, the Egyptian government sold its canal stock to Great Britain in 1875, a move that established unofficial British control over Egypt to protect its shipping interests. In 1881, France turned Tunis into a protectorate. That same year, Egyptian-controlled Sudan, an important link to the Nile, launched a revolution for independence. To suppress the rebellion and beat France, Great Britain invaded

Sudan in 1898. French and British forces almost went to war at Fashoda until the outmanned French troops retreated, leaving Sudan for Britain. Shifting tactics, France worked diplomatically to gain control over Morocco, which became French protectorate in 1909.

Belgium's rule of the Congo region

Central Africa largely remained an unknown mystery to Europe until 1869, when British journalist Henry Stanley embarked on a two-year journey through the Congo River region to find lost missionary David Livingstone. Stanley's remark upon finding the man ("Dr. Livingstone, I presume.") was well publicized in the popular press. Stanley used stories about his journey to encourage British settlement around the Congo, but officials were not interested. Belgium's King Leopold II, however, was interested, and claimed a private colony called the Congo Free State in 1885. Leopold exploited the region for his own financial gain, enslaving many indigenous people and plundering natural resources. Leopold's brutal treatment of the Congolese people earned rebuke from other western leaders, forcing him to turn over control of the colony to the Belgian government in 1908, shortly before he died. The new government of the Belgian Congo was much less harsh; nevertheless, native Congolese had few rights and little control over local policies.

Struggle for European dominance over South Africa

- 1652 — Dutch traders established Cape Town (around the Cape of Good Hope).
- 1700s — Boers (European-descended South Africans) developed their own language, Afrikaans, a combination of various European and African dialects; often fought with native Africans and the Dutch colonial government.
- 1814 — The Dutch ceded Cape Colony to the British; many Boers fled to establish their own colonies: Natal, the Orange Free State, and Transvaal; met strong resistance from native peoples, especially the Zulu.
- 1879 — British forces helped the Boers defeat the Zulu; by this time, the discovery of diamonds and gold in the Boer colonies had peaked European interest in the region.
- 1884 — Germany declared a protectorate over the territory of South-West Africa; in response, British settlers led by Cecil Rhodes moved inland to secure more land (including Rhodesia).
- 1899-1902 — Great Britain and the Boers fought the Boer War, ending in British victory.
- 1910 — Britain united Cape Colony and the Boer colonies to form the Union of South Africa.

Affect of European imperialism on Africa

European imperialism had carved up Africa so much by 1914 that a map of the continent resembled a patchwork quilt. In 1884, officials from various European nations met in Berlin to resolve conflicts over African lands. The Berlin Conference ignored traditional ethnic land boundaries and divided lands based on geographic boundaries that reflected European desires. These divisions contributed to ethnic conflicts for years to come and reflected Europeans' paternalistic and dismissive attitudes toward Africans. Although colonization improved infrastructures such as roads and railroads, it led to a decrease in freedom, independence, and traditional culture among Africans. Even colonial and missionary schools for Africans focused on "civilizing" students by assimilating them into western culture. Throughout the continent, the native people and lands were exploited for European benefit. South Africa's apartheid system represented the most extreme example, as the majority of non-whites had virtually no rights.

British experience in India

For many years, the British East India Company controlled about three-fifths of the Indian subcontinent as a private colony. After Indians rebelled against the company in 1857, the British government took direct control and then set out to take possession of the many independent principalities that lay outside the colony. Many princes became puppet rulers who were required to follow orders from British officials. British settlers established a strong presence in India but remained segregated from the majority of native Indian society, so that two separate and very unequal societies developed. In 1899, British officials established western-style schools for Indians. These schools spread not only western culture to native Indians, but also western ideas about democracy and equality. Many Indian nationalists embraced these ideals and began to push for Indian independence. Although the nationalist movement grew in popularity, the British remained firmly in control of the colony.

European Expansion into Southeast Asia and the Pacific Islands

- 1819 — The British East India Company established a presence in Singapore, soon a major British trading and naval base.
- 1858 — France began seizing control of what would become French Indochina.
- 1865 — American business leaders established a presence in the Hawaiian Islands.
- 1886 — Great Britain took complete control over Burma.
- Late 1800s — Indonesians staged frequent revolts in the Dutch East Indies, leading Dutch officials to reform colonial policies without allowing complete independence.
- 1889 — Officials negotiated an agreement in which Great Britain withdrew from Samoa, the United States established American Samoa, and Germany retained Western Samoa.
- 1893 — Americans led a coup against Queen Liliuokalani, the last Hawaiian monarch.
- 1898 — The United States annexed Hawaii and ended Spanish control over the Philippines through victory in the Spanish American War. Filipinos launched a revolution for independence.
- 1902 — After defeating Filipino rebels, the United States took control of the Philippines, Guam, and Wake Island.

Chinese vs. Japanese Western Policies

Though China and Japan both remained independent of western colonization, the nations experienced different degrees of western influence. Chinese had opened key ports to British ships in the 1700s, but the British introduction of addictive drugs to China led to the Opium Wars (1839-1842). The Treaty of Nanjing ended the conflict, giving Britain control of Hong Kong as well as several key Chinese port cities. The Open Door Policy established free western trade in China. As European nations expanded their presence in China, they tried to pressure an isolated Japan to open its ports as well. The United States increased this pressure by sending a large naval fleet led by Commodore Matthew Perry to Japan in 1853, asking for open ports. Over the next few years, Japan negotiated treaties with several western nations. By the end of the century, Japan was rapidly industrializing, expanding its military and reforming its government. Japan's humiliating defeat of Russian forces in 1905 (over Korean and Chinese territories) held off threats from other western powers.

The First World War and the Russian Revolution

CONTRIBUTIONS TO WORLD WAR I

- Nationalism — The nationalist movements that arose in the 1800s led to the unification of some countries but increased tensions within other more diverse countries. Many groups arose that identified more strongly with ethnic than political ties, increasing calls for homogenous nations. At the same time, national pride among long-time citizens in existing countries increased, fueling intense competition among European countries.
- Imperialism — Nationalistic competition manifested itself most clearly in the struggle for imperial dominance. Colonial expansion provided natural resources that fueled industry, military power, and wealth among European nations. The expansion of European control and influence throughout the globe set the stage for a European conflict to encompass the entire world.
- Militarism — Closely tied to nationalism and imperialism was militarism, the glorification of military power and might. While strong military forces were needed to secure the European empires, militarism fueled romantic notions of fighting for the glory of one's country. By 1914, these feelings increased support for calls to war.

ALLIANCES FORMED BY GERMANY

German leader Otto von Bismarck fueled the push for alliances. Although Prussian-dominated Germany had defeated France in the Franco-Prussian war, Bismarck believed that the humiliated French would seek a rematch. Fearing that France would seek support from Russia, Bismarck struck a preemptive blow by seeking his own alliance with Russia and Austria-Hungary. In the Three Emperor's League, formed in 1881, these three countries pledged to remain neutral if any of the other two went to war. The move served not only to protect Germany, but also to end conflict between Russia and Austria-Hungary over the Balkans. In 1882, Germany entered into the Triple Alliance with Italy and Austria-Hungary. Bismarck reinforced his ties with Russia by signing the Reinsurance Treaty of 1887. The alliances ensured the protection of Germany's southern and eastern borders and weakened France's ability to seek military assistance.

RESPONSE OF OTHER POWERS TO THE GERMAN ALLIANCES

Germany's alliances succeeded temporarily in isolating France diplomatically. France fought back by trying to expand its ties in the 1890s. French leaders undermined the Germany alliance with Russia by coming to the Russians' aid during a financial crisis. This aid resulted in the signing of a military protection agreement between France and Russia in 1894. Meanwhile, German and British competition for overseas colonies was heating up. In 1904, Great Britain and France signed a non-competition agreement, or entente. In 1907, Russia signed onto the agreement, forming the Triple Entente of Russia, Great Britain, and France. Meanwhile, both Britain and France worked out secret agreements with Italy, undermining its public agreement with Germany.

BALKANS

The Balkans became the center of nationalistic conflict and imperialist rivalry after the Congress of Vienna granted Serbia its independence. Many Serbs hoped to expand their country into a larger Slavic state. They especially wanted control of the largely Slavic Bosnia and Herzegovina, which the Congress had placed under the protectorate of Austria-Hungary. When Austria-Hungary annexed Bosnia and Herzegovina, Serbian nationalists became outraged and sought support from Russia, which supported the concept of Pan-Slavic unity throughout Eastern Europe. Russian leaders, however, believed that they would be able to dominate an alliance of Slavic nations in the Balkans. Fueling these tensions was the ongoing rivalry with other nations. Great Britain opposed Russian dominance in the east, fearing Russia would cut off access to the Mediterranean Sea. Germany, meanwhile, announced its own plans to build a railroad that would connect Germany to the Middle East via the Balkans. Germany's rivals joined forces to undermine these efforts. By 1914, the Balkans had become a "powder keg" for potential violence.

Immediate Events Leading to the Outbreak of World War I

By 1914, multiple groups were vying for control over the Balkans, often in secretive and underhanded ways. Extreme Serbian nationalists formed terrorist groups that used violence to advance their political goals. A member of one such group, Gavrilo Princip, assassinated Archduke Franz Ferdinand, heir to the Austria-Hungarian throne, in Sarajevo. Serbian officials quickly arrested several people involved in the assassination plot, but Austria-Hungarian leaders blamed the Serbian leaders themselves for fomenting violence. Austria-Hungary sent a list of demands to Serbia, insisting that the Serbian government help suppress radical groups fighting to undermine Austria-Hungary, fire government officials and teachers who publicly criticized Austria-Hungary, ban anti-Austrian publications, and allow officials from Austria-Hungary to participate in the trials of the accused assassins and conspirators. Serbian leaders agreed to all but the last demand, but they did offer to allow the International Court to oversee the assassins' trials. Austria refused to accept this counteroffer and declared war against Serbia on July 28, 1914.

Alliance Systems

The alliance system quickly turned the conflict between Serbia and Austria-Hungary into a far-reaching war as countries came to the aid of nations with whom they had formal alliances. Even before presenting Serbia with its list of demands, leaders from Austria-Hungary reaffirmed the support of its ally Germany. As soon as Austria-Hungary declared war, Germany joined the cause and mobilized its troops for war. Russia mobilized its troops to aid its ally Serbia, prompting Germany to declare war on Russia on August 1, 1914. Anticipating that France would join its ally Russia, Germany preemptively declared war on France on August 3. Great Britain joined its allies Russia and France in declaring war on Germany after the Germans invaded Belgium on August 4. All of the major European powers were locked into a two-sided battle between the Central Powers, led by allies Germany and Austria-Hungary, and the Allied Powers, led by Great Britain, France, and Russia.

Expansion of the War by 1915

The dominos of the alliance system continued to fall throughout the first year of the war. In late August, Japan joined the Allied Powers mainly because it wanted to stop German colonial expansion in Asia and hoped to seize German-held territories in China and on Pacific Islands. The Central Powers gained a valuable ally when the Ottoman Empire joined their side in October. Although militarily weak, the Ottomans still controlled access to important land and sea routes to the resource-rich Middle East. Italy initially remained neutral, arguing that Austria-Hungary's aggressive maneuvers voided previous pacts between the two nations. In the summer of 1915, Italy finally joined the Allies after being promised that it could retain some Austrian lands. In order to protect the land route between Austria-Hungary and the Ottoman Empire, Germany convinced Bulgarian leaders to join the Central Powers. By the end of 1915, most European countries had joined one side or another.

US's Role in the European War

In 1914, the United States followed a largely isolationist foreign policy. Immediately after fighting began, President Woodrow Wilson declared that the United States would remain neutral, since the conflict was a fight between European nations. Most Americans supported this policy, which was largely responsible for Wilson's re-election in 1916. Behind the scenes, however, the United States gradually increased its support for the Allies. The United States was the world's most heavily industrialized country. As such, both the Allied and Central Powers desired Americans goods. Initially neutral American countries traded with both sides. As the British naval blockade of Germany became more effective and German U-boat activity became more threatening, the United States shifted more of its trade towards the Allies. Despite his campaign promises, Wilson fully expected that US forces would have to join in the fighting.

Economic Mobilization of the War

All participating countries realigned their economies to focus on the needs of war. Countries that were already industrialized held a greater advantage than their nonindustrialized rivals because they already had the infrastructure in place to mobilize for warfare. For example, Russia's lack of industrialization hampered its war efforts, contributing to domestic instability. Most nations either nationalized industries or worked with industry leaders to direct business toward war industries. Governments rationed the private use of materials needed for the war effort and encouraged conservation by ordinary citizens ("meatless Wednesdays," the planting of "victory gardens" to conserve food for soldiers). Even laissez faire capitalist nations such as the United States accepted government direction of the economy during the crisis. When the European war began in 1914, President Wilson ordered the closure of the New York stock exchange to prevent cash-strapped European nations from liquidating assets. His administration would continue to direct economic activity throughout the end of the conflict

Technological Innovations

- U-boats: Unterseebooten ("undersea boats"), double-hulled, torpedo-armed German submarines capable of sinking large ships quietly and escaping quickly
- Chemical Gas: Introduced by Germany in trench warfare, leading to the need for gas masks; caused long-term health problems for many soldiers
- Machine guns: Rapid-fire guns capable of causing massive casualties; became lighter and more portable as the war progressed
- Long-range artillery: Capable of attacking distant targets with great accuracy.
- Tanks: Introduced by Britain; mounted with guns; capable of moving across rough terrain and through defensive barriers such as barbed wire
- Airplanes: Recent invention initially used for observation; evolved into "dogfights," one-on-one air battles, exemplified by Baron Manfred von Richthofen "the Red Baron"

Role of Propaganda

Governments on both sides of the conflict used propaganda to inspire patriotism and rally support for their cause. Propaganda involves manipulating the use of select information, both true and false, to sway public opinion. Even democratic Allied governments established boards to censor and control content in the press, motion pictures, and other forms of communication that might sway public opinion. Each side emphasized casualty reports and exaggerated claims of atrocities carried out by enemies. For example, the Allies portrayed the Germans as violent "Huns" who sexually assaulted women, oppressed religion, and sought to overturn democratic values. Propaganda helped increase volunteerism (before the introduction of drafts) and financial support for the war.

Concentration of Fighting Around Belgium and France

Tiny Belgium declared neutrality at the beginning of the war, but Belgium lay between Germany and France. The Germans wanted to attack and defeat France quickly to avoid having to fight a major two-front war squeezed between France to the west and Russia to the east. Thus, Germany violated Belgium's neutrality and invaded it to get to France, sparking Great Britain's entry into the war. Initially, the German offense worked well, as their forces quickly pushed all the way to the Marne River near Paris. Combined British and French forces were able to hold off the Germans and protect Paris, but both sides dug in. Fighting on the Western Front fell into a stalemate along a line of trenches mainly in France and Belgium that extended from the Netherlands in the north to Switzerland in the south.

European Land Battles

- First Battle of the Marne — September 1914; resulted in Allied victory; halted German advance through France; beginning of stalemate on Western Front
- Battle of Tannenberg — August 1914; Germans inflicted huge defeat against Russian army, which lost half of its troops; followed by German advance into Russia's Polish region
- First Battle of Ypres — October 1914; British forces halted German advance in northern France
- Second Battle of Ypres — April 1915; German offensive advanced in northern France; Germans introduced the use of chlorine gas; ended in Allied victory, although Germans continued to lay siege to city
- Battle of Verdun — February-December 1916; German offensive that ended with virtually no change in territory; marked by huge casualties on both sides
- Battle of the Somme — July-November 1916; British offensive that led to huge German casualties and little Allied advance

Campaigns in the Naval War

Great Britain issued a blockade in the North Sea to prevent Germany from receiving supplies. Germany retaliated by issuing its own blockade and using U-boats to attack ships trying to supply the British. Controversy arose as the British tried to obtain supplies using civilian ships and Germany waged war on passenger as well as cargo ships. In May 1915, U-boats sank the British passenger liner Lusitania, which was carrying war supplies as well as 1,200 passengers who died. The greatest sea battle of the war was the Battle of Jutland, fought in May 1916 off the coast of Denmark. Both British and German vessels claimed victory. However, after Jutland the Germans essentially retreated from naval combat.

Campaign in Gallipoli

The Allies hoped to aid the war on the Eastern Front by forcing the Ottoman Empire out of the war. Doing so would ease pressure on the Russians and allow Allies to get much-needed supplies to poorly equipped Russian troops. The Allies forged a plan to advance through the Dardanelles and take Constantinople. In April 1915, British and French ships began to bombard Ottoman Turks on the Gallipoli Peninsula. The battle dragged on for eight months, with heavy casualties on both sides. Australian and New Zealand forces played a major role in the fighting, an experience that increased patriotism and national pride in those countries. Finally, having achieved little success, the Allies retreated from Gallipoli in January 1916, and the weakened Ottoman Empire remained in the war.

Social and Economic Changes for Women

Women on both sides played major roles in the war. Propaganda campaigns encouraged women to take on economic roles by filling jobs in much-needed industries and carrying out volunteer work for the war effort. Women also played larger roles in the military, serving as nurses and support staff, often in dangerous war zones. The war dramatically changed cultural opinions of what women were capable of doing. In democratic countries, especially the United States and Great Britain, feminists used this change to rally political support for female suffrage. They urged women to support the war effort to prove their loyalty and usefulness to the government, hoping that officials would reward their loyalty with political rights once the war ended. Their tactic would prove successful.

ANTIWAR MOVEMENTS

Despite propaganda efforts, antiwar movements existed in all major countries. Some governments tried to suppress criticism of the war by associating peace movements with socialism and anti-democratic values (aided by the fact that many socialist leaders did speak out against the war, especially during the early days). Antiwar sentiments ran particularly high in the United States. Reasons for opposition to the war ranged from isolationist desires in order to avoid foreign entanglements to religiously inspired pacifism. Notable opponents to the war included reformer Jane Addams. After the United States entered the war, the government used the Espionage Act to deport foreign-born antiwar activists. The Alien and Sedition Acts helped suppress antiwar speech but never completely squelched opposition to the war. As the tide of public opinion turned toward supporting the conflict, social pressure helped limit antiwar ideas that had been common prior to US entry.

EVENTS LEADING TO THE UNITED STATES JOINING THE WAR

- December 1916 — Newly reelected President Woodrow Wilson presented a "peace note" to warring parties to try to end the conflict, but his plea was rejected.
- January 31, 1917 — Germany declared plans for unrestricted submarine warfare.
- February 3 — US officials severed diplomatic relations with Germany.
- February 24 — US officials discovered the Zimmermann Note, a letter from a German ambassador offering to return lands in Arizona, New Mexico, and Texas to Mexico if it would fight for the Central Powers against the United States.
- March 1 — US newspapers published excerpts from the Zimmermann Note, sparking widespread outrage.
- March 12 — President Wilson ordered the arming of US merchant vessels in response to German aggression.
- April 2 — President Wilson delivered a war address to Congress, urging the country to join the Allied effort to make the world "safe for democracy."
- April 6 — The United States declared war on Germany.

UNITED STATES' ENTRY CHANGED THE ALLIED CAMPAIGN PLAN

Prior to US entry, Allied forces had been working to hold off the German advance while relying on German distractions in the Eastern Front. The removal of Russia from the war allowed the Germans to concentrate all of their efforts on the Western Front. Knowing American troops and supplies were on their way, the Allies focused their efforts on holding the line against the German offensive until American forces could arrive in the summer of 1918. Once the US troops arrived, the Allies were able to launch a counteroffensive to drive back the Germans and threaten the other Central Powers. Under pressure, Bulgaria withdrew from the war in September, followed by the Ottomans, Austria, and Hungary. Left on its own, Germany was surrounded and cut off from aid.

List and Describe the Major Events During the War in 1918.

- March 21 — Anticipating US entry into the war, Germany launched a major offensive with hopes of gaining an advantage before the arrival of US aid to the Allies.
- April 25 — British and Australian forces stopped the German advance near Amiens.
- May 23 — Germans bombed Paris.
- May 31 — Battle of Chateau-Thierry; American forces halted the German advance across the Marne River.
- August 8 — Battle of the Somme; Allied counteroffensive forced the Germans to retreat.
- September 27 — Allied forces broke through the Hindenberg Line of German troops.
- October — Allied forces retook complete control of France and Belgium.
- November 9 — German Kaiser Wilhelm II resigned, leading to the formation of a new republican government in Germany.
- November 11 — The war ended with an armistice that took effect at 11 A.M. on the eleventh day of the eleventh month of the year.

Wilson's Fourteen Points

1. No more secret alliances or treaties.
2. Freedom of travel on the seas.
3. Free trade for all nations.
4. Reduction of arms.
5. Diplomatic settling of conflicts over colonies, taking the desires of the indigenous peoples into consideration.
6. Evacuation of Russian lands and settlement of any disputes with Russia; other nations' non-interference in Russia's internal political affairs.
7. Removal of all foreign troops from Belgium.
8. Removal of all foreign troops from France; restoration of French lands in Alsace-Lorraine lost to Prussia in 1871.
9. Realignment of Italian borders with nationalistic considerations.
10. Autonomous rule for the ethnic peoples of Austria-Hungary.
11. Removal of foreign troops from Romania, Serbia, and Montenegro; alignment of the Balkans to promote organization of independent nations.
12. Reorganization of Ottoman Empire.
13. Creation of an independent Poland.
7. Formation of an international body to resolve disputes and promote peace between nations.

Negotiations at the Paris Peace Conference

In January 1919, world leaders met at Versailles to negotiate the formal peace treaty to end the war. The Big Four, leaders of the major Allied Powers, dominated the meeting. The Big Four included US President Woodrow Wilson, British Prime Minister David Lloyd George, French Premier Georges Clemenceau, and Italian Prime Minister Vittorio Orlando. Wilson pushed for a reasonable peace along the lines of his proposed Fourteen Points, but the other Allied leaders (whose countries had suffered much more than the United States) pressed for more punitive actions against Germany. They felt that the Germans had caused the war and should be punished accordingly. Some even resented Wilson's attempts to negotiate terms of peace. Leaders disagreed among themselves about the best way to resolve territorial conflicts and calls for independence among nationalist groups. Eventually two main camps emerged at the conference—those demanding punishment and those wanting reconciliation. In the end, those advocating punitive measures won out.

Treaty of Versailles

Strengths and Weaknesses of the Versailles Treaty

Strengths:

- Established League of Nations to offer nonmilitary resolution of international disputes.
- Granted independence to many territories and people who wanted self-rule.
- Prevented Germany from launching military opposition by weakening its military strength and including measures to prevent military resurgence.

Weaknesses:

- Imposition of reparations against Germany crippled its economy.
- Requirement that Germany take full blame for the war fostered resentment.
- League of Nations as established was a weak organization.
- Provided no way to enforce its provisions, allowing German officials to ignore them eventually, stop making reparations payments, and rebuild its military.

Treaty of Versailles Redrew the European Map

Austria and Hungary had already voluntarily split their alliance. During negotiations at Versailles, both lost lands in their possession. Italy took control of southern Tirol and the city of Trieste from Austria. The new nations of Czechoslovakia and Yugoslavia were carved out of Hungary. Poland also became a new nation. Bulgaria was forced to cede part of its lands to Greece. The treaty broke up the Ottoman Empire, leaving only the country of Turkey to the Turks, and created the administrative regions of Palestine, Transjordan, Syria, and Iraq. Russia lost part of its lands to the newly formed Poland and to Romania, as well as to several nations that seceded from Russia. These new nations included Finland, Estonia, Latvia, and Lithuania.

United States' Failure to Ratify the Peace Agreement

Although President Wilson was disappointed in the punitive aspects of the Treaty of Versailles, he supported it because it included provisions for creating the League of Nations. He fully believed that the League would prevent future wars. Back home, however, many members of the US Senate opposed the treaty because of the League's provisions. They feared that membership in the League would draw the country into needless wars in which the United States had little or no stake. Wilson campaigned to rally support for the treaty, but he suffered a stroke that limited his effectiveness. Eventually, US officials negotiate their own separate peace with Germany, and the Senate never ratified the Treaty of Versailles.

League of Nations

The Covenant of the League of Nations spelled out two main goals: 1) to promote international cooperation and 2) to keep peace among nations by settling disputes and reducing arms. The League consisted of three branches that would work closely with an independent global judiciary called the Permanent Court of International Justice, or World Court, headquartered in the Hague in the Netherlands. The three branches of the League included:

- The Assembly, made up of all member nations, each with one vote
- The Council, made up of nine member nations (later 14), including the five permanent members of Great Britain, France, Italy, Japan, and the United States; other nations would rotate membership
- The Secretariat, the leading executive over the League

Member nations of the League pledged never to initiate war and to resolve disputes in the World Court or before another body. Member nations who did not comply with the League might face economic sanctions or termination of diplomatic relations.

LONG-TERM SOCIAL AND ECONOMIC EFFECTS OF THE WAR

The Great War was the most devastating war the world had ever experienced, with high human and economic costs. As many as 10 million people had been killed, with another 21 million seriously wounded. The war decimated an entire generation. Those who survived faced serious emotional and mental consequences that shaped their outlook on life. Writers later came to call them the Lost Generation, reflecting their lost idealism. Areas where most fighting took place, especially in France, experienced severe damage to infrastructures that would never fully recover until after World War II. Economically, the war weakened all economies. By some estimates, the total cost of war came to more than $300 billion. The reparations required of Germany hampered its economic recovery and contributed to the rise of fascism. Overall, the war left bitterness and resentment that continued to fester for years. Many historians have argued that World War II came about as a result of unfinished business of World War I.

RUSSIA'S ROLE IN WORLD WAR I

Russia began the war as one of the major Allied Powers and was the focus of German efforts on the Eastern Front. The war revealed serious weaknesses in the Russian economy and government, however. The Russian Army, while huge in number, was poorly equipped. A lack of roads hindered the movement of supplies and men, a situation only made worse when the Ottoman Empire cut essential supply lines to the Russians. The Allies had planned on utilizing the sheer numbers of Russian soldiers to distract the Germans from the Western campaign. For that reason, Russia launched an offensive on East Prussia, but the Russian defeat at Tannenberg undermined its ability to fight. Overall, the Russians were never as helpful in fighting the war as the Allies had hoped, but their efforts on the Eastern Front did help divide the German army.

DISSATISFACTION WITH THEIR GOVERNMENT

The war revealed weaknesses throughout the Russian economy. Even though the government had abolished serfdom in 1861, high rents, debt, and taxes kept most Russians extremely poor. Despite reforms, most power still remained vested in the czar rather than the Duma, the legislature. To most Russians, the czar was a remote leader indifferent to their suffering. High casualties and shortages due to blockades gave rise to strong antiwar feelings. By the spring of 1917, many citizens were openly expressing their lack of faith in the government. When the Duma voted for reforms to appease the people, Czar Nicholas II disbanded the legislature. Usually when such political conflicts occurred, the czar used the military to suppress dissent. Now, most soldiers were busy fighting the war. Those stationed at home were so dissatisfied with poor equipment and lack of pay that they joined the protestors. Without the threat of military interference, Duma leaders refused the czar's order to disband. Instead, they forced Nicholas to resign and soon arrested his entire family.

LENIN AND THE BOLSHEVIKS

Vladimir Lenin was the leader of the Bolsheviks, a radical faction of the Petrograd Soviet of Workers' and Soldiers' Deputies, a socialist organization organized to oppose the czarist government. Lenin was a devout student of Marxism, but he believed that since Russia was not as industrialized as the society Marx had predicted would overturn capitalism, it would require a communist government until the people accepted the benefits of pure socialism. Bolsheviks believed that forced economic equality was necessary to bring about political equality. The Bolsheviks demanded an immediate end to Russian involvement in the war, as well as the redistribution of land. They used the slogan "peace, bread, and land" to win over peasants, weary workers, and soldiers. They were opposed by the moderate Mensheviks, who argued for slower reform. When the provisional government established after the czar abdicated declared its intention to keep fighting the war, Lenin prepared his followers to seize control.

October Revolution

Vladimir Lenin and the Bolsheviks became dissatisfied with the moderate provisional government and decided to launch a workers' revolution to force a new direction. On November 7, 1917, (October, according to the Russian calendar) the Bolsheviks led a coup against the provisional government and dissolved the constitutional assembly. The Bolsheviks reorganized themselves as the Communist Party and established a new government based on radical Marxist theories, with Lenin as their leader. Lenin's government withdrew completely from the war and negotiated a peace agreement with Germany that included giving up significant amounts of territory.

Events of the Russian Civil War

The Russian Civil War followed the October Revolution as Mensheviks and monarchists opposed the new Communist government. As fighting broke out in early 1918, many Communist leaders feared monarchists would try to return the imprisoned czar to power. To prevent this from happening, officials executed the czar and his entire family in July 1918, wiping out any link to the Romanov dynasty. The civil war continued for three years. The Communist forces were called the Reds (led by the Red Army) because red had traditionally been the color associated with European socialist groups. Their opponents were called the Whites. They received significant aid from the Allies, who were angry that the Bolsheviks had signed a peace treaty with Germany and feared the spread of communist ideas. By 1921, the Reds emerged victorious. In 1922, they renamed all of the lands under their control the Union of Soviet Socialist Republics, or the Soviet Union.

Affect of the Russian Revolution on World War I

Russia's withdrawal from the war was a major blow to the Allied cause, as it allowed Germany to focus fighting only on the Western Front. Knowing that the United States would soon be entering the war, the Germans launched a major western offensive in an attempt to seize as much territory as possible. By transferring key lands to German control, the Russians allowed for the creation of new independent countries in lands that had once been under their control. The revolution increased fears of socialism in the Allied nations. Since many antiwar activists were also socialists, propaganda began to focus on socialism as anti-democratic and fueled fears that socialists were just trying to plot their own revolutions. After the war, Russian leaders were not invited to participate in the Paris Peace Conference, both as a punishment for their separate peace and as a sign of their declining role in European affairs.

Europe Between the Wars

Warning Signs of Global Economic Trouble

- Lingering effects of World War I—Many economies never returned to their postwar economic position; heavy reparations imposed by the Treaty of Versailles hampered the German economy, which was beset by high inflation and unemployment.
- Agricultural recession—As with industry, many agricultural regions of Europe never returned to their prewar productivity; even in the United States, which had experienced a wartime farming boom as Allies imported US crops, overproduction and high costs of mechanical farming led to an agricultural recession.
- Protectionism—Despite expansion of global trade and interconnection of world economies, after the war several nations imposed high tariffs that limited trade and forced nations that had to trade to buy more goods on credit.
- Overuse of credit and speculation—High production of consumer goods and effective marketing campaigns, especially by US companies, fueled markets for consumer goods; installment plans increased dependence upon credit, which extended to the stock markets as buyers bought more stocks on margin and engaged in risky stock speculation.

New York Stock Market Crash

- Causes — Stock speculation and margin buying drove up stock prices so that many of them were inflated compared to the value of the companies they represented. During the weeks prior to the crash, investors began to show signs of nervousness over economic such warning signs as the agricultural recession, industrial overproduction, and slow-downs in consumer spending. The market experienced several isolated days of heavy losses, including "Black Thursday" on Oct. 24. On Black Tuesday, Oct. 29, 1929, panic started on Wall Street and did not stop. Over 16 million shares sold in massive selling frenzy, with losses exceeding $26 billion.
- Effects — The crash exposed weaknesses in other systems. When the stock market crashed, people could not repay their loans to banks, nor repay loans for stocks bought on margin. Brokers desperate for cash began calling in margins, but people could not pay. Some started worrying about the security of money in banks, leading to a "run on banks." Many banks collapsed.

The stock market crash sparked a cycle of disaster. As banks failed and credit dried up, businesses facing debts cut production, wages, and workers. People had little money to spend, causing the demand for goods to fall further. As demand declined, businesses cut production, wages, and workers further, and the cycle spiraled downward. European countries with already weakened economies suffered first, but the interconnection of markets and banking affected all nations. The continued imposition of protectionist policies, especially the Smoot-Hawley Tariff of 1930 that raised tariffs on US imports up to 50 percent, worsened the situation. The tariff virtually closed US borders to foreign goods and ignited a vicious international trade war. The loss of such trade was devastating and had ripple effects, similar to bank failures. Deflation, which occurs with lower demand and falling prices, wiped out national and personal finances. Prices for goods fell 30-40 percent in the four largest world economies—the United States, United Kingdom, Germany, and France.

ATTEMPTED ECONOMIC AND POLITICAL REMEDIES

Most European countries experimented with increased government control over their economies, including nationalization of banking and key industries. Examples from the major powers include:

- Great Britain — The government granted low-interest loans to industries to promote job growth and raised tariffs.
- France — People demanded changes in government; led to instability as three different governments ruled in 1933 alone; some people began to call for an end to the republic and a return to Napoleon-style dictatorship; leftist workers responded by organizing general strikes, accepting the Popular Front government of socialist Leon Blum; the government created a nationalized bank system and required higher wages and 40-hour work week for laborers.
- Germany and Italy — Both nations embraced fascist military economy to revive economy.
- Soviet Union — The government increased militarization and command economy to direct recovery.

NEW DEAL

The New Deal focused on three main areas: relief, recovery, and reform. It expanded relief efforts by issuing grants to states to feed and clothe people. It provided unemployment insurance to those seeking work, as well as social security for the elderly. The government also funded extensive public works projects to provide jobs and extended loans to help businesses. It also reformed the US economic system by imposing new regulations on banking, the stock market, industries, and agricultural markets. Overall, the US government's role in the economy dramatically increased and would continue to increase, adopting some elements of the modern welfare state and rejecting traditional laissez faire economic policies. However, unlike many European countries, the nation did not adopt fascist or communist systems, nor did the government nationalize industries to the extent of many other nations. As a result, US recovery was slower than in some European countries, but the system fared better in the long run.

LOCARNO PACT

The Locarno Pact was part of a larger attempt to prevent another major war between European powers. In 1925, leaders from Belgium, Czechoslovakia, France, Germany, Great Britain, Italy, and Poland met in Locarno, Switzerland, to work towards peace. The meeting resulted in six main outcomes:

- All delegates pledged that their countries would work to find peaceful, nonmilitary solutions to conflicts with other nations.
- Border disputes between Germany, Belgium, and France were resolved.
- Former Allies clarified to German officials how the League of Nations would use sanctions against non-compliant countries.
- Germany resolved border disputes with Czechoslovakia and Poland.
- France signed separate mutual assistance treaties with Czechoslovakia and Poland.
- Allied troops prepared to leave the Rhineland in 1930 instead of 1935, as had been established by the Treaty of Versailles.

GREAT BRITAIN'S CONFLICTS WITH IRELAND

Needing Irish help to fight the Great War, British officials promised Ireland home rule once the conflict ended. Many Irish nationalists such as Michael Collins demanded complete independence, which resulted in the Easter Rising of 1916. British officials quickly suppressed the revolt and executed the riot instigators, who became martyrs for independence. By 1918, the Irish nationalist party of Sinn Fein won a majority of Ireland's seats in Parliament and then sparked the Irish War of Independence by declaring themselves representatives of an independent Irish republic. Sinn Fein's military branch, the Irish Republican Army (IRA), fought a brutal war that resulted in the Anglo-Irish Treaty that split Ireland into the majority Catholic, self-governing Irish Free State and the majority Protestant British province of Northern Ireland. Some nationalists refused to accept the treaty and launched a bloody civil war. Although nationalists conceded defeat in 1923, the IRA continued to wage terrorist attacks, such as the assassination of treaty-supporter Collins.

Austria and Hungary after World War I

Once mighty Austria-Hungary declined dramatically after the war. The Treaty of Versailles forced it to remain two separate, weak nations. Independent Austria struggled with economic and class conflicts, as many rural Austrians felt dismissed by the one-third of the population that lived in urban Vienna. Constant fighting between socialists and conservatives undermined the effectiveness of the democratically-elected government. Many Austrians began to call for unification with Germany, an action prohibited by Versailles. Hungary also faced economic difficulties after the war, having lost most of its industrialized cities in the postwar treaties. In 1919, communist leader Bela Kun overthrew the fledgling republican government and tried to establish a Soviet-style system. His attempts to nationalize farmlands, followed by failure to redistribute food and a lack of Soviet support, led to widespread anger and the collapse of Kun's government. Military leader Miklos Horthy tried to reestablish stability, but Hungary continued to suffer from economic problems that only worsened during the Great Depression.

Failed democracy in Poland

Most Eastern European countries faced severe economic difficulties after the war that seemed to overwhelm their democratically-elected governments. Faced with hardships, many people became nostalgic for what seemed like stability offered by benevolent dictators. By the end of the 1920s, Bulgaria, Romania, and Yugoslavia all had replaced their democracies with dictatorships. Eventually, even newly formed Poland failed to maintain a democratic government. Although Poland was established as a constitutional democracy, many Polish citizens opposed key provisions of the constitution, leading to bitter political infighting. Beginning its existence as a poor nation made it very difficult for the government to rapidly improve the economy, especially after Germany imposed high tariffs against Polish goods. In 1926, as the government became increasingly unstable, widely admired military leader Marshal Jozef Pilsudski seized control as a dictator, maintaining only a sham form of democratic government.

US and European role in Latin America

The discovery of oil and other valuable resources in Latin America peaked foreign interest in that region. US officials made it clear that they would continue to oppose any new attempts at Latin American colonization by European nations, and most of those countries were reluctant to fight for new colonies following World War I. However, their leaders did recognize the value of economic investment. During the 1920s, European governments invested heavily in Latin American economies, whose leaders welcomed the improvements and jobs such interest usually brought to their nations. However, political coercion often accompanied economic influence, which in turn fueled a backlash of nationalist opposition to foreign investment. Some nations forced European investors out by nationalizing industries, such as when Mexico nationalized its largely British-owned oil industry in 1938. US President Franklin Roosevelt tried to improve relations with his Good Neighbor Policy, which promised limited foreign interference in the domestic affairs of Latin American nations.

Affect of Nationalist Movements in Africa and Asia on British Colonies

The era following World War I witnessed a rise in nationalism within African and Asian colonies, many of which had been pawns in the European power struggles that had led to war. Egypt's Wafd Party led a nationalist revolt against British control that resulted in Egyptian independence in 1922. British forces remained in the country as a protective force, and British officials continued to exert political influence there, as it also did in newly-independent Iraq and Transjordan. Inspired by Egypt's success at winning independence, as well as by Mohandas Gandhi's nonviolent movement against the British in India, many African nationalist movements gained support. Britain retained control over Palestine, which became the center of struggle between Jewish and Palestinian nationalists. Having promised Zionists a homeland in the Balfour Declaration, Britain worked toward the goal of dividing the land into two nations that would serve as homelands for Jews and for Arab Palestinians.

Japan's Interwar Expansion

Japan experienced increased militarism that challenged western resolve following World War I. Although the emperor maintained his throne, generals came to dominate the civilian government, especially after militaristic planning successfully turned around an economic decline in the 1920s. Soon all government policies were geared toward military goals. The generals even instituted their own version of an Asian "Monroe Doctrine," declaring the continent off limits to further western expansion while they were planning on seizing more Asian lands themselves. Japan's invasion of Manchuria in 1931 openly violated the covenant of the League of Nations. Although the western powers protested, Japan merely resigned from the League. Japan continued to take advantage of western focus on the Great Depression and on fascism to seize more Chinese lands. After 1938, Japan used the distraction of the European war to seize lands in Southeast Asia. Although Japanese expansion cut off crucial supply lines to British and French forces, the European powers were too busy defending against German attacks to retaliate against the Japanese.

Joseph Stalin

Vladimir Lenin's death in 1924 sparked a power struggle within the Communist Party. Many people expected Red Army organizer Leon Trotsky to take Lenin's place, but Trotsky faced a serious challenge from rising party leader Joseph Stalin. Trotsky had played a crucial role in the Bolshevik success, but Stalin was the more skilled politician, forging careful alliances and establishing the cult of Lenin to secure his power. The two rivals offered widely contrasting political plans. Trotsky followed a traditional Marxist view of planning for a worldwide workers' revolution, while Stalin wanted to focus solely on building the perfect communist system in the Soviet Union, a goal reflected by his slogan "socialism in one country." By 1928, Stalin emerged as the party (and defacto national) leader. To assure that Trotsky would no longer be a threat to his power, Stalin ordered his rival exiled in 1929 and then assassinated in 1940.

Five-Year Plans

Stalin believed that Lenin's New Economic Policy was too slow in reforming the economy. He was also angered by peasants' refusal to follow many tenets of the NEP. He immediately replaced the NEP with his first Five-Year Plan, an ambitious agenda to shift into a complete command economy with the government making all major economic decisions. Stalin hoped the plan would transform the Soviet Union from a largely agricultural nation into a modern industrial power to show the effectiveness of the command system. He set ambitious five-year economic goals, calling for doubling Soviet production of oil and coal and tripling the production of steel. He also planned for collective farms to produce enough crops to feed the entire population in addition to providing export crops. He planned to invest the income from crop exports into industrial expansion until industry was able to support itself.

Short and Long-Term Effects of the Five-Year Plans

The short-term effects proved disastrous for the Soviet people. When peasants resisted joining collective farms, government troops forced them to do so. Those people who still refused faced imprisonment, exile, or execution. Such heavy-handed tactics succeeded in converting about 90 percent of farmland into collective farms. However, collective farming failed to produce even enough crops to feed the population, much less export enough to fund industry. Widespread famine ensued that left millions dead and future generations suffering ill effects of malnutrition. Industrially, the plan succeeded in expanding production as the government focused most of its economic efforts on heavy industry and military armaments. Factory workers experienced few fruits of their labor, however. Despite the weaknesses of the First Five-Year Plan, Stalin instituted a second one in 1933, with similar results. Overall, the Five-Year Plans made life much worse for average Soviet citizens while strengthening government control.

Stalin's Control over Soviet Society

Russia had a long history of leaders who used secret police and spies to monitor and control political enemies. Joseph Stalin expanded and perfected this system, using terror to control the entire population. He carefully created a cult of personality around his image, even changing the name of the city of Tsaritsyn to Stalingrad. His government tightly controlled the press as well as all forms of art. Artists were allowed to produce only works of "socialist realism" approved by the government. Following the Marxist view that religion was incompatible with communism, the government outlawed all religious faiths, seized church property, and executed or imprisoned church leaders. Stalin often used the threat of imprisonment or execution to maintain order. His oppressive tactics frequently had no clear objective other than illustrating his power and instilling fear of retribution. Several times throughout his reign, he called for purges, or mass killings, of identified enemies of the state. Millions of people were killed or imprisoned for political reasons during Stalin's reign.

Changes Brought by the Soviet Constitution

The constitution proposed by Stalin reorganized the Soviet government into the following branches:

- The Supreme Soviet, the parliamentary body, which met only twice per year and elected members of the Politburo, a small committee in charge of the Communist Party.
- The Council of People's Commissars (later the Council of Ministers), which served as the executive and administrative body

The constitution operated under the pretense of following western-style governments (an attempt to appease western allies in the face of rising fascist enemies), but the established government was a sham. Although the constitution allowed for the election of officials, these elections were tightly controlled and offered only those candidates who had been pre-selected by Communist Party leaders (the only legal political party). The Politburo really controlled the government, as reflected by Stalin's official role as head of the Politburo, from which he ran his dictatorship.

Fascism in Italy

Italian fascism was the creation of charismatic politician Benito Mussolini. Prior to World War I, Mussolini had embraced socialism. During the war, however, he came to support a strong government rooted in extreme nationalism and militarism. After the conflict, he organized the

Fascist Party to advocate his views. As the constitutional monarchy failed to relieve Italy's postwar sufferings, many people embraced Mussolini's promises to return the nation to the glory days of the Roman Empire and prevent it from falling to Soviet-style communism. As the Fascist Party gained popularity, its Black Shirt forces (so-called because of their uniforms) waged violent campaigns to intimidate political opponents. In October 1922, Black Shirts convened a mass meeting in Rome. Viewing this gathering as a security threat, liberal members of Parliament asked King Emmanuel III to use police force against the Fascists. When he refused, most liberals resigned in protest, leaving conservatives in control. To prevent civil war, they convinced the king to name Mussolini as Italy's premier.

Tenets of Fascism

Fascism, from the Latin word fasces (bundle of sticks bound tightly around an ax), was a one-party political system rooted in authoritarian, militaristic, nationalistic government fueled by propaganda and based around a charismatic dictator. Fascism opposed both communism and democracy. Though it supported private ownership of business, fascism called for control of private industry through a military-based economy. Fascist governments tended to be highly bureaucratic, yet efficient in carrying out large-scale projects that reflected the dictator's goals. Fascism relied on "scapegoating," or blaming certain groups of people for all of a nation's problems. In Italy, communists served as prime scapegoats; in Germany it was the Jews. Fascism appealed to middle and upper classes because of its claimed support of private ownership and preservation of traditional class divisions. It relied on helping the wealthy maintain their money and status in exchange for some losses of their individual freedom and the oppression of minority groups. In practice, both fascism and communism were totalitarian forms of government that suppressed most individual rights.

Life in Italy under Mussolini's Rule

Historians often summarize Mussolini's rule by repeating the popular expression that "he made the trains run on time." This quote reflects his government's efficiency in providing much-needed services, while ignoring the high price Italian citizens paid in personal freedom under his rule. Once named premier, Mussolini quickly worked to dismantle all vestiges of democratic rule, which he claimed had been corrupted by socialist influence. He appointed Fascists to all major government positions and pushed through election laws guaranteed to ensure Fascist control of Parliament. The king was relegated to a figurehead, and Mussolini and his Grand Council of advisors ran the government, which quickly devolved into a police state. Mussolini outlawed all other political parties and non-government labor unions and suspended freedom the press, individual speech, and trial by jury. To control the economy without reverting to communism, Mussolini established a corporatist economy, in which 22 corporations headed by a committee of industry leaders and government officials set policy for those businesses that tightly controlled wages and prices.

Weimar Republic

In many ways, the Weimar Republic—the German democratic government established after World War I—seemed doomed to failure from its inception. Officials established a temporary republic following Kaiser Wilhelm's abdication in 1919. In 1920, an assembly convened in the city of Weimar to write a new constitution. The first major act of the Weimar government was approving the Treaty of Versailles, a necessary step for ensuring peace. However, many Germans opposed the treaty because of its harsh reparations and blaming of Germany for the entire war. They believed that Weimar officials did not defend the nation vigorously enough at the Paris Peace Conference. Some citizens considered the German delegates to be traitors. Like most European nations, Germany faced severe economic and social problems following World War I. Reparations made recovery much more difficult for Germany, which experienced runaway inflation and high unemployment. In the face of such problems and with little public support, Weimar officials found themselves unable to compete with communist and fascist alternatives.

Nazi Party

The Nazi Party, or National Socialist German Workers' Party, was one of several extreme ring-wing nationalist groups that organized to oppose the Weimar government. By 1921, charismatic recruit Adolf Hitler had emerged to head the party. Hitler gained fame by leading the Beer Hall Putsch in 1923 and turning his imprisonment into political martyrdom and a platform for his political ideas. As the Weimar Republic weakened, the Nazi Party grew in popularity, growing from 25,000 members in 1925 to 180,000 members in 1930, when the party won numerous seats in popular elections. In 1932, the party won a plurality 230 seats in the Reichstag. President Paul von Hindenberg appointed Hitler as chancellor of his cabinet in January 1933. The following month, Hitler blamed a suspicious fire in the Reichstag on communist conspirators. Declaring martial law, Hitler seized dictatorial powers and used his secret police to suppress all political opposition. The already weakened Weimar government quietly ceded its authority to the Nazis.

Mein Kampf

Hitler wrote Mein Kampf (My Struggle) while imprisoned for his role in the Beer Hall Putsch. Published in two volumes in 1925 and 1927, it became the bible of Nazism. The book offered a frank and detailed explanation of Hitler's political vision. The first volume recounted what Hitler saw as the betrayal of Germany at Versailles and called for revenge against France, which he viewed as the main culprit for Germany's punishment. He also expressed his racist views of Aryans (pure Germans) as a perfect race undermined by "parasitic" Jews. He blamed most of the world's problems on Jews, whom he believed needed to be exterminated. He also called for Germans to expand their living space by seizing eastern lands from hated communists and Slavs. The second volume of Mein Kampf offered very explicit guidelines for how the Nazi Party should use violence and terrorism to achieve its political goals. Hitler's philosophy appealed to many citizens of a country long steeped in both nationalist and anti-Semitic sentiments.

Life in Germany under Hitler

Hitler emphasized his power by taking the title of Fuhrer ("leader") and referring to his government as the Third Reich, or third German Empire. He said the first had been the Holy Roman Empire, the second the Hohenzollern kingdom. He promised that his Third Reich would last at least 1,000 years. Like Mussolini in Italy, he turned Germany into a totalitarian police state, using the Gestapo to suppress individual rights and all political opposition. His militaristic planning succeeded in improving the economy and infrastructure. However, success for many often came at the expense of scapegoated groups, including Jews, gypsies, homosexuals, Jehovah's Witnesses, people with disabilities, and communists. Hitler gradually increased the oppression of these other "inferior groups." The Nuremberg Laws were the first in a series of limitations on Jews, who were stripped of citizenship, as well as their economic and political rights. Eventually, many were sent to concentration camps, mass prisons built for political prisoners.

Developments in the Sciences

World War I brought about significant advances in emergency medicine and improved surgical techniques. The use of chemical weapons led to advances in poison antidotes and increased awareness of how chemicals affected the human body. The war increased ethical debates over the creation and uses of deadly weapons. Some people looked to science to make sense of the war itself. Some embraced Sigmund Freud's theories that the unconscious mind controlled human behavior. Others applied Albert Einstein's theories of relativity to ethical questions, embracing moral relativism over absolute rules and laws traditionally promoted by religion. No wartime dangers proved as deadly as the influenza pandemic that began in the spring of 1918. Commonly called the Spanish influenza pandemic, the outbreak quickly spread throughout the globe due to the movement of troops and goods during the war. The flu was highly contagious and deadly, killing some 20 million people before suddenly dissipating. Scientists continued to study the pandemic to better understand contagious diseases.

MAJOR ARTISTIC MOVEMENTS

Nearly all aspects of the art world reflected changing worldviews brought about by World War I. Artists of varying fields rejected traditional norms, experimented extensively, and reflected changing values in their works. Examples in various fields included:

- Literature was marked by disillusionment of war, reflected by "Lost Generation" writers. Major figures included Gertrude Stein (The Autobiography of Alice B. Toklas), Ernest Hemingway (The Sun Also Rises), F. Scott Fitzgerald (The Great Gatsby), John Dos Passos (Three Soldiers). Writers showed experimentation in forms, such as Franz Kafka's surrealism (Metamorphosis), James Joyce's stream of consciousness (Ulysses), and the work of nontraditional poets such as T.S. Eliot and e.e. cummings.
- Music reflected a rejection of tradition and the creation of new types of music; musicians of the time included Igor Stravinsky and Arnold Schoenberg, along with American jazz artists.
- Visual arts showed new forms, including cubism (Pablo Picasso, Georges Braque), surrealism (Salvador Dali), and Dadaism (Marcel Duchamp).
- Architecture emphasized functionalism (Louis Sullivan, Frank Lloyd Wright).

The Second World War and Contemporary Europe

Ethiopia's Significance in the Rise of Italian Power

Since fascism relied on a military economy, Mussolini prepared his armies for conquest and expansion. He hoped to use his forces to expand Italian colonies and access to natural resources. Ethiopia, located between Italian Somaliland and Italian-controlled Eritre, seemed a perfect target. Since Ethiopians had inflicted a humiliating defeat upon the Italian army in the 1896, Mussolini viewed Ethiopian conquest as a matter of national pride and revenge. As one of the few remaining independent African nations, Ethiopia had no guaranteed protection from other European nations, except for promises from the weak League of Nations. Betting that the League would not bother to defend the tiny nation, Mussolini used the pretense of a border dispute to invade Ethiopia in 1935. King Haile Selasse appealed to the League of Nations for defense, but, as Mussolini predicted, no countries were willing to risk armed conflict to help the Ethiopians. The League did issue economic sanctions against Italy, but with no enforcement power, these sanctions had little real effect.

Spanish Civil War

Spain became the first battleground in the revolt against fascism. In 1931, following several years of military dictatorship, democratic leaders established the Second Spanish Republic. Some reforms issued by the new government angered citizens and fueled support for the Falange, Spain's fascist party led by Francisco Franco. After socialist and communist members of the Popular Front won elections in 1936, civil war broke out between supporters of the Falange, called Nationalists, and supporters of the republic, called Loyalists. Germany and Italy supported the Nationalists. While the Soviet Union supported the Loyalists, few democracies were willing to lend direct aid, lest they spark another global war or appear to be supporting communism. Instead, democratic leaders encouraged private support for the Spanish Republic. Thousands of American, French, and British individuals joined International Brigades to fight with the Loyalists. Despite this aid, the Nationalists won, establishing a fascist government in 1939. However, the civil war had crippled the nation, preventing fascist Spain from becoming a threat to other nations.

German Expansion between 1933 and March 1939

- 1933 — Upon taking office, Hitler announced he was rearming Germany and withdrawing from the League of Nations.
- March 1936 — Using French treaties with the Soviets as an excuse, Germany sent troops into the Rhineland, in violation of the Treaty of Versailles. Other nations offered little protest.
- November 1936 — Germany signed the Anti-Comintern Pact with Japan (later expanded to include Italy), an alliance against the Soviet Union.
- March 1938 — Hitler annexed Austria, which had already come to be dominated by the Nazi Party; British and French leaders expressed concern, but offered little protest.
- September 1938 — In an attempt to prevent war between Germany and Czechoslovakia, British Prime Minister Neville Chamberlain and French Premier Edouard Daladier orchestrated the Munich Agreement, which gave Germany the disputed Sudetenland. Munich would come to symbolize the failure of appeasement.
- March 1939 — Germany invaded Czechoslovakia and seized a portion of Lithuania. British and French officials refused to intervene, hoping that Germany had fulfilled all of its plans for control of Central Europe.

Germany's Conquest of Czechoslovakia and the Outbreak of World War II

Despite hopes for the success of appeasement, most European leaders recognized Poland as Hitler's next target. To prevent Germany from invading Poland, both France and Great Britain pledged to defend the country. Hoping to gain control of the land diplomatically, Hitler tried to forge an alliance with the Poles against the Soviet Union. When that failed, he prepared for invasion, first by securing Italy's help with the Pact of Steel. Then, contrary to his anti-Soviet propaganda, Hitler negotiated the German-Soviet Nonaggression Pact with Stalin in August 1939. They agreed that neither country would attack the other. Secretly, Hitler agreed to give the Soviet Union control over eastern Poland and not to intervene should the Soviets invade the Baltic States. Stalin did not trust Hitler any more than he trusted western democracies, but he hoped to buy time to prepare his army for war. On September 1, 1939, Hitler launched a massive invasion of Poland. On September 3, Great Britain and France declared war on Germany, marking the beginning of World War II.

Progression of the War Between 1939 and 1941

Some people referred to the first few months of the conflict as a "phony war" because little direct fighting took place between German and Allied troops. The blitzkrieg strategy helped Germany secure Poland very quickly. The British navy blockaded German ports and sent troops to help France fortify its borders, including the recently constructed Maginot Line. Meanwhile, the Soviets built up their forces and seized lands in Eastern Europe. The "phony war" phase ended when Germany invaded neutral Denmark and Norway in April 1940 and then seized the Netherlands, Belgium, and Luxembourg. German forces surrounded France and forced the evacuation of British troops at Dunkerque. In June, Italy declared war on Britain and France, helping the Germans defeat northern France by mid-month. Southern French leaders maintained some control by establishing the Vichy government, which collaborated with occupying German forces. Germany then launched air attacks on Great Britain, which proved more resilient than Hitler expected. The Battle of Britain dragged on throughout the fall of 1940 and most of 1941.

US Role in the War Between 1939 and 1941

In 1939, Congress revised the Neutrality Acts to allow US companies to sell munitions to warring nations on a cash-and-carry basis. Since Britain controlled western sea routes, American companies sold arms only to the British. In September 1940, President Roosevelt authorized the exchange of 50 old US warships to the British in exchange for the use of British air and naval bases. At the same time, Congress approved the first peacetime US military draft. In March 1941, Congress passed the Lend-Lease Act, allowing the US to supply Britain with war materials on credit. In 1941, Roosevelt and Churchill announced their mutual support in the Atlantic Charter. Throughout the fall of 1941, US naval forces protected British vessels in the Atlantic. On December 7, 1941, Japan, a German ally, attacked the US naval fleet stationed at Pearl Harbor, Hawaii, to prevent US forces from impeding its plans to conquer Asia. The United States and Britain immediately declared war on Japan, forcing Germany and Italy to declare war on the United States.

Germany's Broken Alliance with the Soviet Union

By the fall of 1940, Germany controlled almost all of Western Europe and began moving to take control of key lands in the Mediterranean, North Africa, and Middle East. By the end of 1941, Germany had seized all of the Balkans except for Turkey, which it allowed to remain neutral. This moved alarmed the Soviets, who had been promised control of the Balkans. They rightfully believed that Hitler was setting the stage for an assault on the Soviet Union. On June 22, 1941, Germany broke the Nonaggression Pact by invading the Soviet Union. The move forced Germany to fight a major two-front war, as the Soviet Union refused to fall quickly. The Eastern Front spanned 2,000 miles of rough terrain, requiring a totally different kind of war plan for German troops. The move also shifted alliances. Great Britain and the still-neutral United States offered aid to the Soviets, though geography and German control of key ports prevented most foreign aid from reaching the country.

Holocaust

Despite being engaged in a global war in 1941, Hitler ordered resources redirected towards his Final Solution for the Jewish "problem." The meticulous planning and execution of the Holocaust was the prime example of fascist bureaucratic planning. Heinrich Himmler, head of the SS (the Nazi military), directed the operation. Initially, SS troops gathered Jews, led them into the woods, and shot them. Considering this system to be inadequate, Nazi leaders met at the Wannsee Conference in 1942 to plan for the conversion of camps for political prisoners into death camps. The SS systematically relocated all Jews to the camps, then sorted them based on a system designed to maximize their benefit to Germany before their ultimate deaths. The weakest immediately went to gas chambers. The strongest became slave laborers, fed very few rations until they either died from starvation and disease or became too weak to work and went to the gas chambers. By the time the Nazi government fell in 1945, more than six million Jews had been killed.

1942 - Turning Point in the War

The entry of United States into the war rejuvenated the Allied effort. In January 1942, representatives of 26 nations met in Washington, D.C., to declare their united alliance against the Axis powers. US naval forces won several key victories in the Pacific, while ground troops prepared for the European conflict. That summer, German troops forced the Soviets to retreat to Stalingrad and lay siege to the city. The Soviets successfully resisted the German onslaught, launching a counteroffensive in November that trapped the ill-prepared German troops, forcing them to remain in the region throughout the harsh Russian winter. Also in November, US General Dwight Eisenhower led a British-American coalition against German troops in North Africa. These Allied offensive moves turned the tide of the war to their sides' favor and revealed weaknesses in Axis strategies. They set up a series of key victories in 1943, including the German surrender at Stalingrad (February) and in North Africa (May).

Allies Achievment of Victory in Europe

Allied successes at Stalingrad and North Africa freed up troops for an attack on Italy. British troops took the island of Sicily in the summer of 1943, forcing Mussolini to resign. When Allied troops landed on the mainland in September 1943, the new Italian government surrendered and declared war on Germany. However, German troops stationed in Italy continued fighting the Allies. With the Soviets keeping most German land troops occupied on the Eastern Front, the Allies prepared for a massive offensive on the Western Front that would divide and surround German forces. They launched "Operation Overlord," an invasion of German-occupied northern France, on June 6, 1944 (D-Day). For the next several months Allied forces fought their way eastward as the Soviets increased their assault, forcing the Germans to retreat westward. The plan succeeded in surrounding German troops. In April 1945, American and Soviet forces crossed the German border. Hitler committed suicide on April 30. On May 8 (V-E Day), Germany surrendered.

End of the Global War

Despite the Allied victory in Europe, the war in the Pacific continued. Although US forces had won significant battles, the Japanese refused to surrender. In February 1945, Stalin promised to direct the full force of his army towards the Pacific campaign in exchange for some key Asian territories following the war. Allied leaders met again in July and demanded Japan's unconditional surrender, which the Japanese refused. While Soviet and American troops prepared for an invasion of Japan, Truman authorized use of the newly created, top-secret atomic bomb. On August 6, 1945, a US plane dropped the first atomic bomb on Hiroshima. Despite the large loss of life, Japanese officials refused to surrender. On August 8, the Soviet Union declared war on Japan and invaded Manchuria. The next day, the United States dropped another atomic bomb on Nagasaki. On August 14, Japan surrendered unconditionally, asking only that the emperor remain as a figurehead. On September 2, 1945 (V-J Day), Japanese officials signed a formal surrender.

ALLIES' WARTIME CONFERENCES

There were two major conferences:

- Yalta — British Prime Minister Winston Churchill, US President Franklin D. Roosevelt, and Soviet leader Joseph Stalin met in February 1945 to prepare for Germany's inevitable defeat. They agreed to divide Austria and Germany into zones of military occupation until a permanent peace agreement was finalized. All parties agreed to allow occupied Eastern European countries to determine their own future, though all agreed that, to insure stability, the new governments should ideally be friendly to the Soviet Union.
- Potsdam — With the death of Roosevelt and replacement of Churchill, Stalin met with new US President Harry Truman and British Prime Minister Clement Atlee to prepare for Germany's future. They agreed on several key principles:
    - Germany would remain a united country following Allied occupation.
    - Germany must give up its military.
    - The Nazi Party would be outlawed.
    - A new German government based on democratic principles would be formed.
    - An international court would try individuals who participated in war crimes.

GERMANY UNDER ALLIED CONTROL

Germany was divided into four Allied-occupied zones: the Soviet-controlled northeastern zone, the US controlled southeastern zone, the French-controlled southwestern zone, and the British-controlled northwestern zone. Because the important capital city of Berlin fell within the Soviet zone, the Allies divided the city into four zones as well. The Soviets controlled the entire eastern half of the city, with each of the other three Allies occupying smaller sections of the western half: France occupied northwestern Berlin, Britain controlled central-west Berlin, and the US controlled southwestern Berlin. The Allied Control Council, made up of delegates from the four occupying nations plus China, oversaw the work of the occupying governments.

NUREMBERG TRIALS

The Nuremberg Trials marked the first major attempt by an international court to try individuals for "crimes against humanity" committed during wartime. The trials focused on 22 Nazi leaders, who generally claimed the defense that they were merely following orders from their superiors. The trials ended with 12 defendants sentenced to death, 7 sentenced to prison terms, and 3 acquitted. More importantly, the trials established a precedent that the postwar world would not tolerate war crimes. The judges who presided over the Nuremberg Trials established that the defense of following orders was no justification for certain acts (like genocide) that were clearly so heinous that no decent human being should obey them.

UNITED NATIONS VS. LEAGUE OF NATIONS

Representatives from 51 countries met in 1945 to organize the United Nations for resolving international conflicts and promoting peace. Unlike the League of Nations, the UN was not designed for the idealistic goal of preventing all wars, although its leaders hoped to limit unjust wars. The UN structure included a series of programs to implement and enforce its goals, resulting in an organization that wielded more power than the League. The UN structure included:

- General Assembly — Made up of all member nations who had equal voting rights, regardless of size or wealth; elected UN Secretary-General.
- Security Council — Made up of five permanent members (Britain, China, France, the Soviet Union, and United States), each with veto powers and 10 temporary members who rotated two-year terms; determined any punitive actions against aggressor nations.
- Trustee Councilship — Controlled territories under UN supervision.
- Economic and Social Council — Sponsored various organizations to promote trade and human rights issues.
- International Court of Justice — Resolved issues of international law; justices elected by General Assembly.

Events in the Cold War

1946 — The Soviet Union installed communist puppet governments in Eastern European countries to protect its borders.

1947 — When communists instigated a civil war in Greece, Harry Truman issued his Truman Doctrine, dedicating the United States to containment, or halting the spread of communism.

1948 — The United States launched the Marshall Plan, a massive infusion of economic aid to rebuild European economies and prevent more from turning to communism. The Soviet Union and its eastern communist allies refused to participate. As the western allies prepared to withdraw from western Germany, the Soviet Union issued a blockade against Berlin, prompting the United States to launch the Berlin Airlift.

1949 — West Germany became the democratically-governed Federal Republic of Germany; East Germany became the communist-governed German Democratic Republic. The Soviet Union tested its first atomic bomb, sparking the arms war.

Twelve western nations organized the North Atlantic Treaty Organization (NATO), a defensive alliance.

1955 — Communist nations formed the Warsaw Pact in opposition to NATO.

1956 — Hungarians unsuccessfully revolted against their government.

1957 — The Soviet Union sparked the Space Race by launching the Sputnik satellite.

1959 — Communists led by Fidel Castro took control of Cuba.

1961 — The Bay of Pigs attack against the Cuban communists failed miserably; East Germany began the construction of the Berlin Wall.

1962 — The United States and the Soviet Union barely avoided nuclear war during the Cuban Missile Crisis.

1963 — Officials approved the Nuclear Test Ban Treaty.

1964 — The Gulf of Tonkin incident increased US involvement in Vietnam.

1969 — US astronauts reach the moon, thereby winning the Space Race.

1972 — Officials approved the SALT I Treaty, part of detente.

1975 — Communists won control of Vietnam.

1979 — Officials approved the SALT II Treaty.

1985 — Soviet leader Mikhail Gorbachev initiated reforms to expand Soviet political and economic freedom.

1986 — Gorbachev ended Soviet aid to satellite nations.

1989 — Communist governments fell in Poland, Hungary, Czechoslovakia, Bulgaria, and Romania; the Berlin Wall fell.

1990 — Germany reunited.

1991 — The Soviet Union dissolved.

LIFE AFTER 1945

AFFECT OF TECHNOLOGY

World War II ushered in many technological advances that were initially created for wartime needs but later adapted to postwar life. Microwaves and computer technology, for example, shaped daily life by allowing the invention of numerous devices to make domestic and work life easier. The Space Race sparked increased education in math and sciences, which led to further advances in transportation and communication. The ability to travel and communicate rapidly and easily helped promote the globalization of world economies and the interconnection of peoples throughout the world. The dawn of the Internet Age has rapidly changed the way people obtain and share information, and it continues to change constantly.

RELIGIOUS TRENDS

Since 1945, participation in religious organizations has generally declined in Europe. The United States has experienced increased diversity in religious participation, as well as increases in the number of people who consider themselves spiritual without belonging to any faith. Most western nations have experienced an increase in traditionally non-western faiths, such as Buddhism, Hinduism, and especially Islam, due mainly to increased immigration from Asia and the Middle East. Catholicism, while on the decline in much of the western world, has seen an increase in Latin America and Africa. Many experts expect Latin America to remain the focal point of the Catholic faith for many years to come.

ADVANCES AND CHALLENGES IN GLOBAL MEDICAL SCIENCE

Scientists have made great advances in the diagnosis and treatment of diseases since 1945. Jonas Salk's development of the polio vaccine in 1952 heralded a new age of fighting viral diseases. Crick and Watson's mapping of DNA in 1953 launched a new era in genetics. Scientists harnessed the power of nuclear energy for the treatment of certain cancers and other diseases. Despite such advances, new medical challenges continue to emerge. Scientists have yet to discover a complete cure for cancer. New diseases, such as AIDS and Ebola, continue to emerge and confound doctors. Overuse of some medicines, especially antibiotics, has also led to the development of "superbugs" that are resistant to known medical cures.

PHILOSOPHICAL MOVEMENTS

Following World War II, many writers and philosophers struggled with moral issues raised by Nazi atrocities. Philosophers such as Hannah Arendt tried to understand how people could carry out war crimes. Arendt coined the phrase "banality of evil" to describe Nazi bureaucrats who implemented the Final Solution simply because it preserved their jobs and promoted their own self-interest without any regard for those harmed by their actions. During the postwar world, many spiritual and political leaders urged people to actively oppose evil rather than passively allow it to exist. Martin Luther King Jr. applied the teachings of Mohandas Gandhi to promote nonviolent civil disobedience. By the 1960s, new philosophical movements were emerging that promoted self actualization and experimentation. By the 1980s, these movements had given way to a backlash of conservatism, following by neoconservative movements.

ARTISTIC MOVEMENTS

Totalitarian governments had oppressed many artistic endeavors, and communist governments continued to do so for many years following World War II. In communist countries, artists used their works as forms of protest, often smuggling them to wider audiences under threat of arrest. In democratic countries, artists expressed their freedom through various genres that experimented with form and style. A new school of artistry emerged in the United States called Abstract Expressionism. Exemplified by painters such as Jackson Pollard, abstract expressionists portrayed images that did not seem to reflect any obvious images from daily life, but rather reflected patterns and styles of creation that expressed such concepts as movement.

POLITICAL AND ECONOMIC DEVELOPMENT OF WEST GERMANY

Leaders from other western nations have often referred to West Germany's development after World War II as the "West German miracle." Using money from the Marshall Plan, West Germany rebuilt its economy to focus on industry and new technological innovations. As early as 1958, Germany had emerged as the leading industrial nation of Western Europe. Germany also succeeded in forming a new democratic government, dominated by the Christian Democratic Party and the Social Democratic Party. Dedicated to its alliance with the United States and Great Britain, along with fierce opposition to the reemergence of extremism, West Germany thrived. The economy experienced a downturn following West Germany's reunification with the much poorer East Germany, but leaders were eventually able to merge the two economies and workforces.

BRITISH WELFARE STATE

Causes:

- Ascendance of the Labour Party in 1945
- Outdated and inefficient industries
- Worker shortages due to wartime deaths
- Housing shortages due to wartime destruction
- Damage to infrastructure from bombings
- Emigration of many scientists and engineers who could help rebuild the economy.

Effects:

- Establishment of a free medical care system
- Nationalization of the Bank of England
- Nationalization of coal mines, railroads, and utilities
- Slow recovery for British economy compared to other western nations

- Inability to adapt as oil and nuclear energy became more important than coal
- Re-emergence of the Conservative Party in 1951

Political developments in France

The Marshall Plan helped France recover economically faster than Great Britain, but not as successfully as Germany, partly because the French government proved highly unstable. After the war, the nation established a weak Fourth Republic. In 1954, the colony of Algiers launched a war for independence, bringing French forces into a conflict many citizens did not want. By 1958, many were calling for withdrawal from Algiers. The issue so divided France that many leaders feared the outbreak of civil war. In 1958, legislative leaders appealed to military hero Charles de Gaulle for aid. De Gaulle called for the creation of a new constitution, launching the Fifth Republic, and negotiated for Algierian independence. He also withdrew French troops from NATO, though remaining a member of the organization, and worked to strengthen ties with West Germany, ending years of German-Franco animosity.

Steps towards European economic integration

Western European nations experienced varying levels of economic recovery after World War II. Most communist nations experienced continued economic problems until the collapse of their political systems. Some political leaders argued that European nations should unite their economies, while remaining politically independent, for the greater good of all. Major steps toward this goal included:

- 1952: Formation of the European Coal and Steel Community, comprised of France, West Germany, Italy, Belgium, the Netherlands, and Luxembourg, to regulate prices, wages, and standards within the industry.
- 1957: Formation of the European Economic Community (Common Market) by Belgium, France, Italy, Luxembourg, the Netherlands, and West Germany to regulate trade practices.
- 1967: Reorganization of the Common Market as the European Community.
- 1993: Reorganization of the European Community as the European Union, which included many former communist nations.

Effect of independence movements on colonialism

In many parts of the world, anti-colonial nationalist movements had been gaining ground prior to World War II. Many colonized people put their movements on hold during the war, hoping their aid to Allies would be rewarded with independence. However, the weakened state of most western powers also weakened their resolve and ability to maintain colonies. Once-mighty Great Britain began to cede its colonies soon after the war, granting independence to India and Pakistan in 1947. Over the next several years, Britain either voluntarily relinquished or was forced to give up most of its Asian and African colonies. French leaders initially resisted giving up their colonies, but the disaster in Algiers followed by rebellion in Indochina eventually led them to give up many French overseas possessions. Increasingly, western nations sought influence with other countries through economic investment, ideological alignment, and humanitarian aid.

CLEP Practice Test

Want to take this practice test in an online interactive format?
Check out the online resources page, which includes interactive practice questions and much more: **mometrix.com/resources719/clepwescivii**

1. Europe's Thirty Years' War was popularly known as

a. a war of economy.
b. a war of religion.
c. a war of power.
d. a war of commerce.
e. a war of reform.

2. Regarding the Treaty of Westphalia, all but which of these is factual?

a. It politically recognized the Swiss Confederacy (Switzerland) as independent.
b. It politically recognized the United Provinces of Holland as independent.
c. It accomplished the preparation for the politics in Europe to become secularized.
d It provided for reparations to France, which had undergone severe war damages.
e It was met with opposition by the Pope, but it was nonetheless signed.

3. Which of the following statements is correct regarding the Hapsburg Empire after 1648?

a. The Hapsburg Empire shared postwar stability and homogeneity with Prussia.
b. The Hapsburg Empire had military forces known for functioning smoothly after the war.
c. Following the war, the Hapsburg Empire presided over a significant number of Muslims.
d. After the war, the Hapsburg Empire included various languages and cultural groups.
e. After the war, the Hapsburg Empire included various religious and political groups.

4. Which statement is true regarding the political philosophies of Thomas Hobbes, Bishop Bossuet, Cardinal Richelieu, and John Locke?

a. Hobbes, Bossuet, and Richelieu disagreed with Locke on the right to rule a country.
b. The English, Hobbes and Locke, disagreed with the French, Bossuet and Richelieu.
c. Hobbes and Richelieu concurred and were opposed to Bossuet and Locke who agreed with each other.
d. Hobbes, Bossuet, Richelieu, and Locke all agreed about what gave the right to rule.
e. Hobbes, Bossuet, Richelieu, and Locke each disagreed individually about this issue.

5. Which of these statements is not accurate concerning events between 1640 and 1660 surrounding the English Civil War?

a. Parliament's army led by Oliver Cromwell defeated King Charles I's army.
b. Following a victory, Puritans eliminated all Presbyterians from Parliament.
c. The Rump Parliament annihilated the monarchy and the House of Lords.
d. King Charles I was executed the same year the monarchy was wiped out.
e. All of these statements are accurate regarding events surrounding the English Civil War.

6. Which of the following statements is *incorrect* regarding England's Glorious Revolution?

a. One outcome of this revolution was the crowning of William and Mary as leaders.
b. One outcome of the revolution was Parliament's writing an English Bill of Rights.
c. One reason that this revolution occurred was fighting between Whigs and Tories.
d. One reason that this revolution was called "glorious" was its minimal casualties.
e. The English Bill of Rights influenced America's Constitution and Bill of Rights.

7. What did Peter the Great of Russia *not* do with respect to the West in the late 1600s?

a. He influenced Russia's government officers and upper class to speak in the French language.
b. He influenced Russia's government officers and upper class to wear more Western fashions.
c. He influenced wealthy Russians to import Western art and educate their children in Europe.
d. He extended the already strong influences Russia had been deriving from Western cultures.
e. He built a new capital, St. Petersburg, and established state control over the Orthodox Church.

8. Which of the following statements is *not* true regarding the Huguenots?

a. The policies of King Louis XIV caused many Huguenots to leave France.
b. The Huguenots were French Catholics who were driven out by Protestants.
c. Many Huguenots who left France settled in England, helping its economy.
d. Many Huguenots who left France settled in Prussia, boosting its economy.
e. Huguenots settling in the USA contributed to the ancestry of 11 presidents.

9. Of these English words or names, which set is not a legacy of the Dutch Republic and language?

a. Manhattan, Harlem, Brooklyn, Yankees
b. boss, coleslaw, waffle
c. Santa Claus, cookie, bundle
d. knapsack, cruise, skate
e. All of these words come from Dutch.

10. Which of these statements is inaccurate regarding the Dutch Republic in the 17th century?

a. The Dutch Republic was centrally governed by its strongest province, Holland.
b. During the 17th century, the Dutch had great naval and economic world powers.
c. At that time, the Dutch were trading in Asia, Africa, North America and the Caribbean.
d. Religious tolerance and the Dutch Golden Age in artwork were hallmarks of the time.
e. Amsterdam was a world banking center; Grotius and others formed the center of international free trade.

11. By the turn of the 15th to 16th century, the languages predominating in the western hemisphere show which countries performed the most colonization worldwide. Among the following, which *includes* a country that was *not* one of these major colonists?

a. Portugal and Spain
b. The Netherlands
c. England and France
d. None of these
e. All of these

12. Which statement is accurate regarding the dominance of world powers in Europe by the 18th century?

a. France and England had equal dominance over each half of Europe (East and West).
b. France overpowered England and became the single dominant world power in Europe.
c. France dominated Western Europe on land, and England experienced naval dominance.
d. France was overpowered by England which became the dominant power in Europe.
e. France and England vied for power over Europe, but neither of them was successful.

13. Which of these statements correctly summarizes the economic philosophy of mercantilism as practiced by Britain, France, and other nations from the 16th-18th century?

a. A country needed only to access wealth, whose potential was without limits.
b. A country needed to export as many goods as it could sell to other countries.
c. A country needed to engage in as much free trade as possible with all other countries.
d. A country needed to balance its sale of exports with its purchase of imports.
e. A country needed to focus on buying and selling rather than on colonization.

14. Among the commodities produced in North America for which Britain and France competed in the 18th century, which of these is *least* associated with North America?

a. Furs
b. Fishing
c. Rich soil
d. Sea access
e. Sugar cane

15. Among the commodities produced in the West Indies for which Britain and France competed in the 18th century, which of these is *least* associated with the West Indies?

a. Cotton
b. Coffee
c. Fishing
d. Tobacco
e. Sugar cane

16. To what does the name of the War of Jenkins' Ear refer?

a. A war between England and Spain in the West Indies
b. A war fought over a strain of corn grown in the US
c. A war fought by England and France about Austria
d. A war in which England and Prussia fought against France and Austria.
e. A war begun in the American Ohio Valley against the French

17. Which statement best describes the significance of the American Revolution?

a. It enabled the formation of a major world power, the United States of America.
b. It caused considerable additions to the number of people speaking English in Canada.
c. It produced legal documents expressing major Enlightenment philosophies.
d. It created a direct influence on the development of the French Revolution.
e. It accomplished all of these, which all have similar historical significance.

18. Which is an accurate statement regarding Eastern vs. Western civilizations' respective development in mathematics and science?

a. The Western world surpassed the Eastern world in these disciplines from the Middle Ages through the 17th century.
b. The Eastern world surpassed the Western world in these disciplines from the Middle Ages through the 17th century.
c. The Eastern and Western worlds were roughly equal in these disciplines in the Middle Ages through the 17th century.
d. The East exceeded the West in these areas in the Middle Ages, but the West had overtaken them by the 17th century.
e. The West exceeded the East in these areas in the Middle Ages, but the East had overtaken them by the 17th century.

19. Who was the first scientist of record to posit a heliocentric rather than a geocentric universe?

a. Ptolemy
b. Copernicus
c. Galileo
d. Kepler
e. Newton

20. Of the following choices, which one arranges these early proponents of the scientific method in the correct chronological order?

a. Leibniz, Pascal, Descartes, Bacon
b. Descartes, Bacon, Leibniz, Pascal
c. Bacon, Descartes, Pascal, Leibniz
d. Pascal, Leibniz, Bacon, Descartes
e. Bacon, Pascal, Descartes, Leibniz

21. Which of these best explains deism?

a. God exists and maintains a hands-on involvement in day-to-day events and individual lives.
b. God exists and set things in motion, but does not perform miracles or act on everyday lives.
c. God may or may not exist; there is no evidence to prove or disprove this, so nobody knows.
d. God does not actually exist, but is simply a concept created by human beings who need to believe in a higher being.
e. God exists, but only in the minds of the individual human beings who conceive of this entity.

22. Of the following, which answer best describes ideas that Charles Montesquieu presented in his books?

a. Criticism of the monarchy and the Catholic Church
b. Natural laws that all political systems must observe
c. The necessity of checks and balances in government
d. The need for separation of powers in government
e. All of these describe ideas about which Montesquieu wrote.

23. Regarding the European Enlightenment philosophers, which statement is correct?

a. These philosophers were mainly English, rather than French, as England's government needed more changes to fit with Enlightenment ideas.
b. These philosophers were all French, rather than English, as England's government needed more changes to fit with Enlightenment ideas.
c. These philosophers were more English, rather than French, as England's government needed fewer changes to fit with Enlightenment ideas.
d. These philosophers came from both France and the United Kingdom, but the French were more motivated by a repressive government.
e. These philosophers came from both France and the United Kingdom, but the English were more motivated by a repressive government.

24. For which of the following was Voltaire known?

a. Publishing the satirical picaresque novella Candide
b. Writing the political treatise The Spirit of the Laws
c. Editing the West's first 28-volume Encyclopedia
d. Writing his books Émile and The Social Contract
e. Publishing his Essay on Crimes and Punishments

25. *The Wealth of Nations* was written by which United Kingdom author?

a. David Hume
b. Edward Gibbon
c. Adam Smith
d. Jeremy Bentham
e. Mary Wollstonecraft

26. Of the following, who was *not* known as an "enlightened despot"?

a. Emperor Joseph II of Austria
b. Catherine the Great of Russia
c. Frederick the Great of Prussia
d. Louis XVI the King of France
e. All were "enlightened despots".

27. Which of these accomplishments was not one of many by Benjamin Franklin?

a. Proving that lightning is one form of electricity
b. Organizing firefighters and starting public libraries
c. Inventing bifocal spectacles and a type of stove
d. Having founded the University of Pennsylvania
e. All of these were accomplishments of Franklin.

28. Which of the following advantages did Great Britain possess to facilitate the Industrial Revolution?

a. Its mining of coal
b. Its mining of iron
c. Its transportation
d. Its individualism
e. All of these were.

29. In which country do historians consider the 18th century "agricultural revolution" to have begun?

a. America
b. France
c. England
d. Russia
e. Germany

30. Which of the following was *not* an outcome of the enclosure movement in England?

a. Fewer sheep farms
b. Fewer small farms
c. Less common land
d. More productivity
e. Fewer total farmers

31. Which factor was *not* related to the growth of industry during the 18th century?

a. Growing profits among landowners
b. The invention of the spinning jenny
c. The urbanization of many farmers
d. Growth of Manchester and Liverpool
e. All of these factors were related to it.

32. Of the following, which is *not* true regarding the development of the textile industry?

a. The Watt steam engine contributed to cloth production.
b. The Watt steam engine contributed to iron production.
c. The Watt steam engine, iron, and steel led to railroads.
d. The railroads both resulted from and added to industry.
e. These statements are all true.

33. Which of these was *not* one of the less-desirable effects of the textile industry's growth?

a. Europe's businesses supported slavery in America.
b. Steam-powered machines encouraged child labor.
c. Cotton planters in the Southern US made profits.
d. All of these were less-desirable effects of industry.
e. None of these was a less-desired effect of industry.

34. The expression "the pits," meaning something really bad, was originally used to describe

a. streets full of sewage in England's cities during the Industrial Revolution.
b. the numerous coal or iron mines in England where many people worked.
c. English factories blowing coal soot into the air in the 19th - 20th centuries.
d. the English tar pits, a popular name for asphalt pits of surfacing bitumen.
e. the filthy barracks of the factories in England where many workers lived.

35. Which is *not* a true statement regarding England in the 18th-19th centuries?

a. At that time, Britain had the same kind of democracy we think of in America today.
b. Movement to political/urban/industrial reform began in England just as industry did.
c. Britain had more interaction among its classes then than in other European countries.
d. Britain had less interaction among its classes than the United States did at that time.
e. Industrialization brought higher wages and a middle class, but also much suffering.

36. To what did the Reform Bill of 1832 in Great Britain pertain?

a. The right of Catholics to hold seats in Parliament
b. The abolition of slavery within the British Empire
c. The beginning of sanitary procedures in the cities
d. The right of the males in the middle class to vote
e. The limitation of workdays to 9 hours for children

37. In 1874, Britain's Parliament passed a law prohibiting

a. children under age 13 from working more than 9-hour days.
b. children aged 13 to 18 from working more than 69 hours a week.
c. men from working for more than ten hours in one work day.
d. women and boys under age 18 working more than 10 hours a day.
e. men, women, and children from working more than 8 hours a day.

38. Which statement is *not* true regarding the Chartist movement in Great Britain?

a. It expressed the desire of the people to establish a People's Charter.
b. It included the demand that women in Britain have the right to vote.
c. It included the signatures of millions of British subjects on petitions.
d. It included the demand for MPs to be paid as a way to prevent graft.
e. It was the first movement ever of the working class on a mass scale.

39. Of the following, which was/were *not* associated with the organizing of labor in England?

a. The group known as the Luddites
b. The Amalgamated Society of Engineers
c. Social reformer Robert Owen
d. The Grand National Consolidated Trades Union
e. These all were associated with the organizing of labor.

40. Which is an *incorrect* answer regarding the Luddites?

a. This group constituted a British social movement.
b. This group was made of artisanal weavers.
c. This group was opposed to new textile machines.
d. This group was famous for destroying machines.
e. This group's name is now used for skilled artists.

41. Which of these was *not* a factor in industrialization taking longer to develop in the rest of Europe than in England?

a. Fewer decent roads in Europe than England
b. Costly tolls along rivers in the rest of Europe
c. More cultural individualism in Great Britain
d. Laws in the rest of Europe restricting traders
e. Europe's many wars between 1790 and 1815

42. Regarding the French Revolution, which of the following statements is most accurate?

a. The French Revolution was very important to France, but not internationally.
b. The French Revolution had and still has a major impact on the entire world.
c. The French Revolution, though very dramatic, was basically a simple event.
d. The French Revolution is notable for affecting the world more than France.
e. The French Revolution is not accurately described by any of these answers.

43. Which of these was *not* a major contributor in setting the stage for the French Revolution?

a. The condition of the national economy in France and its progression in pre-war years
b. King Louis XVI's historical financial requirements and progression in pre-war years
c. France's assisting Prussia in the War of Austrian Succession, which soon backfired
d. France's aid to Prussia in the War of Austrian Succession got Great Britain involved.
e. All these factors were major contributors in setting the stage for the French Revolution.

44. Before the French Revolution began, who were members of the First Estate?

a. Members of the clergy
b. Members of the nobility
c. Bourgeoisie and peasants
d. None of these
e. All of these

45. Before the French Revolution began, who were members of the Second Estate?

a. Members of the clergy
b. Members of the nobility
c. Bourgeoisie and peasants
d. None of these
e. All of these

46. Before the French Revolution began, who were members of the Third Estate?

a. Members of the clergy
b. Members of the nobility
c. Bourgeoisie and peasants
d. None of these
e. All of these

47. The Abbé Emmanuel Sieyès published a pamphlet in 1789. In it he wrote, "What is the _____ Estate? *Everything.* What has it been in the political order up to the present? *Nothing.* What does it ask? *To become something."* Which word correctly fills in the blank in the first sentence?

a. First
b. Second
c. Third
d. Fourth
e. Fifth

48. What was one difference between France's Declaration of the Rights of Man and Citizen and America's Declaration of Independence?

a. France's declaration did not declare the right to liberty.
b. France's declaration did not assert the right to property.
c. France's declaration did not declare the equality of all people.
d. France's declaration did not give power to the people.
e. None of these differed in the two declarations.

49. Which of the following provides the correct chronological order of the groups governing France (with or without a monarch) between 1789 and 1795?

a. The National Assembly, the National Convention, the Legislative Assembly, the Directory, the Committee of Public Safety, the Paris Commune
b. The Directory, the National Convention, the National Assembly, the Legislative Assembly, the Paris Commune, the Committee of Public Safety
c. The Legislative Assembly, the Committee of Public Safety, the Directory, the Paris Commune, the National Assembly, the National Convention
d. The Committee of Public Safety, the Paris Commune, the Directory, the Legislative Assembly, the National Convention, the National Assembly
e. The National Assembly, the Legislative Assembly, the Paris Commune, the National Convention, the Committee of Public Safety, the Directory

50. After returning to Paris in 1799 and becoming France's emperor, Napoleon accomplished a number of things. Which of the following was *not* one of these accomplishments?

a. Giving order and stability to the country
b. Allowing the Pope to nominate bishops
c. A Civil Code abolishing primogeniture
d. Granting equality and rights to peasants
e. Taking most newspapers out of circulation

51. Events between 1793 and 1795 caused which of the following to happen in Poland?

a. Poland ceased to exist as a country until after World War I.
b. It fomented a revolution like ones in America and France.
c. Poland became stronger by becoming an ally with Austria.
d. Poland completely severed all its connections with Russia.
e. Poland became a territory owned by Prussia.

52. Which of these was *not* an outcome of the French occupation of Egypt under Napoleon?

a. The Rosetta Stone was discovered.
b. Slavery in Egypt was abolished.
c. Religious taxation was abolished.
d. British Lord Nelson was defeated.
e. Torturing prisoners was abolished.

53. Among the following, all *but* which mainly approved of the French Revolution?

a. Thomas Jefferson
b. The London Corresponding Society
c. The British government
d. The Society of United Irishmen
e. All of these approved of the French Revolution.

54. Among the following, which was/were against the French Revolution?

a. The London Corresponding Society
b. The Alien and Sedition Acts
c. The British government
d. The Society of United Irishmen
e. All of these were against the French Revolution.

55. In which of these countries that Napoleon invaded in the early 19th century did he suffer the worst defeat?

a. Prussia
b. Spain
c. Portugal
d. England
e. Russia

56. Which of the following countries was *not* a member of the Quadruple Alliance?

a. Russia
b. Prussia
c. Austria
d. France
e. England

57. What was *not* one of Napoleon's motives for offering the Louisiana Purchase to the United States?

a. A recent defeat in Haiti in a war of slaves against French masters
b. A way to recoup financial losses incurred by his European wars
c. A way to start over again to establish another empire in America
d. All of these were motives for Napoleon to sell Louisiana to the United States.
e. None of these motivated Napoleon to sell Louisiana to the United States.

58. Which of these groups included France as a member?

a. The Concert of Europe
b. The Quadruple Alliance
c. The Congress of Vienna
d. All of these included France.
e. None of these included France.

59. Which one is *not* a true statement regarding the Crimean War?

a. The Crimean War made Russia lose control of Christian shrines in the Ottoman Empire.
b. The Crimean War involved Russia, the Ottoman Empire, England, France, Austria and Prussia.
c. An outcome was that English ships were permitted to trade in the Black Sea.
d. An outcome was that French ships were permitted to trade in the Black Sea.
e. Florence Nightingale prevented many deaths from diseases during the Crimean War.

60. Which statement is true regarding social reactions to the Enlightenment and the French Revolution in Europe in the 19th century?

a. The well-educated upper class embraced Enlightenment ideals and the majority of them became liberals.
b. The bourgeoisie wanted to protect their newfound wealth, so the majority of them became conservatives.
c. Both the upper and middle classes reacted to these occurrences by primarily becoming liberals.
d. Both the upper and middle classes reacted to these events by primarily becoming conservatives.
e. None of these statements is true regarding reactions to the Enlightenment or French Revolution.

61. The author of *On Liberty* was

a. John Stuart Mill.
b. Edmund Burke.
c. John Locke.
d. Friedrich Hegel.
e. Thomas Carlyle.

62. Who was *not* associated with the Romantic literary movement in England?

a. William Wordsworth
b. George Gordon, Lord Byron
c. Ralph Waldo Emerson
d. Samuel Taylor Coleridge
e. Percy Bysshe Shelley

63. Of the following, which was *not* related to the Greek Revolution of 1821?

a. The Ottoman Empire
b. The poet Lord Byron
c. The Treaty of London
d. The French and Russians
e. These were all related to the Greek Revolution of 1821.

64. Among the countries where Napoleon III tried to expand France's control, which did he *not* actually colonize?

a. Asia
b. Italy
c. Africa
d. Mexico.
e. None of these

65. Which of these men, while influential in fostering Italian nationalism, was the least successful in actually furthering the unification of the Italian states in the 19th century?

a. Count di Cavour
b. Giuseppe Garibaldi
c. Giuseppe Mazzini
d. None of these was successful.
e. All of these were successful.

66. Which of the following was *not* associated with Otto von Bismarck?

a. Kaiser Wilhelm I
b. Seven Weeks' War
c. Franco-Prussian War
d. The Berlin Decrees
e. Modern Germany

67. Which of the following words are associated with commerce in the German states in the mid-19th century?

a. Zollverein
b. Realpolitik
c. Schleswig
d. Holstein
e. Reichstag

68. Which changes were most apparent in Europe and beyond by the turn of the 19th to the 20th centuries?

a. Advances in the study of the sciences
b. Longer life expectancies of people
c. Nationalism in nations and minorities
d. Transportation enabled by railroads
e. These were all changes that occurred.

69. Of the following men who contributed to the automotive industry in the 19th and 20th centuries, which one was *not* specifically an inventor, developer, or manufacturer of engines and/or cars?

a. Karl Benz
b. Henry Ford
c. Rudolf Diesel
d. Gottlieb Daimler
e. John D. Rockefeller

70. Jane Addams' Hull House is an example of which of the following turn-of-the-century cultural developments?

a. Higher Criticism movement
b. Social Gospel movement
c. Darwinism
d. Freudianism
e. Salvation Army

71. Between the years of 1846 and 1932, approximately how many people emigrated from Europe to North America, Canada, and South America?

a. 20 million
b. 30 million
c. 40 million
d. 50 million
e. 60 million

72. Which of these is *not* true regarding the Second Industrial Revolution?

a. The number of Germany's factories more than quadrupled during that time period.
b. The United States and Germany were tied as leaders of industry during that time.
c. The oil industry was one of the most significant components of industrial growth.
d. The steel industry was one of the most important components of industrial growth.
e. While big companies had previously existed, this was when modern "mega" businesses grew.

73. Chronologically, which came first?

a. Transatlantic radio transmission
b. The first Zeppelin airship
c. The Morse telegraph
d. The Wright airplane
e. The telephone

74. As a consequence of the second Industrial Revolution, the percentage of the urban population in Great Britain from 1800 to 1900

a. doubled.
b. tripled.
c. quadrupled.
d. increased by fifty percent.
e. increased by 75 percent.

75. In England, the population of the city of London alone increased by ___ times from 1800 to 1900.

a. two and a half
b. three and a half
c. four and a half
d. five and a half
e. six and a half

76. As a consequence of the second Industrial Revolution, the population of Berlin increased by more than ___ times between 1800 and 1900.

a. Five and a half
b. Ten and a half
c. Fifteen and a half
d. Twenty and a half
e. Twenty-five and a half

77. Which of these was *not* an example of the urban development required by rapid urbanization resulting from the Industrial Revolution?

a. The establishment of police departments
b. Gladstone's Reform Act of 1884
c. The formation of Departments of Health
d. The heating of homes and water with gas
e. Indoor plumbing and new sewer systems

78. Great Britain's Public Health Act of 1875

a. mandated the construction of hospitals in cities.
b. provided for home health nurse visits in cities.
c. provided for free clinics to be built in the cities.
d. required all new homes to contain indoor plumbing.
e. stipulated that all of these provisions be made.

79. In 1884, the Prime Minister of England gave the right to vote to __ of the adult men in the country.

a. 40%
b. 50%
c. 60%
d. 70%
e. 80%

80. Which of the following is *not* true about urban life around the turn of the 19th-20th centuries?

a. Most people living in cities experienced a lower standard of living.
b. Most city dwellers had poor living conditions by today's standards.
c. By working fewer hours, urban people had more leisure time.
d. Tourism became popular because people could afford it.
e. All over the Western Hemisphere, bicycles became a popular craze.

81. Increasing emphasis on education in the late 19th century meant that adult illiteracy was virtually wiped out by 1900 in all but which of the following countries?

a. France
b. Russia
c. England
d. Germany
e. Scandinavia

82. In the 1860s, who proved the theory that bacteria were sources of infection?

a. Marie Curie
b. Robert Koch
c. Louis Pasteur
d. Albert Einstein
e. Gregor Mendel

83. The ideas of which of the following men presented challenges to traditional Christian beliefs?

a. Sigmund Freud
b. Charles Darwin
c. Charles Lyell
d. Thomas Malthus
e. All of these men

84. Who founded the school of thought known as Social Darwinism?

a. Charles Darwin
b. Friedrich Nietzsche
c. Rudyard Kipling
d. Herbert Spencer
e. Andrew Carnegie

85. Which of the following is *not* true regarding the British Empire?

a. By the 20th century, the British Empire controlled over 25% of the world's population.
b. The Rhodes Scholarships program is a legacy of the British Empire.
c. African country Zimbabwe was formerly named after Cecil Rhodes.
d. Great Britain is much smaller than the American state of California.
e. All of these statements are true statements regarding the British Empire.

86. Which of these is *not* a consequence of the British Empire?

a. The freedom that is currently found in America
b. The freedom that is currently found in Jamaica
c. Problems of hostile groups that coexist in India
d. Problems of hostile groups in African countries
e. The freedom that currently exists in Hong Kong

87. Among the following countries, which was *not* a British colony until the 20th century?

a. Kenya
b. Sudan
c. Nigeria
d. Algeria
e. S. Africa

88. Among the following countries, which was a French colony until the 20th century?

a. Canada
b. Algeria
c. Indonesia
d. Mozambique
e. South Africa

89. Among the following countries, which was a Dutch colony until the 20th century?

a. Indonesia
b. Indochina.
c. Mozambique
d. South Africa
e. New Zealand

90. Among the following countries, which was a Portuguese colony until the 20th century?

a. Indochina
b. Indonesia
c. South Africa
d. New Zealand
e. Mozambique.

91. In which of these countries did linguistic minorities not rebel against an English-speaking majority?

a. Wales
b. Ireland
c. Scotland
d. Brittany
e. Québec

92. In the mid-1880s, Germany colonized territories which now form all but which of the following countries?

a. Tanzania
b. Cameroon
c. Mauritania
d. Togoland
e. Namibia

93. The Berlin Conference (1885)

a. convened in order to resolve imperialist claims in Germany.
b. convened to settle imperial claims in Germany by England.
c. divided African colonies among various European powers.
d. convened to settle competition between Germany and France.
e. settled differences among world powers regarding Germany.

94. The Triple Entente (1907) was made between

a. Britain, Russia, and France.
b. Germany, Austria, and Russia.
c. Germany, Austria, and Italy.
d. Britain, Russia, and Germany.
e. Britain, Germany, and France.

95. Labor unions were legalized in England in

a. 1866.
b. 1871.
c. 1884.
d. 1891.
e. None of these

96. Labor unions were legalized in France in

a. 1866.
b. 1871.
c. 1884.
d. 1891.
e. None of these

97. Labor unions were legalized in Germany in

a. 1866.
b. 1871.
c. 1884.
d. 1891.
e. None of these

98. The first national labor union in America was formed in

a. 1866.
b. 1871.
c. 1884.
d. 1891.
e. None of these

99. The tradition of referring to liberals as "left-wing" and to conservatives as "right-wing" has its origins in

a. the American Revolution.
b. the British Parliament.
c. the Continental Congress.
d. the Berlin Conference.
e. the French Revolution.

100. Approximately how many military deaths were caused by World War I?

a. 7 million
b. 13 million
c. 37 million
d. 27 million
e. None of these

101. Which of these was *not* a result of the First World War?

a. The USA. became a major world power.
b. Russia became a world Communist center.
c. The stage was set for the Second World War.
d. Europe's moral superiority was reinforced.
e. Religious doubt and pessimism developed.

102. The catalyst to the onset of World War I was the assassination of Archduke Franz Ferdinand by

a. Austrian terrorists.
b. Russian nationalists.
c. Serbian nationalists.
d. German terrorists.
e. French nationalists.

103. Regarding World War I, "It must be a peace without victory....Only a peace between equals can last." Who said this?

a. Woodrow Wilson
b. David Lloyd George
c. Georges Clemenceau
d. Adolf Hitler
e. Wilfred Owen

104. Which of the following is *not* true regarding the United States and World War I?

a. The United States did not enter into the war until 1917.
b. US troops participated in the battle for slightly more than a year.
c. The sinking of the Lusitania motivated Woodrow Wilson to enter the war.
d. The Zimmermann Telegram motivated Woodrow Wilson to enter the war.
e. None of the First World War was fought in America.

105. After the First World War, which of these countries did *not* result from the dissolution of the Austro-Hungarian Empire?

a. Czechoslovakia
b. Yugoslavia
c. Hungary
d. Austria
e. Poland

106. After the First World War, which of these countries did *not* result from the dissolution of the Ottoman Empire?

a. Turkey
b. Syria
c. Egypt
d. Iran
e. Iraq

107. Which was *not* a factor contributing to the Russian Revolution in 1917?

a. Lack of arms
b. Lack of food
c. An absent Tsar
d. Linguistic heterogeneity
e. These were all factors.

108. Of the following, which is *not* true regarding the Russian Revolution of 1917?

a. Riots broke out in the cities of Russia that year.
b. Rasputin affected the Tsar's wife in his absence.
c. Loss of the Russo-Japanese War contributed to the revolution.
d. Nicholas II reorganized the government in 1917.
e. Demonstrators stormed the Winter Palace in 1905.

109. Who is generally regarded by historians as having killed the most people in Russia in the first half of the 20th century?

a. Vladimir Lenin
b. Joseph Stalin
c. Leon Trotsky
d. Sergei Kirov
e. None of these

110. "In the whole history of the...nation...it has never been so united as today and...it will remain united in the future." Who said this?

a. Adolf Hitler
b. Benito Mussolini
c. Winston Churchill
d. Franklin D. Roosevelt
e. None of these said this.

111. "We shall fight on the beaches, we shall fight on the landing grounds, we shall fight in the fields and in the streets; we shall fight in the hills. We shall never surrender." Who said this?

a. Adolf Hitler
b. Benito Mussolini
c. Winston Churchill
d. Franklin D. Roosevelt
e. None of these said this.

112. "More than an end to war, we want an end to the beginning of all wars." Whose quotation is this?

a. President Woodrow L. Wilson
b. President Franklin D. Roosevelt
c. Prime Minister Winston Churchill
d. Hungarian Zionist Theodor Herzl
e. None of these made this statement.

113. Which is true regarding the United States' entry into the Second World War?

a. The US wanted neutrality from the 1930s until 1941.
b. Winston Churchill's persuasion secured aid from the United States.
c. Congress' Lend-Lease Act aided the UK and Canada.
d. Japan's attack on Pearl Harbor triggered US entry.
e. All of these are true regarding US entry into WWII.

114. What was the largest Nazi extermination camp of the Holocaust?

a. Auschwitz
b. Treblinka
c. Dachau
d. Sobibor
e. Buchenwald

115. Which of the following groups of peoples were imprisoned and murdered by the Nazis in their death camps?

a. Jewish people
b. Slavic people
c. Gypsy people
d. people with disabilities
e. All of these

116. In the Cold War, which was *not* an instance of attempts to contain Communism?

a. The enactment of the Marshall Plan
b. The policies of the Truman Doctrine
c. The activities of the Berlin Airlift
d. The 1961 building of the Berlin Wall
e. The Cuban Missile Crisis of 1962

117. Who was *not* a major contributor to social changes, especially among young people, in the second half of the 20th century?

a. Elvis and the Beatles
b. Charles de Gaulle
c. Camus and Sartre
d. Rachel Carson
e. Simone de Beauvoir

118. Which of the following is *not* associated with the end of the Cold War?

a. The Soviet war in Afghanistan
b. Polish Solidarity organization
c. Fall of Germany's Berlin Wall
d. South Africa abolishing apartheid
e. These are all associated with the end of the Cold War.

119. Which is *not* true regarding the European Union?

a. It was established through the Treaty of Rome in 1957.
b. It was first called the European Economic Community.
c. It accepted Turkey as a member without any conditions.
d. It was called the Common Market and removed tariffs.
e. It was instrumental in the adoption of the euro currency.

120. What statement would historians be least likely to agree with about Western civilization?

a. By the beginning of the 21st century, Western civilization has not been as influential as others.
b. The philosophical beliefs associated with communism have their origins in Western civilization.
c. The philosophical beliefs associated with democracy have their origins in Western civilization.
d. The great technological and educational advances in modern life are from Western civilization.
e. One sign of great changes from 1648 to 2000 is that there was no such idea as a nation in 1648.

Answers and Explanations

1. B: The Thirty Years' War (1618-1648) in Europe was known as a "war of religion." It was fought among Lutherans, Catholics, and Calvinists in central Europe. It was not called a "war of economy" (a) and moreover was not fought over economic issues. It was not called a "war of power" (c), even though it was fought over issues of political power. Indeed, power was more important to this war than was religion, for which this war was named; however, since church and state were not yet separated at this time, religion and politics were so intertwined that political plotting and the ensuing warfare always involved religious issues as well. As with economy, commerce (d) was not used to describe this war. Although the treaty ending this war did cement changes to religious practices that were begun by the Protestant Reformation, the war itself was never designated as a "war of reform" (e).

2. D: It is not a fact that the Treaty of Westphalia provided for reparations to France, or even that France had undergone war damages. In fact, the majority of the Thirty Years' War was fought in central Europe, and none of it was fought in France at all, so this answer is untrue. It is a fact that this treaty gave political recognition to the independence of the countries that are now Switzerland (a) and Holland (b). The Treaty of Westphalia also prepared the way for political secularization of Europe (c). In addition, this treaty marked the decrease in the Pope's influence over Europe: He stated he was against the treaty, but the signing parties paid no attention to his objections (e).

3. C: Following the Thirty Years' War, the Hapsburg Empire, ruled by the monarchy of the Hapsburg royal family, included many Muslims from Hungary after it was freed from the rule of the Turkish Ottoman Empire. It is not correct to say that the Hapsburg Empire was stable or homogenous like Prussia following the war (a). Unlike Prussia, the Hapsburg Empire was made up of a diverse population. This heterogeneity made the empire unstable for the majority of its existence until it ended after World War I. The diversity in the Hapsburg Empire caused major differences among its members in languages and cultures (d) and in religious and political beliefs (e). As a result, even the empire's military forces did not run smoothly (b) as they were made up of people from various regions with different backgrounds, customs, and attitudes.

4. A: Thomas Hobbes was an absolutist who believed that a leader should have absolute power to protect the populace from their own baser instincts. (The title of Hobbes' famous book, *Leviathan,* refers to such an absolute ruler.) Bishop Bossuet, who was the tutor to King Louis XIV, not only agreed with absolutism, but moreover believed in the divine right of kings in the tradition of the Carolingians and Charlemagne. Cardinal Richelieu, who was French Secretary of State and King Louis XIII's chief minister, had similar conservative views and had established the political and religious practices which Bossuet then maintained and furthered. In contrast to these three, the English Enlightenment philosopher John Locke believed not in a ruler's divine or absolute right to lead, but in a leader's earning the right to lead by observing the natural human rights to life, liberty, and property. Moreover, Locke believed in the right, and even the duty, of the people to overthrow a ruler who violated these human rights. Thus (b) is not true: the two Frenchmen did agree, but the two Englishmen did not agree with one another. Locke and Bossuet did not agree, so (c) is untrue. Since Locke held a different view than the other three, (d) is not true that they all agreed. And it is not true that each of these four held a different opinion (e). Primarily Locke's view was different from that of absolutists such as Hobbes. In addition, Bossuet and Richelieu not only endorsed absolute power, but moreover believed in the divine right of kings to rule.

5. E: After Parliament impeached many of Charles I's ministers, destroyed Charles' judiciary system, and voided the taxes Charles had imposed independently of Parliament, all in 1640, Charles' attempt to secure the arrest for treason of five MPs triggered the English Civil War. Parliament (the "Roundheads") formed the New Model Army with Oliver Cromwell as its leader, and they defeated King Charles I's armed forces (a), the Cavaliers. Following this, the victorious Puritans removed all Presbyterians from Parliament (b). The remains were known as the Rump Parliament, which in 1649 eradicated both the monarchy and the House of Lords division of Parliament (c). In the same year, Charles was executed (d). After more MPs were eliminated, Cromwell and the Bare Bones Parliament ran the country with fairly stable conditions until Cromwell died in 1658. By 1660, public opinion in England held that the monarchy should be reinstated.

6. C: The Whigs and the Tories in England did disagree at one point, but by the advent of the Glorious Revolution, Whigs and Tories in Parliament agreed about the revolution. The Whigs had wanted to stop King Charles II's brother James II from succeeding to the throne because James was Catholic while the Tories supported Charles II. Once James II did succeed to the throne, he exempted Catholics from laws that had prevented them from serving in the armed forces, the court system, and local government. This led both Whigs and Tories in Parliament to reunite against what they saw as a common enemy: the reversion of England from Protestantism to Catholicism. Thus the Glorious Revolution was neither a conflict between Whigs and Tories nor a result of any such conflict. Parliament invited the Dutch Republic's William III of Orange, James II's nephew, and William's wife Mary, James' oldest daughter, to overtake the English throne. William accepted the offer and invaded England. This did lead to the crowning of William and Mary (a). Another result was the drafting by Parliament of the English Bill of Rights (b). One reason this revolution was called "glorious" was its minimal casualties (d). [Note: This revolution is often called "bloodless" which is not entirely accurate. However, compared to other revolutions, there were few battles, relatively little blood was shed, and few people died.] Since James ultimately fled the country, William's invasion met with little resistance. This revolution was also called "glorious" because it ended absolute rule in England and can be said to be the start of modern Parliamentary democracy in England. It is true that the English Bill of Rights influenced America's Constitution and Bill of Rights (e); in fact, it had a major influence on these documents: The English Bill of Rights prevented rulers from making laws without the approval of Parliament; the American counterpart to this is the provision that Presidents cannot pass laws without the approval of Congress. The English Bill of Rights also provided protection to citizens against "cruel and unusual punishment" and "excessive bail," both provisions also found in America; and it established the right of citizens to take up grievances with the government, also a right in America.

7. D: He did not extend already strong influences of Western culture to Russia. Rather, he instituted more Western influences in Russia, which until his reign had *not* been deriving much cultural influence from the West at all. Peter changed this. He did cause the influential people in Russian government and upper classes to make it fashionable to speak French (a), to wear Western clothing styles (b), to import fine art from Europe and send their children to Europe to be educated (c). In addition, he built St. Petersburg to be Russia's new capital, located in the western part of Russia near Europe, and in imitating Western governmental practices, he established state control over the Russian Orthodox Church (e). He also imitated Western organizational strategies with respect to the armed forces and the economy, with the result that he strengthened both of these.

8. B: The statement that is not true regarding the Huguenots is (b): The Huguenots were French Protestants, not Catholics, and they were driven out by Catholics, not Protestants. This was largely due to the policies of King Louis XIV (a). In 1685, he revoked the 1598 Edict of Nantes, which had provided for a modicum of religious toleration. Thereafter, Louis XIV effectively pushed many

Huguenots out of the country. In retrospect, historians find that because the Huguenots were very hard workers and possessed many important skills, this excision of them was detrimental to France. Thousands of fleeing Huguenots settled in England, with their work in watchmaking and other industries strengthened England's economy (c). Fewer, but still thousands, of Huguenots settled in Prussia (then the territory of Brandenburg-Prussia) at ruler Frederick William's invitation, where they also contributed to the economy with their industrious habits (d). In addition, many Huguenots migrated to America, making significant contributions. In fact, there are 11 US presidents with Huguenots among their ancestors (e). These are: George Washington, John Quincy Adams, John Tyler, James Garfield, Theodore Roosevelt, William Howard Taft, Herbert Hoover, Franklin Delano Roosevelt, Harry S. Truman, George H.W. Bush, and George W. Bush.

9. E: These words and names all come from Dutch. New York's Manhattan, Harlem, and Brooklyn were all named by Dutch settlers from their language, and the etymology of Yankees is the Dutch name Jan Kees. The word "boss" meaning an employer or a controlling politician comes from Dutch [the word *baas* meaning "master"], as do "coleslaw" [*koolsla* in Dutch] and "waffle" [*wafel* in Dutch] (b). The name of "Santa Claus" is from the Dutch *Sinterklass,* as are the words "cookie" [*koekje* in Dutch] and "bundle" [*bundel* in Dutch] (c). "Knapsack" is derived from the Dutch word *knapzak;* "cruise" comes from the Dutch *kruisen,* and "skate" developed from the Dutch *schaats.*

10. A: In the 17th century, the Dutch Republic was really a loose confederacy composed of states which had sovereignty. Holland was the strongest province in this Republic, but it did not centrally govern the other sovereign states and could not even control them. The Dutch did enjoy world power status economically and nautically during the 17th century (b). This ended in the 18th century when England and France overpowered the Dutch. The Dutch East India Company was formed for trading in Asia, and Dutch merchants settled and also traded in South Africa, as well as conducting trade in North America and the Caribbean at this time (c). Two hallmarks of this period in the Netherlands were religious tolerance, such that it became a haven for many Europeans who escaped religious persecution in their countries by moving there, and the Dutch Golden Age of art (d), exemplified by artists such as Rembrandt, Vermeer, Frans Hals, and Jacob van Ruisdael. During the 17th century, the city of Amsterdam was a world center for banking, and Hugo Grotius and other Dutch philosophers were proponents of international free trade (e).

11. D: None of these choices *includes* a country that was *not* one of the major colonists; in other words, all countries included in these choices were major colonizers. Portugal's colonizing can be seen in Brazil, where the official language is Portuguese, while Spain's is seen in Mexico, Central America, and the majority of South American countries, where Spanish is the main language spoken (a). The colonizing of the Netherlands (b) is shown in South America's sovereign state of Suriname whose language is Dutch, and in South Africa where the Dutch language Afrikaans among others) is still spoken. England's colonization is seen in the fact that English is the language in the United States and in the majority of Canada, while France's colonization is seen in the use of French as the official language of the Canadian province of Québec, and in the widespread use and influence of French in the American state of Louisiana (c). Since (d) is the correct answer, (e), all of these, is incorrect.

12. C: After wars in the 17th and 18th centuries, France was the dominant power in Western Europe, while England was dominant over the waterways via its powerful navy. Hence France and England did not equally control Eastern and Western Europe (a). France never overpowered England nor controlled Europe alone during this period (b). However, neither was France overpowered by England (d) at this time, except on the water, and England was not the only power controlling Europe. It is also not accurate to say that neither of these two countries succeeded in gaining power over Europe (e) at this time; both were successful in different arenas (France over Western

Europe's land and England over the seas around and related to Europe). While France continued to be a major European power, its colonial power was seriously deteriorating by the end of the French and Indian War in America and the Treaty of Paris, but England's naval dominance persisted into the 20th century. (Both France's and Spain's attitudes of denial about their loss of colonial strength were motivating factors in their alliance with colonial Americans in the Revolutionary War against England)

13. B: Proponents of this economic philosophy believed that a county should sell as many exported goods to other countries as possible to attain wealth. The basis of mercantilist philosophy was the belief that the wealth available in the world was of a finite amount; therefore answer (a) is incorrect. A practice consistent with mercantilism was to eschew free trade in favor of profits; therefore answer (c) is incorrect. Mercantilists did not believe in balancing imports and exports or sales and purchases (d); rather, they believed in selling as much as possible while buying as little as possible from other countries in the interest of self-sufficiency. Mercantilists also did not believe that commerce was exclusive of colonization (e); to the contrary, colonizing colonies abroad was viewed as securing a "captive audience" of customers, since once an area became a nation's colony, that nation could trade more easily in and with that region.

14. E: The commodity least associated with North America is sugar cane. This crop was grown in more tropical climates such as the Caribbean. British and French merchants competed for North America's animal pelts (a), waters rich in edible fish (b) such as cod, rich soil (c) for growing crops, and coastal areas with seaports (d) for easy access to waterways

15. C: The commodity least associated with the West Indies in the 18th century was fishing. Though Caribbean natives fished their own coral reefs locally, they did not trade in fish, as the plantations there at the time focused on growing cash crops such as cotton (a), coffee (b), tobacco (d), and sugar (e) for export. (The development in the southern US of cotton and tobacco as major cash crops benefited when these were brought from the West Indies and other countries and found to grow well in the soil of the American South.)

16. A: The War of Jenkins' Ear was a war between England and Spain which started in 1739 when British Prime Minister Walpole conceded to Parliament's demands and sent troops to the West Indies, as well as to Gibraltar. Its name came from the fact that in 1731, a Spanish privateer cut off the ear of Robert Jenkins, captain of an English merchant vessel. Jenkins is said to have presented his severed ear to Parliament, adding to anti-Spanish sentiment in Britain and, along with other incidents, contributing to war with Spain. Thus Jenkins' "ear" does not refer to an ear of corn (b). The following year (1740), the War of Jenkins' Ear merged with the War of Austrian Succession, which was a war fought by England and France about Austria (c). France supported Prussia's actions against Austria, which was historically France's enemy. England wanted Austria to continue to control the Netherlands rather than for France to take over the Netherlands. These factors led to war between England and France. Within four years the conflict came to include American territory when the French backed Spain in the war against England. The War of Austrian Succession was concluded by the 1748 Treaty of Aix-la-Chapelle. In the Seven Years' War (1756-1763), Prussia allied with Britain and Austria allied with France against each other (d). Concurrently with the Seven Years' War in Europe, the French and Indian War (1754-1763) began in America when George Washington's troops fired on French troops in the Ohio Valley (e). In both Europe and America, the fighting ended with the 1763 Treaty of Paris.

17. E: The American Revolution's historical significance is equally described by all of these statements. The war enabled the American colonists to secure their independence from Britain and form the United States, which is now a major world power (a). Because many Loyalists to the

United Empire moved from America to Canada in opposition to the revolution, there were suddenly many people in Québec speaking English where there had formerly been mainly French-speaking people (b) [so much so that the Constitutional Act of 1791 divided this province into Upper and Lower Canada, with separate legislatures, as a solution to the language difference]. The American Revolution produced documents such as the Declaration of Independence, the Constitution, and the Bill of Rights, which expressed many of the most important philosophies of the Enlightenment (c). Between the fact that the French allied with the Americans (out of their enmity for the British), helping America to win the war, and the fact that America's success in gaining independence demonstrated Enlightenment philosophy in action, the American Revolution also directly influenced the French in beginning the French Revolution (d) six years after the American Revolutionary War ended.

18. D: The East had far exceeded the West during the latter part of the medieval period. The Arabs were known for developing algebra, the system of Arabic numerals, and other scientific/mathematical systems still used today. However, by the 17th century the West had overtaken the East. Major factors in this turnabout were the invention by Gutenberg of movable type and the printing press in the West during the 16th century, and the prohibition of its use by Muslims in the East, also during the 16th century. The advantage of printing enabled the West to advance scientifically past the East. Therefore the Western world did not remain in the lead in these areas throughout the period described (a). Neither was the West ahead of the East beginning in the Middle Ages (b). Since progress in each hemisphere varied according to each time period, they were not roughly equal in their scientific development for the entire time (c). Answer (e) is the opposite of correct answer (d) and thus is incorrect.

19. B: The first scientist of record to posit a heliocentric universe, i.e. planets revolving around the sun, rather than a geocentric one, i.e. the sun and everything else revolving around Earth, was Copernicus [1473-1543], the multitalented Polish scholar. Ptolemy (a) [c. 90-c. 168] was the ancient Greek philosopher who, along with Aristotle and others, believed the universe revolved around Earth, and this view is often named after him as the Ptolemaic universe. Galileo (c) [1564-1642] lived after Copernicus and was the first to examine the heavenly spheres with a telescope, and he published a book discussing the opposing Ptolemaic and Copernican world views. Kepler (d) [1571-1630] was a German mathematician and astronomer who believed with his contemporary Galileo in the heliocentric universe. He also first proposed the idea of elliptical planetary orbits. Englishman Isaac Newton (e) [1642-1727] not only explained why Kepler's idea of elliptical orbits was correct with his explication of gravity; he moreover developed the system of calculus whereby he proved mathematically that the universe was indeed heliocentric.

20. C: Englishman Sir Francis Bacon lived from 1561-1626, and championed the inductive method of reasoning. Frenchman René Descartes lived from 1596-1650, and was responsible for the deductive method of reasoning. His statement of the ontological principle "Cogito ergo sum," which in Latin means "I think therefore I am," is particularly famous. Frenchman Blaise Pascal lived from 1623-1662, and created an important theory of chance and probability, invented a calculator, and was known for Pascal's Wager regarding belief in the existence of God. German Gottfried Leibniz lived from 1646-1716, and, like Pascal, invented a calculator; he apparently came up with calculus separately from Isaac Newton; and in his *Théodicée*, he argued that our world with its inclusion of both good and evil is the best possible world, as a world with only good or only evil would not be as balanced.

21. B: Many of the philosophers of the 18th century's Enlightenment were deists. Deists believe that God does exist and that God created the world and set it in motion, but thereafter is not directly involved in everyday events or the lives of individuals. This belief promotes the concept of humanity's free will and rejects the concept of predetermined fates. Answer (b) that God not only exists, but is active personally in daily life, is closer to an expression of theism than of deism. Answer (c) that God may or may not exist, and without proof nobody knows for sure, is closer to an expression of agnosticism than of deism. Answer (d) that God does not exist is closer to an expression of atheism than of deism. Answer (e) that God only exists in the minds of humans who came up with this concept is somewhat closer to an expression of existentialism than of deism.

22. E: All of these answers describe ideas Montesquieu wrote of in his books. His 1721 book *Persian Letters* used his rhetoric to make indirect criticisms of France's monarchs and of the Catholic Church system (a). In 1748, he published *The Spirit of the Laws,* in which he wrote of "natural laws" or "laws of nature." These natural laws were a concept in which Enlightenment philosophers believed. This concept meant that every living being was subject to natural laws which gave them basic rights, such as the rights to live, to be free, and to pursue happiness. Enlightenment philosophers believed that all government systems must observe these natural laws (b). They further believed and stated that any government that interfered with these laws and their attendant rights should be overthrown, and moreover that it was the people's responsibility to overthrow such a government. In *The Spirit of the Laws,* Montesquieu also wrote of the need for systems of checks and balances in governments (c) so that one division of a government cannot overpower other divisions. In this book, he also wrote about the need for separation of powers in governments (d). Montesquieu's ideas had a significant influence on the American architects of the US Declaration of Independence and the US Constitution, James Madison and Thomas Jefferson. The Declaration of Independence refers to our "inalienable rights" according to the Enlightenment's natural laws, and the Constitution established both separation of powers and checks and balances by dividing our government into three branches and dividing Congress into two parts.

23. D: There were many thinkers and authors of the Enlightenment from both France and the United Kingdom England and Scotland especially), and those in France were more motivated to call for change in their government since it was more of an absolute monarchy than England's. French philosophers advocating change saw England's system of both the monarchy and Parliament making decisions as an example of the greater freedom experienced in France. There were not many English Enlightenment philosophers, and England's government did not need more changes to fit with their ideas (a). These philosophers were not all French, and those who were French did not exist because their country needed fewer changes compared to England's government (b). There were not more Enlightenment philosophers in England even though their government was less restrictive than France's (c). While Enlightenment philosophers came both from France and from the United Kingdom, at the time England's government was not more repressive than France's (e).

24. A: Voltaire wrote *Candide* (1759) as well as *Zadig, Micromégas, Dictionnaire Philosophique,* and many other books, as well as *Treatise on Toleration* (1763), a good number of plays, poems, and a great many letters. *The Spirit of the Laws* (b) was written by another Enlightenment author, Charles Montesquieu, and his ideas in this book directly influenced the United States' new government. The first 28-volume *Encyclopedia (or Classified Dictionary of the Sciences, Arts, and Trades)* (c) was edited by another French Enlightenment figure, Dénis Diderot, who in common with Voltaire wrote criticisms of the Church, though he is now better known for the *Encyclopedia.* (Note: Although Diderot, and not Voltaire, edited the *Encyclopedia,* Voltaire did contribute so many articles to Diderot's *Encyclopédie* that Voltaire's own *Dictionnaire Philosophique* was composed largely of those articles.) *Émile* and *The Social Contract* (d) were written by Jean-Jacques Rousseau, a friend of Diderot and a very important Enlightenment writer. *Émile: or, On Education* was a seminal work still read and taught today in education courses, and was the book Rousseau felt was his most important. *The Social Contract*, Rousseau's book of political philosophy, is believed by others to be his most important work. His essays *Discourse on Inequality* and *Discourse on the Arts and Sciences* are also famous. The work *Essay on Crimes and Punishments* (e), published in 1764, was written by Cesare Beccaria, an Italian Enlightenment philosopher and politician whose work influenced prison reform.

25. C: Scottish economist Adam Smith wrote *The Wealth of Nations,* a book so influential that it can be said to have laid the foundation for the economic philosophy of capitalism, which is now practiced throughout the Western hemisphere and beyond. David Hume (a), along with Adam Smith, is a well-known figure of the Scottish Enlightenment. His published works include *Enquiry Concerning Human Understanding* (1748), *An Enquiry Concerning the Principles of Morals* (1751), *Natural History of Religion* (1757), *Dialogues Concerning Natural Religion* (1779, posthumously), and many others. English historian Edward Gibbon (b) is famous for *The Decline and Fall of the Roman Empire* (1776). English philosopher Jeremy Bentham (d) is best known for the political philosophy of utilitarianism. Bentham's secretary, James Mill, collaborated with him in developing utilitarianism and James Mill's son, John Stuart Mill, was a major advocate of this philosophy, publishing the book *Utilitarianism* (1863). English philosopher, writer, and feminist Mary Wollstonecraft (e) wrote *A Vindication of the Rights of Women* (1792), one of the first books of feminist philosophy. Her daughter, Mary Wollstonecraft Godwin, married the famous Romantic poet Percy Bysshe Shelley, and she wrote the very famous and popular novel *Frankenstein* (published anonymously in 1818 and published under her married name, Mary Shelley, in 1831).

26. D: King Louis XVI of France was not known as an "enlightened despot." Louis XVI was an absolute monarch who reigned from 1774 to 1792. The term "enlightened despot" refers to rulers who, although they were still monarchs with absolute power, did initiate some reforms consistent with Enlightenment philosophy during their reigns. These included Austria's Emperor Joseph II (a), who ruled from 1765-1790. While he was Catholic himself, Joseph granted freedom of religion to Protestants in his 1781 Edict of Toleration, as well as removed the confinement to ghettos of Austrian Jews, eliminating the requirement of their wearing yellow stars, and permitted university enrollment by Jews. He promoted education, so much so that by the end of the 18th century more Austrian children were in school than in any other European empire or nation. In addition, Emperor Joseph II freed the serfs in Austria. He also overrode the Pope's authority regarding church real property, selling around a third of the convents and monasteries in the Austrian Empire and using the proceeds to fund hospitals. Russian Empress Catherine II, or Catherine the Great (b) ruled from 1762-1796. She challenged the death penalty and the use of torture in the penal system. She also disagreed, like Emperor Joseph II of Austria, with the feudal practice of forcing peasants to work as serfs for lords owning land. Catherine divided Russia into fifty separate provinces. She corresponded with Enlightenment writers Voltaire and Diderot. Prussian ruler Frederick the Great (c), who reigned from 1740-1786, also admired the ideas of the Enlightenment, even inviting Voltaire to live in his country for three years. While the country's main religion was Lutheran at the time, Frederick the Great permitted Catholics and Jews to settle in Prussia. Within limits, he allowed his subjects freedom of speech. During his reign, he worked to improve the efficiency of the Prussian legal system and set up a bureaucracy to manage government beyond his time. (Note: the reforms advocated by these enlightened despots were important, even though their efforts were relatively unsuccessful at the time due to the continuing strength of European aristocracy.)

27. E: These were all things Franklin accomplished. By experimenting with conduction during storms, he proved that lightning is one form of electricity (a). He invented the bifocal lens for glasses, which corrects for both nearsightedness and farsightedness a. great boon for aging adults!), and invented the Franklin stove (c) as well as other inventions. He founded the University of Pennsylvania (d). He also organized firefighters and started public libraries (b). Additionally, Franklin founded the American Philosophical Society and went to France from 1776-1785, encouraging the French to help the American colonists in their revolution against England. (He was quite successful as French allies helped Americans to win the war.) These are only a few of the myriad things that Benjamin Franklin accomplished in his life.

28. E: All of these were advantages Britain enjoyed during the Industrial Revolution. England had naturally large seams of coal (a) and iron ore (b), which people had mined for a long time, and there was thus a strong tradition in England of mining. Britain also had a well-developed network of waterways (rivers and canals) and roadways to be used for transportation (c) of the products of industry as they developed. In addition, the British culture in the 17th and 18th centuries emphasized individualism (d), which facilitated private enterprise. By the middle of the 1700s, the British government had very little involvement in private-sector businesses, giving great freedom to entrepreneurs.

29. C: The 18th century "agricultural revolution" is considered to have begun in England. A number of innovations by English inventors enabled the industrialization of agriculture; hence, the agricultural revolution led to the Industrial Revolution. Included among these innovations were Jethro Tull's use of metal plows for planting and Charles "Turnip" Townsend's discovery of the principle of crop rotation. The advances of the Industrial Revolution in England spread to continental Europe and eventually throughout the world. Therefore these innovations came later to France (b), Germany (e), and Russia (d), by the early 19th century. In America (a), industrialization began a bit earlier, but only in the Northeast because of its rivers, which were needed as Americans relied on water power at the time. After the Civil War, industrialization spread throughout the United States once steam was substituted for water as a power source in the late 1860s.

30. A: The existence of fewer sheep farms was not an outcome of the enclosure movement in England. As demand for wool increased and sheep farming became more profitable, the number of sheep farms in England increased. Previously, much land in England had been shared. For example, many farmers could let their cattle graze on land owned by others and/or get hay by mowing meadows owned by others. During the enclosure movement, this practice was largely ended (c) by the fencing of properties. As large sheep farms took up much of this newly enclosed land, small farmers were put at a great disadvantage, with many small farms ceasing to exist (b). Although small farms were lost, farming itself in England gained productivity (d) through the enclosure movement. While a majority of the English population had farmed as an occupation in 1700, by 1800 fewer than half of the population was engaged in farming (e) due in part to there being more large farms and fewer small farms (as well as to urbanization and other factors).

31. E: All of these factors are related to the growth of industry in the 18th century. As a result of the agricultural revolution (see question #29) and the enclosure movement (see question #30), landowners gained larger profits (a) from larger crop. This prosperity meant landowners could afford to invest in burgeoning businesses, such as the textile industry. The construction of cotton textile factories was enabled by the invention of the spinning jenny (b). This device changed the process of spinning cotton from being done by hand to being done by machine so that much greater production in a much shorter time was possible, allowing cotton cloth to be mass-produced in factories. The budding textile industry created job openings, and many people in England (and later in other countries) moved from working on farms in the country to working in factories in the cities (c). As a result of this trend of urbanization, cities like Manchester and Liverpool in England grew substantially in population (d).

32. E: All of the statements are true regarding the development of the textile industry. James Watt's invention of the steam engine in England provided a source of power for new cotton mills (a). Soon the steam engine was also applied to the process of making iron (b). The production of iron and steel together with the steam engine enabled England to build its first railroad (c). By the middle of the 19th century, many cities in England were connected by railroads, and in another 70 years there were railroads in America, Canada, Europe, Asia, Africa, and Siberia. The railroads resulted from industry and feeders of industry (d) as their existence created additional demand for metal, oil, and machine power.

33. C: Cotton planters in the Southern US made profits, is not one of the less-desirable effects of the textile industry's growth. Making profits was good for the economy of the Southern states and for the US in general. However, the business American producers of raw cotton got from European countries like England and France did support those producers' use of slaves (a), which was a less-desirable effect of the industry. Another less-desirable effect was the increase in child labor (b). Since machines were powered by steam rather than by men, women and children could run these machines, with the result that soon there were children working in textile factories all over the nations of the Western world. Since (c), profits for the cotton planters, was not a less-desirable effect, (d), all of these, and (e), none of these, are both incorrect answers.

34. B: The expression "the pits" was originally used to describe the mines in England where many people worked. "The pits" was originally a synonym for "the mines" because they were, in fact, dug deep in the ground; as mining work was hard, unpleasant, and very dangerous, "the pits" also came to signify any very unpleasant experience. As a result of the Industrial Revolution, rapid urbanization created many problems in the suddenly overcrowded cities, which were unprepared as there were no laws mandating sanitation or clean air practices. English city streets did often fill with sewage (a), but they were not referred to as "the pits." Factories in England's cities did commonly use coal as fuel for steam engines, and the soot from burning coal was spewed into the urban atmosphere (c), but these factories were not called "the pits." There are no such things as English tar pits (d) because there are no tar pits in England. Such pits or lakes of asphalt, created by bitumen leaking up to the surface land, are found in California and Texas in the United States; in Trinidad and Tobago in the Caribbean; in Peru and Venezuela in South America; and in Russia, Poland, and Iran, but not in England. During the Industrial Revolution, many people who moved from small villages to big and growing cities did live in barracks of the factories where they worked (e), but these barracks were not called "the pits."

35. A: In the 18th-19th centuries, Britain did not have the kind of democracy that we think of in America today. Despite this, Britain did have more interaction among its classes than other cities in Europe had at the time (c). However, Britain did not have as much interaction among its classes as Americans had at the time (d). While the Industrial Revolution benefited people in that they earned more money, and in Britain a middle class emerged where formerly there were only royalty and commoners, there was also much suffering (e) brought on by poor work conditions, such as unhealthy factories, excessive work hours, employer abuse, overcrowding, lack of sanitation, and air pollution in industrialized cities. These poor conditions served as impetus for reform movements starting in England, just as the industrialization causing the conditions had started there (b).

36. D: The Reform Bill of 1832 in Great Britain pertained to the right of the males in the middle class to vote. As the middle class was a new development in Great Britain, the right of only nobles to vote was a holdover from the times of much greater privilege for aristocrats and very little for commoners. Indeed, the Reform Bill of 1832 was passed first by the House of Commons while the House of Lords rejected it. When workers protested with mass meetings, strikes, and riots, King

William IV, fearing a revolution, put pressure on the House of Lords until they passed this bill. The right to vote allowed middle-class Englishmen to elect MPs who would further the interests of the middle class. These elections allowed further significant reform to take place. The right of Catholics to hold seats in Parliament (a) was granted in 1829. The abolition of slavery within the British Empire (b) occurred in 1833. The beginning of sanitary procedures in the cities (c) and towns was instituted by the Public Health Act of 1848. The limitation of workdays to 9 hours for children (e) was accomplished by the Factory Act of 1833.

37. C: In 1874, Britain's Parliament passed a law prohibiting men from working for more than ten hours in one work day. Children under age 13 were prohibited from working more than 9-hour days (a) by the Factory Act of 1833. Children aged 13 to 18 working more than 69 hours a week (b) was also made illegal by this Factory Act of 1833. Women and boys under age 18 working more than 10 hours a day (d) was banned by the Factory Act of 1847. There was no law passed by 1874 limiting work days to 8 hours (e). In fact, the majority of industrialized nations in the world would not have an 8-hour work day passed into law until the 20th century.

38. B: In the Chartist movement, people were not demanding women's suffrage. They were demanding (among other things) that all adult *men* be given the right to vote. This movement did express the desire of the people to have their own charter (a), as exemplified in the petitions signed by millions of people (c) in this movement, which also called for members of Parliament to receive salaries to discourage corruption in politics (d). The Chartist movement was the first movement in history by members of the working class on such a massive scale (e). The Chartist movement helped to motivate Parliament to pass the Factory Acts (see question #37).

39. A: The group *not* associated with organizing labor in England was the Luddites, who opposed machines as threats to their jobs. The Amalgamated Society of Engineers (b) was one of the early labor unions formed in England. This union charged its members a small amount of dues weekly to provide them with unemployment insurance. Robert Owen (c) was a proponent of social reform and an organizer in England who founded the Grand National Consolidated Trades Union (d). His focus in starting this union was to campaign for an 8-hour workday. Because the Luddites (a) were not a group associated with organizing labor unions, (e), these all were associated with organizing labor, is incorrect.

40. E: The name "Luddite" is now used as a generalization, but not regarding skilled artists. Rather, it is used to describe anybody who reacts negatively against any kind of new technology and/or is opposed to technical progress. (For example, when personal computers or cell phones first became popular, people might have called someone who hated and refused to use them a Luddite.) The Luddites were a social movement in Britain (a) composed of skilled artisans who used handlooms to weave cloth (b) and who were opposed to the new machine looms (c). These machines could be run by low-paid, unskilled workers, so Luddites feared they would lose their higher-paying, skilled jobs as more manufacturers converted to machines, whereby they could produce far more fabric in a shorter time and also pay lower wages to more employees. The Luddites were known for sabotage such as breaking mechanized looms (d) and destroying wool and cotton mills. (Note: The name Luddite is derived from the name Ned Lud, or Ned Ludd, a man who may or may not have existed in the village of Anstey, Leicestershire. According to legend, he destroyed some stocking knitting frames around 1779. Once stories of this alleged event had spread, it became a popular English joke whenever such equipment was sabotaged to say, "Ned Ludd did it." This joke reflects the fact that machine saboteurs were usually of necessity anonymous. The Luddite movement began in 1811-1812 and took its name from this possibly imaginary hero.)

41. D: Laws restricting trade in Europe were not a factor in the slower development of industrialization in Europe compared to its earlier and faster development in England. Factors contributing to later and slower development in continental Europe than in Britain included the fact that transportation of goods was easier in Britain because it had more good roads (a) and was the first to develop railroads. In addition to having fewer decent roads, the European continent also had tolls charged on routes running along rivers (b), making trading cost more and discouraging merchants. Great Britain's culture at the time favored individualism (c) and, hence, private enterprise. America followed Britain's example in this respect, while Continental Europe placed less value on individual achievement and enterprise at that time. Of all these factors, one of the biggest to delay industrialization in Europe was the series of wars between 1790 and 1815 (e), which caused much damage, interfered with new industries, and distracted the people and governments from industrial and business pursuits.

42. B: The French Revolution not only had an impact on the entire world, but it continues to do so today. For example, Benito Mussolini, dictator of the Italian Fascist Party (He formed the party in 1919, it was voted into power in 1924, and Mussolini had full control of Italy's political system by 1926.), stated that his politics were in direct opposition to "the fundamental principles laid down in 1789," a reference to the French Revolution. And Communist China's Chou En-Lai, when asked about the consequences of the French Revolution, also in the early 20th century, he replied, "It is too soon to say." These examples show the far-reaching impact of this war. Therefore it is not true that (a) this war only affected France. The French Revolution was certainly dramatic, but it is very inaccurate to say it was a simple event (c); it reality the war and the events surrounding it were extremely complex. While this war did have an effect on the whole world, it cannot be said that this effect was greater than its effect on France itself (d). In addition to its major international significance, the French Revolution still had its major impact in France. Because (b) is an accurate statement, (e) is incorrect that none of the answers is an accurate description.

43. E: All these factors contributed to conditions allowing the French Revolution to begin. France's economy (a) was suffering due to the many wars in which the country had been involved, and the economy was continuing to deteriorate. King Louis XVI had always required a lot of money, and the poor economy and the costs of war exacerbated his demands (b). France's support of Prussia in the War of Austrian Succession was soon to backfire against France (c) when an ally became an enemy: France's help strengthened Prussia as a European power, and subsequently Prussia allied with England against France (just as, conversely, Austria also changed its alliance from England to France from one war to the next). Another consequence of France's aid to Prussia in the War of Austrian Succession was the involvement of England (d) in the war. Once France and England, which were both world powers, were involved in the war, this increased the cost of war as it was raised to an international level.

44. A: The First Estate was made up of the clergy. Before the French Revolution, there were three social classes or "Estates" in France. The Church did not pay taxes to the government. This was not a source of concern among the rest of French society for many years. However, in the years leading up to the war, there were members of the clergy who were socially prominent and had developed arrogance regarding their positions. Many clergy members of lower positions sided with proponents of revolution. Members of the nobility (b) were the Second Estate, and bourgeoisie and peasants (c) were the Third Estate. Since (a) is correct, (d), none of these, and (e), all of these, are incorrect.

45. B: Members of the Second Estate were nobles. In France, those in this class were divided into "nobles of the sword," who were descended from long lines of aristocrats; and "nobles of the robe," who were not noble by ancestry but had bought their social status. Neither division was necessarily rich. However, the nobility did not pay many taxes and possessed significant influence. They were also landlords who collected dues, such as rent, from peasants living on their land. Some of the nobles supported the revolution and some were against it. Members of the clergy (a) were the First Estate. Bourgeoisie and peasants (c) were the Third Estate. Since (b) is correct, (d), none of these, and (e), all of these, are incorrect.

46. C: Bourgeoisie (middle-class professionals and businessmen) and peasants were members of the Third Estate. By the eve of the French Revolution, the bourgeois owned about 20% of the land in France. Many of them were also frustrated in their desire to buy offices in the *parlements* (high courts) to attain "noble of the robe" status (see question #45) because such offices were not numerous or affordable enough for them to purchase. Their frustration was a significant motivation as the war began among members of the Third Estate. Members of the clergy (a) were the First Estate. Members of the Second Estate were (b) nobles. Since (c) is correct, (d), none of these, and (e), all of these, are incorrect.

47. C: The Abbé Sieyès' pamphlet, published just before the French Revolution began, was entitled "What Is the Third Estate?" Sieyès' writing reflected the prevalent sentiments felt by the middle and lower classes in the Third Estate. Some of these people (the bourgeois) had money, but no power in the government, and none of the privileges of the nobility. Others (the peasants) did not possess money, political power, or privilege. They paid more taxes than the other two classes. On top of paying taxes to the King, they were forced to pay tithes to the church, and food that peasants had hunted was confiscated by nobles at times as nobles were allowed to hunt on land that peasants owned. Compounding this was the fact that many Third Estate members--for example, those working in city factories and gardeners working in urban settings--had undergone a 62% rise in cost of living but only a 22% rise in wages, both in only four years (from 1785-1789), which meant they could no longer afford to live on their income. Thus they found their current system of government unfair and demanded change. The First (a) Estate was made up of clergy. Those of lower ranks in this class tended to side with revolutionaries leading up to the war, but those of higher ranks did not. The Second (b) Estate was made up of nobility—those who had inherited it and those who had bought it. Like the First Estate, this class had mixed attitudes toward revolution. Some were against it as they wanted to conserve their current status. Because members of the upper classes had been exposed to Enlightenment philosophy, other nobles were in favor of revolution as they were interested in the monarchy becoming less absolute as it had in England's example. Thus the Third Estate was the group most unanimously in support of the revolution. In pre-war France, there was no such thing as a Fourth (d) or Fifth (e) Estate; there were only three.

48. D: One difference between France's and America's declarations was that France's did not give power to the people. In America's declaration, individuals united by a common cause were named as having power, but France's declaration stated that "all authority rests essentially in the nation." Thus, according to some historians, nationalism in the modern sense began with the French Revolution and its Declaration. France's declaration did declare the right to liberty (a) just as America's did. Both countries' declarations also asserted the right to property (b). Both declarations also stated that all citizens were politically equal (c). Because (d) is a difference between the two, (e), none of these was a difference, is incorrect.

49. E: The National Assembly, the Legislative Assembly, the Paris Commune, the National Convention, the Committee of Public Safety, and the Directory. In 1789, the Third Estate renamed itself the National Assembly and invited the First and Second Estates to join it. King Louis XVI, by then lacking the power to oppose this, ordered the First and Second Estates to join the National Assembly, but revolution broke out soon after this. The National Assembly passed laws eradicating the *ancien regime.* The Legislative Assembly had been formed by 1791, in which year the French constitution dictated that the King shared power with the National Assembly, and could veto acts passed by the Legislative Assembly but his veto could be overridden by the Legislative Assembly. This is like the United States' system with respect to the President and Congress. The Legislative Assembly in France came to replace the National Assembly. In 1792, the Legislative Assembly was mobbed by revolutionaries known as "sans-culottes" (meaning "without fine clothes"). For a time, the revolution was then run by the Paris Commune instead of the Legislative Assembly. The Paris Commune was led by revolutionary George Danton. Within a month of the invasion of the Legislative Assembly, following many executions by the Paris Commune, the National Convention took the Legislative Assembly's place and eliminated the monarchy. Within four more months, Louis XVI was guillotined. The National Convention, however, suffered from internal divisiveness. When Austria, Britain, the Dutch Republic, Portugal, Prussia, and Spain all fought against the French Revolution in an effort to bring back the French monarchy, first Danton and then Robespierre were in charge of the Committee of Public Safety, which succeeded the National Convention. This 12-man Committee performed many more executions, by guillotine as with Marie Antoinette, and by mass drownings using retired ships, during the notorious Reign of Terror. In 1794, public sentiment turned against the Paris Commune's and Committee of Public Safety's radical members as the populace tired of the revolution. Three months after ordering Danton's execution, Robespierre was executed himself. In 1795, the National Convention, which still existed even while the Committee of Public Safety had taken over its leadership, drafted a new constitution for the country. Included in this new constitution was a legislature under the oversight of a five-man Directory. This Directory continued until it was eliminated by Napoleon in 1799.

50. B: The item that was not one of Napoleon's accomplishments was allowing the Pope to nominate bishops. Napoleon, as emperor, reserved the right to nominate bishops. However, he did give the Pope the right to depose existing bishops in his 1801 Concordat with the Roman Catholic Church. He also got rid of the new calendar instituted in the revolution, which had been extremely unpopular and included a ten-day week, began with 1792 as year one and renamed the months, in 1806, restoring the Christian calendar in recognition of Christianity's importance in France. After so many years of wars and then the revolution, Napoleon did give France more order and stability (a) at this time. The Civil Code he established got rid of the old tradition of primogeniture (c) whereby first-born sons had always automatically inherited most of their fathers' estates. Napoleon's shift of emphasis from such inheritance to earning one's assets via merit, which he also instituted in the military and government, made him popular with the people, and some historians have deemed him to have been another type of "enlightened despot" during this time period. Napoleon's Civil Code also gave the peasants legal equality and the rights of equals (d). Napoleon had started by appointing a three-man consulate to lead France, but within five years of surviving an assassination attempt he averred that in order to maintain control in the country. He also obtained the French vote to become emperor. In the same way, Napoleon subsequently ended the circulation of the majority of French newspapers (e) to reduce public threats to his power. The few remaining papers had to get government approval of their articles before printing them.

51. A: What happened in Poland between 1793 and 1795 was that it ceased to exist as a country until after World War I. This was due to the desires of Russia, Austria, and Prussia to acquire more territory and to quash revolutionary and nationalist sentiments and philosophies developing in Poland at the time. These three countries parceled Poland into territories such that it no longer existed as a separate nation. Poland, thus, did not get a chance to start a revolution during those years (b). Therefore, Poland also was not made stronger by allying itself with Austria (c). Because of the territorial aggression of Russia, as well as of Austria and Prussia, Poland was not able to sever all of its ties with Russia (d) at that time. Poland did not become a territory exclusively owned throughout by Prussia (e), but became subdivided into territories occupied by Russia, Austria, and Prussia. Poland did not become a distinct nation again until after World War I.

52. D: Lord Nelson being defeated was not an outcome of France's occupation of Egypt under Napoleon. This leader of the British navy defeated the French navy in Aboukir Bay, which ended the French occupation of Egypt. Before it ended, though, the period of occupation brought certain reforms to Egypt. These included the abolition of slavery (b), of religious taxation (c), and of the practice of torturing prisoners (e). Napoleon also introduced many scientists to Egypt, which resulted in the discovery of the Rosetta Stone (a). This stone, by its inclusion of the same texts in both Egyptian hieroglyphics and the ancient Greek language, enabled hieroglyphs to be translated for the first time since ancient history.

53. C: The British government did not mainly approve of the French Revolution. Even with Parliament declaring it no longer an absolute monarchy, Britain's government was still a monarchy and monarchic governments despised the French Revolution. Thomas Jefferson (a), who wrote the American Declaration of Independence, mainly approved of the revolution, even while he thought the revolutionaries tended to go overboard. The London Corresponding Society (b) was a group that kept abreast of revolutionary ideas and tended to approve of the French Revolution. The Society of United Irishmen (d) was for Irish nationalism and against the British government in general, and this group approved of the nationalist character of the French Revolution. Since (c) did not approve of the French Revolution, (e), all of these approved of it, is incorrect.

54. B: The Alien and Sedition Acts passed in the United States were against the French Revolution in that parts of these acts were meant to stop the immigration of revolutionaries from France to America. The London Corresponding Society (a) was a group interested in and in favor of revolutionary matters, and its members tended to approve of the French Revolution. The British Government (c), being a constitutional monarchy, but still a monarchy, opposed the revolution. It also suppressed the Society of United Irishmen (d), a group who supported Irish nationalism and were therefore also in favor of the French Revolution's nationalistic ideas. Since only (b) were against the French Revolution, (e), all of these were against it, is incorrect.

55. E: Of the countries listed, Russia was where Napoleon suffered the worst defeat in the early 1800s. When he invaded Prussia (a)*, he forced that country, as he did others, to adopt a number of significant and beneficial reforms. Among these was the fostering of nationalism. This backfired because Prussia became stronger as an outcome of Napoleon's invasion. When he invaded Spain (b), his attack triggered guerilla warfare in that country, and combating the guerillas cost him dearly. Also, Napoleon's invasion of Spain was on the way to his destination of Portugal (c), a country which Napoleon wanted to stop from conducting trade with England (d). England sent troops to Spain to aid the guerillas. So Napoleon was unable to end Portuguese commerce and relations with England. But of all these unsuccessful attempts, the worst was in Russia (e). As this country was readying for war in 1812, Napoleon had about a million of his troops invade. The Russian strategy responding to this invasion is known as a "scorched-earth policy," the tactic it would later use in 1940 against Hitler's troops. The Russians retreated from the French forces, but burnt their land behind them as they went. This stopped French armies from subsisting off Russian land. Eventually it began to snow in Russia; Napoleon's troops were now farther from their home and supplies, and it was freezing. They began to retreat from these unfavorable conditions, and as they did the Russians turned from a defensive position to an offensive one, attacking the retreating French. This was Napoleon's worst defeat of the countries listed.

(Note: Russia, Prussia, Austria, and England formed the Quadruple Alliance in 1813; Napoleon was defeated in Leipzig, in what is now Germany; and the Quadruple Alliance's troops invaded Paris in

1814. Napoleon abdicated his throne and sought exile in Elba, the island off Italy. Between 1814 and 1815, the Congress of Vienna increased Prussia's and Austria's territories and formed new buffer states, including Belgium. After Napoleon escaped from Elba and returned to Paris to try to reclaim his leadership, his troops were defeated at Waterloo, Belgium in 1815. This time Napoleon was exiled on the island of St. Helena, where he died in 1821. *Napoleon's nephew, Louis Napoleon, was named Emperor Napoleon III in 1852, and was captured and suffered a permanent defeat in the Franco-Prussian War of 1870. When thinking of Prussia, Napoleon III should not be confused with his uncle Napoleon.)

56. D: The country that was not a member of the Quadruple Alliance was France. The purpose of this alliance's formation in 1813 was to combat Napoleon and France. The alliance consisted of Russia (a), where Napoleon had recently been badly defeated; Prussia (b), where Napoleon had forced reforms during his invasion which ultimately backfired on him by making Prussia more nationalistic and a stronger force; Austria (c), which had had territory in the Netherlands and Northern Italy taken from it as well as privileges taken from the Catholic Church in Switzerland by the French revolutionary army before Napoleon's rise to power; and England (e), a longtime enemy of France which Napoleon wanted to destroy by stopping other European nations from trading with it.

57. C: Napoleon's sale of Louisiana to America was not a way for him to start over to establish another French empire in America. In fact, just before the Louisiana Purchase, Napoleon had lost a war waged by slaves in Haiti against their French masters (a). He was discouraged enough by this loss that he was no longer interested in trying to conquer parts of America again. Since Napoleon was not motivated to conquer American territories and since he had lost great amounts of money through all of his European wars, he decided to recoup some of this financial loss via proceeds from the sale of Louisiana (b), especially since the USA, involved in aggressive westward expansion, wanted this territory as it included the Mississippi River, a direct route to the Gulf of Mexico and thence to the ocean. Since (c) was not one of Napoleon's motives, (d), all of these were, and (e), none of these, are incorrect.

58. A: The Concert of Europe included France as a member. The Quadruple Alliance (b) consisted of Russia, Prussia, Austria, and England, and was formed in 1813 to combat Napoleon. The Congress of Vienna (c) convened from 1814 to 1815, both to restructure Europe after defeating Napoleon, to keep any one European nation from taking control of Europe, and to keep the peace. In an effort to forestall animosity in France, the Congress of Vienna invited France to join the Quadruple Alliance. Once France did join in 1815, the group now consisting of all five countries was called the Concert of Europe. Since only (a) included France, (d), all of these, and (e), none of these, are incorrect.

59. B: It is not true that the Crimean War involved Austria or Prussia; this war involved only Russia, the Ottoman Empire, England, and France. One reason for this war was that the countries of the Ottoman Empire had given France authority over their Orthodox Christian shrines, and Russia thought this authority should be theirs; when Russia lost this war, it had to relinquish its claims to control over these shrines (a). Another reason for the war was that Russia occupied parts of what is now Romania, compromising the commercial activities of England and France in the eastern part of the Mediterranean. Russia's loss of the war meant that it had to agree to England's (c) and France's (d) ships trading in the Black Sea. During this war, British nurse Florence Nightingale (e) successfully demanded more sanitary conditions in the field hospitals set up during combat, with the result that many fewer soldiers, who would have otherwise died, perished of diseases caused by poor sanitation. Florence Nightingale also elevated the social position of female nurses, as well as being a pioneer for more modern methods of nursing, and attended to wounded British soldiers during the war.

60. E: None of these statements is true regarding social reactions to the Enlightenment and the French Revolution in Europe in the 19th century. A majority of the upper class reacted against these movements by becoming conservatives, not liberals (a). They believed that change was better affected by building on tradition, which must be preserved and respected, than by completely breaking with tradition, which could only result in anarchy as witnessed after the French Revolution. The bourgeois, on the other hand, did not mostly become conservatives (b) to protect their newfound wealth. Rather, once they had begun to profit from the advances of the Industrial Revolution, they were interested in increasing those profits. They tended, therefore, to agree with the Enlightenment's and French Revolution's ideas about the freedom of individuals to attain property, prosperity, and happiness and not to be restricted by government in their activities to gain these benefits. So a majority of the middle class became liberals. Since more of the upper class became conservative and more of the middle class became liberal in the 19th century, (c) is incorrect that both classes primarily became liberals, and (d) is incorrect that both classes primarily became conservatives.

61. A: The author of *On Liberty* was John Stuart Mill (1806-1873), the English philosopher and political economist. He was a Classical economist, a Utilitarian, and an important liberal influence. His book, *On Liberty* (1859), was the most famous liberal written work of its time in England and was influential outside of the country as well. Edmund Burke (b) (1729-1797) was also English, but was conservative, and is known to some as "the father of modern conservatism." He was admired by both conservatives and liberals for his ideas and writing. Of his works, a well-known one is *Reflections on the Revolution in France* (1790). John Locke (c) (1632-1704), also an English philosopher, was regarded as one of the most important influences of the Enlightenment. Friedrich Hegel (d), or Georg Wilhelm Friedrich Hegel (1770-1831), was a German Idealist and historical philosopher who introduced the concept of the dialectic. He had a widespread influence on both those who agreed with him and those who did not. Thomas Carlyle (e) (1795-1881) was a Scottish historian, writer, and teacher associated with the Victorian era of English literature and is best known for his influential essays.

62. C: Ralph Waldo Emerson was not associated with the Romantic literary movement in England as were the others. Emerson (1803-1882), an American philosopher who wrote essays and poems, was known as a leader of the Transcendentalist Movement. Some of his most famous essays include *Nature, Self-Reliance,* and *The Over-Soul.* Emerson was influenced by the work of Scottish author Thomas Carlyle, who himself derived considerable influence from the German Romantic movement. William Wordsworth (a) (1770-1850) was a major English Romantic poet. His works include "Lines Composed a Few Miles above Tintern Abbey" a. lso known to students of literature as "Tintern Abbey"); "I Wandered Lonely as a Cloud" (popularly known as "Daffodils"); and "Ode: Intimations of Immortality." Wordsworth famously co-published with Samuel Taylor Coleridge (d) the book of poetry *Lyrical Ballads* (1798), which included both Wordsworth's *Tintern Abbey* and Coleridge's *The Rime of the Ancient Mariner.* Wordsworth's *Prelude,* a long autobiographical and philosophical poem, was published posthumously by his widow. George Gordon, Lord Byron (b) (1788-1824) was also a major English Romantic poet. His works include *She Walks in Beauty, Childe Harold's Pilgrimage,* and *Don Juan.* Samuel Taylor Coleridge (d) (1772-1834), who was a friend and collaborator with Wordsworth, is best known for *The Rime of the Ancient Mariner* and *Kubla Khan* and co-published *Lyrical Ballads* (1798) with Wordsworth. Percy Bysshe Shelley (e) (1792-1822) was a major English Romantic poet who wrote, among others, *Ode to the West Wind* and *Prometheus Unbound.*

63. E: These all were related to the Greek Revolution of 1821. The Ottoman Empire (a), which was primarily Muslim, ruled Greece before this revolution. Nationalists and liberals in Greece started the revolution to become independent of this empire. The English Romantic poet Lord Byron (b) was among many Europeans who were interested in the Greek Revolution, not only out of agreement with the Romantic ideals of nationalism and liberty, but also out of a desire for a revival of the classical Greek democracy. In 1830, the Treaty of London (c) gave Greece independence from the Ottoman Empire but specified that it have a monarchy). The French and Russians (d) as well as the English had vested interests in the Mediterranean because of the trade routes they relied on there, so these countries all provided aid to the Greek revolutionaries.

64. B: The country Napoleon III never actually colonized was Italy. He did promise the prime minister of Piedmont-Sardinia in 1858 that he would help Venetia and Lombardy, Italian provinces, to gain independence from the Austro-Hungarian Empire. However, Napoleon had his troops retreat from the fighting before the Italian provinces could be freed. In Asia (a) and Africa (c), France did succeed in colonizing some areas, and it kept these colonies until the middle of the 20th century. In Mexico (d), Napoleon III won a war and captured Mexico City in 1864, placing Prince Maximilian in charge. However, America was displeased with France's occupation of Mexico, and after the Civil War in America, Napoleon III was afraid of war with the United States and removed his forces from Mexico in 1867. Since (b) is correct, (e), none of these was never colonized by France is incorrect.

65. C: Giuseppe Mazzini was the least successful. Though he was known as the most radical and aggressive 19th-century nationalist and his efforts definitely did raise Italians' consciousness regarding nationalism and freedom, Mazzini and his Young Italy movement still were consistently unsuccessful in starting a revolution or unifying Italy. Count (Camillo Benso) di Cavour (a) was more moderate than Mazzini and did much to further Italian nationalism. In fact, when the Kingdom of Italy was formalized in 1861, Cavour was its first prime minister. Giuseppe Garibaldi (b) was largely instrumental in unifying the Italian states. In the 1859 Austro-Piedmontese War—the same war in which Napoleon III had promised to help Count di Cavour, then prime minister of Piedmont-Sardinia, in freeing Venetia and Lombardy from the Austro-Hungarian Empire, but withdrew his troops before accomplishing this (see question #64)—Garibaldi had been a leader of volunteer soldiers. The next year, Garibaldi and his "Red Shirt" soldiers started a campaign in Southern Italy. With the support of local revolutionaries, they won Sicily and set up a new government in Naples. At the same time, Count di Cavour also deployed soldiers to the south who occupied the Papal States. When King Victor Emmanuel II headed south as well, Garibaldi gave his captured territory to the King. This led to the formation of the Kingdom of Italy. Since only (c) is correct, (d), none of these was the least successful and (e), all of these were the least successful are both incorrect.

66. D: The Berlin Decrees were not associated with Otto von Bismarck. These were laws passed by Napoleon in 1806, prohibiting subjects of his empire from trading with England. Kaiser Wilhelm I (a) was associated with Bismarck in that he appointed Bismarck as prime minister of Prussia in 1862. (Bismarck had previously been the Prussian ambassador to France and Russia.) Prussia's Parliament had a majority of liberals who opposed Wilhelm's intentions to create a stronger military force. The Prussian Parliament, therefore, also opposed Bismarck's plans. He circumvented this opposition by attacking and defeating Denmark, taking authority over the duchy of Schleswig from Denmark and giving it to Prussia. The neighboring duchy of Holstein was taken from Denmark and given to Austria. This caused disagreements between Prussia and Austria. To resolve these, Bismarck incited the Prussian army to fight the Seven Weeks' War (b), in which it defeated Austria, clearly establishing Prussia's domination of central Europe. Prussia then annexed

Frankfurt, Hanover, Hesse, and Nassau, forming the North German Confederation. Bismarck was also responsible for starting the Franco-Prussian War (c) by falsifying an insult to the French, ostensibly by the Kaiser. When France declared war in 1870, the southern German states united with the North German Confederation to fight France. This union resulted in the birth of modern Germany (e), with the Kaiser as its ruler and Bismarck as its Chancellor.

67. A: Of the German words listed, Zollverein had to do with commerce in the German states in the mid-19th century. It was the name of the system of free trade used among the German states, which was facilitated by the railroads. Realpolitik (b) was Otto von Bismarck's term for politics based on reality and pragmatism, rather than on ideals or theoretical concepts. Bismarck believed in doing what was realistically possible rather than trying to achieve impossible goals. Schleswig (c) and Holstein (d) were the names of two northern territories, populated partly by Germans, which had been annexed by Denmark until Bismarck attacked and defeated Denmark, giving Schleswig to Prussia and Holstein to Austria; then Bismarck also secured Holstein from Austria in the Seven Weeks' War of 1866. Reichstag (e) is the German word for "Parliament," which was created for the North German Confederation, although it had little control compared to Bismarck and Kaiser Wilhelm. (See also answer explanation to question #66.)

68. E: These were all changes that occurred at the turn of the 19th to 20th centuries in Europe and elsewhere in many countries. Developments in the sciences (a) meant that these were taught quite differently in schools in 1899 than they were in 1859—a relatively short period of time. Because of these advances, including those in medicine, sanitation, and the economy, people were living longer than before (b). The rise of nationalistic sentiments was widespread in many countries, especially in the later 19th century, and these sentiments of unity and identity also extended to minorities (c) such as the Welsh and the Irish in the United Kingdom and the French Canadians in Canada. By the end of the 19th century the railroads were well established, facilitating transportation of goods and travel by people (d).

69. E: While a major contributor to the automotive industry, John D. Rockefeller was not specifically an inventor, developer, or manufacturer of engines and/or cars. He was an American industrialist and philanthropist who founded and owned the Standard Oil Company from 1870-1897. Rockefeller transformed the petroleum industry, and in so doing, his company profited so much that he was often regarded as the richest man in history. In his time, Rockefeller was the richest man in the world and also the first billionaire in America. German Karl Benz (a) is generally credited with being the first to obtain a patent on a gas-powered automobile and founded the Mercedes-Benz auto manufacturing company. German Gottlieb Daimler (d) is credited with inventing the first high-speed petroleum engine, the first motorcycle, and the first motorboat. He and his partner Wilhelm Maybach designed the "Grandfather Clock engine," developed many other internal combustion engines, and formed the Daimler Motoren Gesellschaft (Daimler Motor Company), which later merged with Karl Benz's motor company. Rudolf Diesel (c), also from Germany, invented the diesel engine in 1897. American Henry Ford (b), who founded the Ford Motor Company, was responsible for a great many inventions, including the Model T and Model A automobiles, as well as the idea of creating assembly lines for the mass production of cars. His innovations allowed the majority of average consumers to be able to buy cars by the early 20th century.

70. B: Jane Addams' Hull House is an example of the Social Gospel movement, a Protestant intellectual movement dedicated to the "salvation of humankind" through improving the quality of life for the poor by reform of public health, education, and labor, which it was believed would in turn improve the quality of their moral and spiritual lives. This movement was Addams' inspiration for founding Hull House, a settlement house in Chicago devoted to helping poor residents of inner-city slums by providing health care, education, and day care. The Higher Criticism (a) movement was a development in literary analysis that focused on the sources of literary works, i.e. their authorship, time, and place of origin, which at the turn of the century was applied specifically to the examination of Biblical texts. Darwinism (c) was a belief in Charles Darwin's theory of evolution, which was controversial when he introduced it and has remained so despite paleontological evidence to support it. Freudianism (d) was a belief in the psychoanalytic/psychodynamic theories of Sigmund Freud, who stated that we are all motivated by unconscious impulses; that our personalities are made up of three basic structures, each with its own function; and that our personalities are formed by our experiences in infancy and early childhood with our parents. While parts of Freud's theory have since been discredited, a majority of his concepts remain today as integral parts both of the field of psychology and of daily life. Even in these days of managed care dictating brief, solution-based therapy wherein his long-term, in-depth techniques are not feasible, Freud is still considered to be the father of modern psychoanalysis. The Salvation Army (e) was founded by William and Catherine Booth in 1878. This organization is another example of turn-of-the-century social reform. Its orientation is both religious and social. Like Addams' Hull House, the Salvation Army is dedicated to helping those suffering from poverty, homelessness, addiction, and other forms of neediness. It is still very active today in the United States, Canada, and Great Britain.

71. D: Between 1846 and 1932, more than 50 million people emigrated from Europe, all of them settling in the United States, Canada, Argentina, and Brazil. According to census figures, these immigrants did not number only 20 million (a), 30 million (b), or 40 million (c). While they did number over 50 million (d), there were not 60 million of them (e).

72. B: It is not true that the US and Germany were equal in leading industry. Although Germany's factories did more than quadruple in number (a) during the Second Industrial Revolution, evidencing enormous growth, the United States was still the world leader of industry. The oil (c) and steel (d) industries were two of the most important contributors to additional industrial development. Though large corporations (such as the British East India Company) had previously existed, the Second Industrial Revolution beginning in the late 19th century was the time when "mega" corporations, as we are now familiar with them, came into being (e) all over the Western Hemisphere, but particularly in the United States, due in large part to the immigration of millions of Europeans (see question #71).

73. C: The Morse telegraph was patented by Samuel F. B. Morse in the United States in 1837. He sent the first telegram in 1838 over two miles of wire in New Jersey. In 1844, he sent another telegram farther, from Washington, D.C. to Baltimore, Maryland. By 1861, the Morse/Vail telegraph (Alfred Vail was Morse's assistant) had replaced the Pony Express as it reached from the East Coast of the country to the West Coast. The first intercontinental telegraph cable between America and England was laid in 1867. Alexander Graham Bell was born and raised in Scotland. After college he moved with his family to London, and then to Canada. Bell was invited to America to train instructors of the deaf in Massachusetts and Connecticut in the Visible Speech System. He subsequently taught at Boston University, maintaining his residence in Canada during the summers. Bell obtained a patent for the first telephone (e) in 1876. By 1900, telephones were commonly used in larger cities. The zeppelin airship (b) was patented in 1899 by German Count Ferdinand von Zeppelin in the United States. Guglielmo Marconi was born, raised, and educated in Italy and was interested in and experimented with electricity from an early age. As a young adult he traveled to London and thence to America. After experimenting and demonstrating wireless radio signals at local distances, Marconi worked on sending wireless signals across the Atlantic (a), accomplishing this in 1901 and 1902. American brothers Wilbur and Orville Wright made their first test flights of their airplane, the Wright Flyer, in 1903 (d). Though other inventors had built and even test-flown aircrafts predating this, the Wright brothers were the first to come up with controls enabling flight with a fixed-wing airplane. Within two more years they had developed their plane for practical use, and fixed-wing crafts became the standard.

74. A: From 1800 to 1900, the percentage of Great Britain's population that lived in cities doubled (i.e. it increased by 100%). In 1800, the urban population in England was 40% of the total population; by 1900, it was 80% of the total population, or double what it was 100 years before. It was not triple (b) or three times what it had been, or quadruple (c) or four times what it had been. It did not increase by 50% (d), or by 75% (e), but by 100%.

75. E: Between 1800 and 1900, the population of the city of London increased by six and a half times, going from around 1 million to 6.5 million. It did not increase by only two and a half (a) times, three and a half (b) times, four and a half (c) times, or even five and a half (d) times. (Note that this question and answer are different from the previous question and answer, #74, which refers to how much of the entire country of England's population was living in all the cities in England combined. This question refers only to England's capital and biggest city, London, and how much its population grew during the century.)

76. C: As a consequence of the second Industrial Revolution, the population of Berlin increased between 1800 and 1900 by more than fifteen and a half times. In 1800, the population of Germany's capital and biggest city was around 172,000. By 1900, it had grown to 2.7 million. This equals 15.6976...times, or rounded up, 15.70 times—more than 15 and a half times its size a century earlier. Therefore this city's population did not increase by only five and a half (a) times or ten and a half (b) times. However, it also did not grow by as much as twenty and a half (d) or twenty-five and a half (e) times.

77. B: The development that was not a direct example of urban development was Gladstone's Reform Act of 1884. This law, passed by England's Prime Minister William Gladstone, a liberal, gave the right to vote to a majority of adult men in the country. Police departments were established (a) on a formal basis to enforce laws and keep the peace in cities that were much larger than in the past. Health Departments were formed (c) to see that apartment dwellers lived in sanitary conditions that would not contribute to disease, also because of the growth of urban populations. The innovation of piping water and gas into homes for heating interiors (d) allowed urban citizens to be warm and to take hot baths indoors without building and maintaining fires. In addition, sewer systems were developed in big cities to solve the problem of urban sanitation, and the invention and implementation of indoor plumbing (e) allowed people to flush away refuse rather than dumping it in the streets or rivers as they had previously done.

78. D: Great Britain's Public Health Act of 1875 required that all new homes contain indoor plumbing. Due to rapid urbanization, there were epidemics of cholera and typhus in the cities, and this law's purpose was to reform sanitation conditions. This law did not mandate the construction of hospitals in cities (a). It did not provide for home health nurse visits in cities (b). It did not provide for free clinics to be built in the cities (c). In addition to requiring that new residences contain indoor plumbing and drain systems, this comprehensive Public Health Act also required that the water supply not be contaminated b. y, for example, residue from gas production); that cities have outdoor lighting and pavements; that the city authorities could provide public recreation areas and public clocks; and other provisions in the interest of public health and well-being. Since only (d) is a part of this law, (e), all of these, is incorrect.

79. C: In 1884, William Gladstone, the liberal Prime Minister of England, passed the Third Reform Act, also known as the Representation of the People Act, giving the right to vote to 60% of the adult men in the country. This was done by extending voting rights from boroughs (or towns or cities) to the countryside, thus increasing the electorate. All men who paid a minimum yearly rent for land or who owned land valued at the same minimum amount (£10) were allowed to vote. Though this act did not provide universal suffrage, as women and the other 40% of men still could not vote, it was still an improvement. As 60% of adult men now could vote due to this act, the figures of 40% (a), 50% (b), 70% (d), and 80% (e) of adult men are all incorrect.

80. A: The answer that is not true about urban life around the turn of the 19th-20th centuries is that most urban dwellers experienced a lower standard of living. In fact, although it is true that many city dwellers had terribly poor living conditions by today's standards (b), it is also true that because of the improvements and conveniences brought about by industrialization, as well as the higher wages brought by industrial jobs, most people in the cities experienced a higher standard of living than previously. At this time, most urban employees worked roughly10 hours a day for six days a week. While this may sound like a lot of work hours to some people today, it was actually a decrease compared to pre-reform law levels, when people could be made to work many more hours. (See also answer explanation to question #37.) Because they were no longer working most of their waking hours, people in cities had more time to spend on leisure activities (c). In addition to more time for having fun, people also had more money to spend on it, as was evidenced by the growth of tourism (d). Another indicator of greater amounts of time and money to spend on leisure was that bicycles became a fad all over the Western Hemisphere (e).

81. B: The country where adult illiteracy was not virtually wiped out by 1900 was Russia. This was because education was not emphasized as much in Eastern Europe in the late 19th century as it was in France (a), England (c), Germany (d), and Scandinavia (e), where adult illiteracy was indeed almost gone by 1900. In these countries, compulsory primary education became common in the late 1800s and early 1900s. In these countries and in the United States, more people enrolled in colleges and universities at this time than in the past. The increased literacy in Western and Northern Europe created a greater demand for newspapers, magazines, periodicals, and books. However, in Russia, there was still a 79% rate of illiteracy in 1900.

82. C: Louis Pasteur proved the germ theory between 1860 and 1864. This theory had existed in various forms throughout history, including ancient times. However, Pasteur was the one to prove by his experiments that it was true. In 1898, the chemist Marie Curie (a) discovered the element of radium, found in uranium ore. She and her husband, Pierre, were awarded the Nobel Prize in 1903 for their research into the properties of this radioactive element. Doctor Robert Koch (b) isolated the microorganisms that cause anthrax (in 1877), tuberculosis (in 1882), and cholera (in 1883). He was awarded the Nobel Prize in 1905 for his identification of the tuberculosis organism. Pasteur and Koch are regarded, along with Ferdinand Cohn, as the founders of microbiology. Albert Einstein (d) published an article in 1905 stating his theory of relativity, which came to change the very way we view reality in the physical world. Gregor Mendel (e) conducted experiments with plants from 1856-1863 and identified the processes by which genetic traits are inherited. He read the paper he wrote formulating his laws of inheritance in 1865 at two meetings of a natural history society, and his work was published in 1866. Mendel's discoveries were not given much attention until after his death, but in the early 20th century his work was rediscovered and replicated, and he became known as the "father of modern genetics."

83. E: The ideas of all of these presented challenges to traditional Christian beliefs. Sigmund Freud (a) (1856-1939), who created psychoanalysis, emphasized the importance of relationships with parental figures to children's developing psyches, as well as the importance of largely unconscious processes in determining human behavior. As Freud maintained that God was a father-figure and a human projection (projection being one of the ego's defense mechanisms he described), he influenced the secularization of society during his time. Charles Darwin (b) (1809-1882) presented his theory of evolution (he published *On the Origin of Species* in 1859 and *The Descent of Man* in 1871), which challenged strictly literal interpretations of the Bible by showing that "creation" took much longer and was more gradual than depicted in Genesis. (Of course, reading the scriptures only literally as fundamentalists insist is quite a limited approach. If symbolic meanings and literary devices are considered in reading these works, then Darwin's theory does not need to conflict with them.) Darwin was informed also by *Principles of Geology*, published in1830 by Charles Lyell (c), who pointed out that based on geological evidence, the earth could not possibly be the age stated in Genesis if one were to read it literally. Another writer who influenced Darwin's thinking was the classical economist Thomas Malthus (d) (1766-1834), who stated that population growth has the potential to increase far beyond the earth's potential to supply food. This concept complements the idea of natural selection when there is not enough food to feed as many offspring as are born.

84. D: Social Darwinism was founded by Herbert Spencer (1820-1903). Spencer applied ideas from the theory of evolution created by (a) Charles Darwin (1809-1882) to social and cultural systems. Whereas Darwin was a naturalist and discussed his theories in terms of human and other animal species, Spencer was a philosopher and a political and sociological theorist who applied some of Darwin's ideas to these areas. After reading Darwin's *On the Origin of Species,* Spencer coined the term "survival of the fittest," which can be seen as similar to Darwin's concept of natural selection. Philosopher (b) Friedrich Nietzsche (1844-1900) rejected both religion and rationalism in favor of emotionalism and accessing our "will to power." One of his best known books is *Also Sprach Zarathustra* (1883) [in English, Thus Spoke Zarathustra], in which he included the concept of the *Übermensch* ("overman," or, as some called it, "superman"). Because Nietzsche believed that the strongest individuals should be in charge, Social Darwinism can be related to his philosophy. At the same time for different reasons, Social Darwinism can be applied to the poet (c) Rudyard Kipling (1865-1936), who introduced the idea of the "white man's burden" to help and raise up the subjects of imperialism in India and other colonies. Another public figure of the same time period who wanted to help those less fortunate was (e) Andrew Carnegie (1835-1919). Carnegie, a multimillionaire, was a proponent of a "gospel of wealth," believing that rich people should help poor people by giving them ways to better themselves. One of a number of ways Carnegie realized this belief was by building libraries in many American communities.

85. A: By the beginning of the 20th century, it controlled over 20% of the world's population, not 25%. (Over 20% is still a remarkable proportion.) It is true that the British Empire began the program of Rhodes Scholars and Scholarships (b), which still exists today. This program was named after its founder, Cecil Rhodes, an important person in England's imperial rule of South Africa who wanted certain African colonial students to get educations in England and then come home to help their fellow Africans learn to adopt British culture. The African country of Zimbabwe was also previously named Rhodesia after Cecil Rhodes (c). It is true that despite the impressive size of the British Empire's conquests between the 19th and 20th centuries, the actual landmass of the country of Great Britain is much smaller than the US state of California (d). Because (a) is not true, (e), all of these, is incorrect.

86. C: Problems of hostile groups that coexist in India are not a consequence of the British Empire. Like America (a), Jamaica, (b), and Hong Kong (e), India is a country which enjoys freedom as aftermath consequence of the former British Empire. Problems of hostile groups in African countries (d) are a result of the former British Empire and other countries (such as France and Portugal) that colonized in Africa as these European imperialists set artificial boundaries, creating nations within which hostile groups were forced to coexist even though their cultural traditions and customs were incompatible. As these boundaries remain, the problems within African countries have continued beyond the days of British rule.

87. D: Algeria was not a British colony until the 20th century, but a French colony. By 1945, Algeria's population contained a million people descended from French settlers. Kenya (a), the Sudan (b), Nigeria (c), and South Africa (e) were all British colonies until the 20th century.

88. Algeria was a French colony until the 20th century. (See also answer explanation to question #87.) Canada (a) was a British colony. (France did some colonizing in Canada, as is still evidenced by the use of the French language in part of the province of Québec, but all of Canada was made British property by the 1763 Treaty of Paris.) Indonesia (c) was a Dutch colony. Mozambique (d) was a Portuguese colony, and South Africa (e) was a British colony.

89. A: Indonesia was a Dutch colony until the 20th century. Indochina (b) was a French colony and is called Vietnam today. The African country of Mozambique (c) was a Portuguese colony. South Africa (d) and New Zealand (e) were both British colonies.

90. E: Mozambique an African nation, was a colony of Portugal until the 20th century. Indochina (a), now known as Vietnam, was a French colony. Indonesia (b) was a colony of the Netherlands. South Africa (c) and New Zealand (d) were both British colonies.

91. D: In Brittany linguistic minorities did not rebel against an English-speaking majority, but against the French-speaking majority of France. (Brittany is an English translation of the French name Bretagne. Located in northwestern France, this Celtic nation was once called "Little Britain". Its inhabitants' traditional language was Breton.) In Wales (a), Welsh-speaking minorities rebelled against the English-speaking majority. In Ireland (b), Irish Gaelic-speaking minorities rebelled against the English-speaking majority. In Scotland (c), linguistic minorities who spoke Scots Gaelic, also called Highland Gaelic a. different branch of the Celtic languages than Welsh and Breton, descending from Middle Irish like Irish Gaelic and Manx), rebelled against the English-speaking majority. In Québec (e), Canada, French-speaking minorities rebelled against the English-speaking majority.

92. C: Mauritania was not colonized by Germany in the mid-1880s. It was a French colony at that time. The "Scramble for Africa" or the "Race for Africa" was a competition among European powers for African territories that occurred during this time period. Tanzania (a), Cameroon (b), Togoland (d), and Namibia (e) were all areas taken by Germany, which kept England from exerting greater dominance of the continent.

93. C: The Berlin Conference (1885) divided African colonies among various European powers. This conference was an attempt to avoid war among the major world powers over African colonies, though it was ultimately not very successful as these powers were not satisfied with the divisions and did not observe the terms of the agreement. The conference was suggested by Portugal and convened by German Chancellor Bismarck. The competition over Africa during this time period was known as the "Scramble for Africa" or the "Race for Africa." The Berlin Conference was not (a) convened to resolve imperialist claims in Germany, but in Africa. It was not (b) convened to settle imperial claims in Germany by England, but to settle imperial claims in Africa by a number of European countries, including Austria-Hungary, Belgium, France, England, Denmark, Spain, Portugal, Italy, Russia, the Netherlands, Sweden-Norway, and the Ottoman Empire. (The United States was invited by Bismarck to attend, but did not participate.) It was not (d) convened to settle competition between Germany and France, but among all the countries named above in the explanation to wrong answer (b). It was not convened (e) to settle differences among world powers regarding Germany, but regarding Africa.

94. A: The Triple Entente (1907) was made between Britain, Russia, and France. The Three Emperors' League (1873) was made among (b) Germany, Austria, and Russia. The Triple Alliance (1882) was made among (c) Germany, Austria, and Italy. The Triple Entente (a) and the Triple Alliance (c) were both agreements among countries that ended up fighting one another in World War I. (Not long thereafter, Italy switched sides in the war, and the Ottoman Empire allied with Germany and Austria-Hungary.) During the time period leading up to the start of war in 1914, there were no alliances among (d) Britain, Russia, and Germany or among (e) Britain, Germany, and France. In addition to those already named, other alliances made in the late 1800s and early 1900s included the Dual Alliance (1879) between Austria and Germany; the Franco-Russian Alliance (1894); the British-Japanese Alliance (1902); and the Entente Cordiale (1902) between Great Britain and France. Both the number of alliances and the fact that the members of two of them became enemies in World War I are signs of the discord among European powers that contributed, among many other factors, to the war.

95. B: Labor unions were legalized in England in 1871 to improve conditions for employees, including pay, work hours, workplace conditions, and benefits such as paid vacations, mandatory breaks, and workers' compensation. England was the first European country to legalize unions due to its history of liberalism and industrialization. In 1866, (a) America's first nationalized union, the National Labor Union (NLU), was formed. In 1884, (c) France legalized labor unions. In 1891, (d) Germany legalized labor unions. Since (b) is correct, (e), none of these, is incorrect.

96. C: Labor unions were legalized in France in 1884. In 1866, (a) America's first nationalized union, the National Labor Union (NLU), was formed. In 1871, (b) England legalized labor unions. In 189, (d) Germany legalized labor unions. Since (c) is correct, (e), none of these, is incorrect.

97. D: Labor unions were legalized in Germany in 1891. In 1866, (a) America's first nationalized union, the National Labor Union (NLU), was formed. In 1871, (b) England legalized labor unions. In 1884, (c) France legalized labor unions. Since (d) is correct, (e), none of these, is incorrect.

98. A: The first national labor union in America was formed in 1866. The National Labor Union (NLU) began in 1866, and ended in 1872. It set the stage for subsequent organizations such as the Knights of Labor, the AFL, and the American Federation of Labor. In 1871, (b) England legalized labor unions. In 1884, (c) France legalized labor unions. In 1891, (d) Germany legalized labor unions. Since (a) is correct, (e), none of these, is incorrect.

99. E: The tradition of referring to liberals as "left-wing" and to conservatives as "right-wing" has its origins in the French Revolution. At the onset of the French Revolution, delegates to the National Assembly from France's Third Estate sat on the left side, and delegates from the First and Second Estates sat on the right side. Because the Third Estate was made up of middle- and lower-class citizens who were pro-revolution while the other two estates were made up of clergy and nobility who favored conservation of the Ancien Régime, the term "left" came to be associated with liberals and "right" with conservatives. These terms did not come from (a) the American Revolution or from (c) the Continental Congress which was convened by America's thirteen colonies to run the country during the American Revolution. They also did not come from (b) the British Parliament. They did not originate in (d) the Berlin Conference, which convened from 1884-1885 to divide Africa among European powers vying for control of that continent.

100. B: World War I caused approximately 13 million military deaths, not (a) 7 million. 37 million (c) is the approximate number of total casualties, including not only deaths but also those wounded and those missing in action, not 27 million (d). Since (b) is correct, (e), none of these, is incorrect.

101. D: That Europe's moral superiority was reinforced was not a result of World War I. As an outcome of the war, the idea of Europe's moral superiority was actually undermined. Other outcomes of the First World War included the attainment of world power status by the USA. (a); the arrival of Russia as a world Communist center (b); the preparation of the way to World War II (c); and the development of attitudes of increasing religious and philosophical doubt and pessimism (e) among the world's involved nations, as well as major cultural changes in many countries.

102. C: The catalyst to the onset of World War I was the assassination of Austria's Archduke Franz Ferdinand by Serbian nationalists. The Austrians suspected the Serbian government of aiding these nationalists and made demands of Serbia that would bring that country under the control of Austria. When Serbian officials refused, Austria declared war on Serbia. While the Archduke's assassination was not done by Russians (b), Russia declared war on Austria in defense of Serbia. Being allied with Austria, Germany (d) then declared war on Russia in retaliation. Two days later, Germany also declared war on France, and France (e) declared war on Germany the next day, not only in response to Germany's declaration of war, but also to fulfill its promise to defend Belgium's neutrality since Germany had invaded Belgium the same day it declared war on Russia. All of these events started the First World War and also established the initial two opposing groups: the Allied powers, consisting of Russia, France, and Great Britain; and the Central Powers, consisting of Germany, Austria-Hungary, Bulgaria, and the Ottoman Empire.

103. A: The statement about "peace without victory…between equals" was made by American President Woodrow Wilson. Wilson wanted to maintain neutrality in this war and only reluctantly entered the war in 1917, when it seemed inevitable due to Germany's actions against the US As a result of America's later entry, it did not suffer the enormous casualties that France or England did. At the Versailles peace talks, England was represented by (b) David Lloyd George, who was more inclined to want to punish Germany than Wilson. France was represented at these talks by (c) Georges Clemenceau, and he and his country were even more desirous than England of avenging their tremendous war losses (approximately five and a half million soldiers) against Germany. Adolf Hitler (d) reacted to Germany's mortification in the Versailles Treaty by wanting revenge as well. Thus none of these three men from England, France, or Germany would have spoken in favor of a "peace without victory" or a "peace between equals" given their attitudes. Wilfred Owen (e) was a brilliant British poet and soldier. He wrote poems about the war from his first-hand combat experience. His poetry had great impact and he is still famous for it. Owen was killed in action in 1918. (Ironically, the report of his death reached his home in the UK on Armistice Day.) Owen's poems spoke of the horrors of war; they were bitter and very sad, but in none of them did he call for any kind of a peace, focusing instead on the shocking realities of war itself.

104. B: It is not true that US troops were in battle for slightly more than a year. American soldiers actually saw combat for less than a year. It is true that (a) the US did not join the war until 1917. It is true that (c) the sinking of the British ship *Lusitania* in 1915 motivated Wilson to join the war, as 128 passengers on this ship were American. The *Lusitania*'s sinking was also a motivation because it was a prime example of the unrestricted submarine warfare Germany had been conducting on any and all ships bound for the United Kingdom—warfare which President Wilson had already demanded more than once that Germany not commit, to no avail; and additionally because England and America were allies. It is true that (d) the Zimmermann Telegram in 1917 further motivated Wilson to join the war. This telegram was from Germany to Mexico, encouraging Mexico to ally with Germany if the US joined the war, and moreover saying if it did, Mexico would get the states of

New Mexico, Arizona, and Texas from America after the war. The telegram was intercepted by a British agent and given to the US government. This intelligence infuriated American attitudes against Germany even more than before. It is also true that (e) none of the First World War was fought in America, most likely due in large part to it joining the war so late.

105. E: The country that did not come out of the dissolved Austro-Hungarian Empire after World War I was Poland. In 1772, 1793, and 1795, Poland was partitioned such that it disappeared from the European map and Russia, Prussia, and Austria each owned parts of its land mass. During the war, US President Woodrow Wilson called for Poland's reconstitution in Point 13 of his 14 Points, and the Allied powers agreed. After Germany surrendered in1918, Poland regained its independence as the Second Polish Republic. After the war, the Austro-Hungarian Empire ended, leaving the separate countries of Czechoslovakia (a)*, Yugoslavia (b), Hungary (c), and Austria (d). *(What was then Czechoslovakia is currently divided into the Czech Republic and Slovakia.)

106. C: The country that did not result from the dissolved Ottoman Empire was Egypt. Egypt, part of the Ottoman Empire, was occupied by Napoleon in 1798, and regained by joint British and Ottoman forces in 1801. It was occupied by Great Britain in 1882, but remained officially an Ottoman province until 1914, when it entered the war on the side of the Central powers and Great Britain officially annexed it. The individual countries resulting from the Ottoman Empire after World War I were Turkey (a), Syria (b), Iran (d), and Iraq (e).

107. E: These were all factors contributing to the Russian Revolution in 1917. The Russians had spent three years in World War I, often without arms (a). Russia had not yet industrialized to the degree that other countries in the war had, so it could not manufacture enough weapons. With so many Russian men fighting in the war instead of working on their farms, there was a loss of crop production resulting in food shortages (b) both for people in Russia and for Russian soldiers. In addition, Tsar Nicholas II was at the front attempting to run the Russian war effort. Because he was far from the capital of St. Petersburg, some people blamed his absence (c) for the roughly two million Russian deaths sustained in the war. Moreover, there were more than a hundred different language groups in the Russian Empire (d) at the time. Many of these groups identified more with their own ethnicity than with any feelings of Russian nationalism, making the country more divided than united. All of these things added to the Russians' dissatisfaction and unrest, contributing to revolution.

108. D: It is not true that Nicholas II reorganized the government in 1917. In that year, Tsar Nicholas II was forced to relinquish his control of the government by a combination of demonstrators and soldiers who had joined the demonstration. A provisional government was set up to replace him. It is true that (a) riots broke out in the cities of Russia in 1917, expressing the discontent of the Russian people. It is true that (b) Rasputin affected the Tsar's wife in his absence. While Nicholas was away at the war front, Rasputin, a demented peasant monk, was exerting his influence on Nicholas' wife Alexandra, adding to the undermining of the Tsar's power and discrediting the government and the Romanov dynasty. In 1905, the huge country of Russia lost the Russo-Japanese War (c) to the tiny nation of Japan. This was the first loss of a European military power to an Asian one. It is also true that demonstrators marched on the Winter Palace, the governmental headquarters, in1905 (e), and almost 100 of them were killed by soldiers. This demonstration showed the extent of Russians' dissatisfaction with the government, to the point of risking injury or death to oppose the existing regime, which culminated twelve years later in the Russian Revolution.

109. B: Joseph Stalin is regarded as having killed the most people. While there is no agreement on an exact number, he is estimated to have had tens of millions of people murdered to eliminate all those he considered possible threats. Stalin's predecessor, Vladimir Lenin (a), had his secret police murder around 200,000 people during the Bolshevik regime. Leon Trotsky (c) was an assistant and advisor to Lenin. He helped Lenin overthrow the previous provisional government that succeeded Tsar Nicholas II. As Lenin's employee, Trotsky was an accomplice to the secret police's executions ordered by Lenin, but is not regarded as being solely responsible for these killings as Lenin was the dictator. Sergei Kirov (d) was the chief of the Communist Party in Leningrad and was assassinated during Stalin's Great Purges. Since (b) is correct, (e), none of these, is incorrect.

110. A: Adolf Hitler said this of Germany in 1941, during the Second World War. (In the last ellipsis, he additionally said "…thanks to National Socialism, it will remain united in the future.") Between the First and Second World Wars, many European countries shifted from democracies to dictatorships. In addition to Hitler in Germany, Benito Mussolini (b) founded the Fascist Party in Italy and was an absolute dictator during this time. Winston Churchill (c) was Prime Minister of England at the time, representing one of the countries that did not turn to dictatorship. Outside of Europe, the United States continued to have a democracy with Franklin Delano Roosevelt (d) as president. Since (a) is correct, (e), none of these said this, is incorrect.

111. C: Winston Churchill, the British Prime Minister during World War II, said this. Despite their desire for and appropriation of absolute power, neither Hitler (a) nor Mussolini (b) made this statement of resolution never to give up fighting. American President F.D. Roosevelt (d) did not speak of refusing to surrender, but rather of finding a lasting peace (see also question #112). Since (c) is correct, (e), none of these said this, is incorrect.

112. B: President Franklin D. Roosevelt wrote this in 1945 regarding World War II, between his meeting in February with world leaders at Yalta and his death on April 12, less than a month before V-E Day. It was part of a speech he never had a chance to deliver, and is now carved into the wall of the FDR Memorial. Forming the United Nations was one of FDR's causes to maintain world peace in the future. President Woodrow L. Wilson (a) said of the First World War, "It must be a peace without victory….Only a peace between equals can last." Prime Minister Winston Churchill (c) is more often quoted about World War II as stating "We shall fight….We shall never surrender", than as calling for peace. Austro-Hungarian Theodor Herzl (d), who founded the Zionist movement to attain Jewish statehood for Israel, is popularly quoted from his book *Old New Land (Altneuland)* with his statement, "If you will it, it is no dream" (referring to Israeli statehood). Herzl imagined a Palace of Peace to be built in Jerusalem to settle conflicts among countries. He did not anticipate difficulties between Palestinians and Israelis or between Jews and Arabs in general. His books and speeches were focused on Zionism rather than on war and peace. Since (b) is correct, (e), none of these, is incorrect.

113. E: All of these are true regarding US entry into WWII. The United States decisively preferred to maintain a neutral position from the mid-1930s until 1941 (a) when Japan attacked Pearl Harbor, Hawaii. Even though the American public attitude was supportive toward Great Britain in 1940, the US still did not want to be involved in the European war. However, the UK's Prime Minister, Winston Churchill, was very persuasive (b), and he convinced the American government to trade its old warships to Great Britain for military bases in Newfoundland and the West Indies, as well as convincing the US to provide war supplies to Britain, which would pay America for them after the war. The US Congress passed the Lend-Lease Act (c) enabling this transaction to take place. While America's formal position on the war was still one of neutrality, it also aided England and Canada at the same time. The end of US neutrality was when Japan, an ally with Germany, attacked America's Pacific Fleet in Pearl Harbor, Hawaii on December 7, 1941 (d); the next day America declared war on Japan. Shortly thereafter, Hitler declared war against the US by Germany.

114 A: Auschwitz in Poland was the largest Nazi extermination camp of the Holocaust. More than a million people were killed at Auschwitz. Treblinka (b) and Sobibor (d) were also sites where the Nazis built death camps. Dachau (c) and Buchenwald (e) were concentration camps. While many people also died there, these were differentiated from death camps in that their primary purpose was to extract forced labor from their prisoners, while the primary purpose of death camps was to kill their prisoners. While Hitler's main target was the Jews due to his rampant anti-Semitism and his belief that the "final solution" to the "Jewish question" was to kill all the Jews, who were murdered in the largest numbers, many other people were killed in these camps as well (see also question #115).

115. E: All of these people were imprisoned and murdered by the Nazis in their death camps during World War II. Hitler's paranoia was that Jewish people (a) were "...the universal poisoners of all peoples, international Jewry." Therefore they were his primary target as he wished to exterminate all of them and, to this end, instituted mass genocides. However, Slavic people (b) such as Polish and Russian people were also imprisoned and murdered as the Nazis considered them inferior to the "master race" of Aryan Germans. Gypsy (c) or Romany people were also considered undesirable and executed. In addition, the Nazis wanted to eliminate all people with developmental disabilities (d) as part of his effort to "purify" society. The Nazis also killed Christians who had opposed Nazism or who had helped to conceal Jews from Nazi storm troopers who rounded them up and sent them to work camps or death camps.

116. D: The 1961 building of the Berlin Wall was not an instance of attempts to contain Communism. It was rather an act on the part of Soviet Communists to keep people in countries occupied by the Soviets from going west to non-Soviet areas, and to mitigate the influence of America in East Germany. Instances of attempts to contain Communism include (a) the Marshall Plan, in which the US gave over $12 billion to European countries between 1948 and 1951, to aid their postwar reconstruction. Not only did this European Recovery Program help European countries' economies; it also helped the American economy by enabling Europeans to spend money on goods imported from the US Moreover, while there was no official exchange of these funds for political affiliations, the Marshall Plan's aid did reinforce America's political influence in Western Europe. The Truman Doctrine (b) was another instance of attempts to contain Communism. In 1947, President Harry S. Truman stated, "I believe it must be the policy of the United States to support free peoples who are resisting attempted subjugation by armed minorities or by outside pressures." In demonstration of this belief, Truman ordered approximately $400 million in aid to Greece and Turkey, in the form of both money and military support, to help anti-communists in those countries. In 1948, when the Soviets created a blockade of the passageway between West Berlin and West Germany, the Berlin Airlift (c) was another instance of attempts to contain Communism. America flew up to 13,000 tons a day of goods into West Berlin, continuing this practice for a whole year. This not only gave aid to the people there; it also was a show of power by the Allies and of their determination to prevent Soviet control of West Berlin. The year of the Berlin Airlift resulted in the Soviets' reopening the way to West Germany. Following this confrontation between the Allies and the Soviets, a second confrontation came with (e) the Cuban Missile Crisis in 1962, between US President John F. Kennedy and Soviet Premier Nikita Khrushchev. After a Communist revolution in Cuba, Kennedy gave Khrushchev a deadline to stop building missiles on the island of Cuba and to get rid of existing missiles there; Khrushchev agreed. Historians state that if he had not complied, and Kennedy had invaded Cuba, there would probably have been a war between the United States and Russia.

117. B: Charles de Gaulle, who led the Free French forces as a General in World War II, was the first President of the French Fifth Republic, which he founded in 1958. He was President from 1959-

1969. While de Gaulle did many beneficial things for France, including for its economy, by 1968 much of the public was tired of his government's style, which by then was considered heavy-handed, overly traditional and repressive, especially by students, who initiated demonstrations and strikes in 1968, almost overturning de Gaulle's government. Though he recovered from this blow, offering to accede to some of the demonstrators' demands and also winning the 1968 election, he resigned and retired in 1969, after his referendum for government reform was rejected. De Gaulle is not considered a major contributor to social change among youth. Elvis Presley and the Beatles (a) both contributed in a major way to social change among youth with rock and roll music—Elvis in the 1950s and the Beatles in the 1960s. The popularity of their music helped, along with television, to establish the youth culture as dominant in the Western world and especially in America. Teens and young adults became more distinct from other age groups, identified by their styles of dress, use of colloquial language, and different cultural customs. Albert Camus and Jean-Paul Sartre (c) were both French writers of the Existentialist genre. They had a strong influence on young readers. Their beliefs that life is inherently absurd and meaningless, that individuals create their own meaning in life, that the individual alone is responsible for his or her existence, and even that nothing exists outside of one's own consciousness, became popular with youth disaffected with their elders' traditions and beliefs in the face of a changing world. American marine biologist and naturalist Rachel Carson (d) published her book *Silent Spring* in 1962, describing the potential consequences of the loss of animal and plant life on Earth if we continued to abuse our environment. Her book led to a national ban of DDT and other toxic pesticides, the formation of the Environmental Protection Agency, and is considered to have begun the worldwide movement of environmentalism. French feminist author Simone de Beauvoir (e) published her book *The Second Sex* in 1949, calling attention to the male domination of Western culture and the unequal status of women. This book is considered one of the foundations of modern feminism and greatly influenced subsequent social reform on behalf of women.

118. E: These are all associated with the end of the Cold War. The Soviet-Afghan war (a) was very unpopular and costly. It undermined the Soviet economy and the Soviet populace's loyalty to Communism, contributing significantly to the end of the Soviet Union and the Cold War. The Polish labor organization Solidarity (b) (*Solidarność*) led by Lech Walesa won the 1989 elections in Poland, further weakening the Communist Party. The same year, Hungary opened its Austrian borders and legalized non-communist political parties. As a result many anti-communists began demonstrating in East Germany and the Berlin Wall was soon dismantled (c). This wall had been a major symbol of the Cold War; its fall was another step toward the end of the Cold War. Following an attempt at a coup against Mikhail Gorbachev, Boris Yeltsin attained heroic status for resisting the coup and Gorbachev resigned after being mortified in his betrayal by those he had himself appointed. With Gorbachev's resignation on December 25, 1991, the Soviet Union and the Cold War were both ended. The end of the Cold War had great impact worldwide, influencing the abolition of apartheid in South Africa (d) in 1993; therefore, this event is also associated with the end of the Cold War.

119. C: It is not true that the EU accepted Turkey as a member without any conditions. Turkey applied for membership in the EU in 1987. The Union accepted its application, but did not give it candidate status until 1999. Membership negotiations began in 2004, and continue in 2009. The EU did require Turkey to abolish the death penalty in order to become a member of the group. It is true that the 1957 Treaty of Rome established the EU (a), and that upon its formation it was called the European Economic Community (c) or EEC. At that time it was also known as the Common Market, and its western members removed tariffs on goods traded by other states having membership (d). It is also true that the EU was responsible for proposing that Western Europe should share a common currency, among other proposals, in the 1991 Treaty of Maastricht; by

2001, the majority of Western European countries had adopted the euro (e) as their official currency.

120. A: Historians today would be least likely to agree that Western civilization has not been as influential as other civilizations. To the contrary, historians tend to believe that by 2000, the history of Western civilization makes it one of the most, or the most, influential civilization in the world. Historians do agree that (b) communism originated in Western civilization, as did (c) democracy. They also note that significant modern advances in technology, such as telephones, televisions, radios, automobiles, airplanes, and computers; and in education, in the form of Western universities, all took place in Western civilization (d). Historians would certainly agree that one example of the many radical changes that Western civilization has seen from 1648 to 2000 is that in 1648, there were no nations because the idea of a nation had not yet been conceived (e). Other great changes in this time period include the change from one basic view of the world that most people had in 1648, centered on God's power, to the extensive multiplicity of world views, beliefs, and ideas existing in the 2000s; the decrease in work hours and increase in leisure hours from 1648 to 2000; and the improvement in standards of living over this period of time.

How to Overcome Test Anxiety

Just the thought of taking a test is enough to make most people a little nervous. A test is an important event that can have a long-term impact on your future, so it's important to take it seriously and it's natural to feel anxious about performing well. But just because anxiety is normal, that doesn't mean that it's helpful in test taking, or that you should simply accept it as part of your life. Anxiety can have a variety of effects. These effects can be mild, like making you feel slightly nervous, or severe, like blocking your ability to focus or remember even a simple detail.

If you experience test anxiety—whether severe or mild—it's important to know how to beat it. To discover this, first you need to understand what causes test anxiety.

Causes of Test Anxiety

While we often think of anxiety as an uncontrollable emotional state, it can actually be caused by simple, practical things. One of the most common causes of test anxiety is that a person does not feel adequately prepared for their test. This feeling can be the result of many different issues such as poor study habits or lack of organization, but the most common culprit is time management. Starting to study too late, failing to organize your study time to cover all of the material, or being distracted while you study will mean that you're not well prepared for the test. This may lead to cramming the night before, which will cause you to be physically and mentally exhausted for the test. Poor time management also contributes to feelings of stress, fear, and hopelessness as you realize you are not well prepared but don't know what to do about it.

Other times, test anxiety is not related to your preparation for the test but comes from unresolved fear. This may be a past failure on a test, or poor performance on tests in general. It may come from comparing yourself to others who seem to be performing better or from the stress of living up to expectations. Anxiety may be driven by fears of the future—how failure on this test would affect your educational and career goals. These fears are often completely irrational, but they can still negatively impact your test performance.

Elements of Test Anxiety

As mentioned earlier, test anxiety is considered to be an emotional state, but it has physical and mental components as well. Sometimes you may not even realize that you are suffering from test anxiety until you notice the physical symptoms. These can include trembling hands, rapid heartbeat, sweating, nausea, and tense muscles. Extreme anxiety may lead to fainting or vomiting. Obviously, any of these symptoms can have a negative impact on testing. It is important to recognize them as soon as they begin to occur so that you can address the problem before it damages your performance.

The mental components of test anxiety include trouble focusing and inability to remember learned information. During a test, your mind is on high alert, which can help you recall information and stay focused for an extended period of time. However, anxiety interferes with your mind's natural processes, causing you to blank out, even on the questions you know well. The strain of testing during anxiety makes it difficult to stay focused, especially on a test that may take several hours. Extreme anxiety can take a huge mental toll, making it difficult not only to recall test information but even to understand the test questions or pull your thoughts together.

Effects of Test Anxiety

Test anxiety is like a disease—if left untreated, it will get progressively worse. Anxiety leads to poor performance, and this reinforces the feelings of fear and failure, which in turn lead to poor performances on subsequent tests. It can grow from a mild nervousness to a crippling condition. If allowed to progress, test anxiety can have a big impact on your schooling, and consequently on your future.

Test anxiety can spread to other parts of your life. Anxiety on tests can become anxiety in any stressful situation, and blanking on a test can turn into panicking in a job situation. But fortunately, you don't have to let anxiety rule your testing and determine your grades. There are a number of relatively simple steps you can take to move past anxiety and function normally on a test and in the rest of life.

Physical Steps for Beating Test Anxiety

While test anxiety is a serious problem, the good news is that it can be overcome. It doesn't have to control your ability to think and remember information. While it may take time, you can begin taking steps today to beat anxiety.

Just as your first hint that you may be struggling with anxiety comes from the physical symptoms, the first step to treating it is also physical. Rest is crucial for having a clear, strong mind. If you are tired, it is much easier to give in to anxiety. But if you establish good sleep habits, your body and mind will be ready to perform optimally, without the strain of exhaustion. Additionally, sleeping well helps you to retain information better, so you're more likely to recall the answers when you see the test questions.

Getting good sleep means more than going to bed on time. It's important to allow your brain time to relax. Take study breaks from time to time so it doesn't get overworked, and don't study right before bed. Take time to rest your mind before trying to rest your body, or you may find it difficult to fall asleep.

Along with sleep, other aspects of physical health are important in preparing for a test. Good nutrition is vital for good brain function. Sugary foods and drinks may give a burst of energy but this burst is followed by a crash, both physically and emotionally. Instead, fuel your body with protein and vitamin-rich foods.

Also, drink plenty of water. Dehydration can lead to headaches and exhaustion, especially if your brain is already under stress from the rigors of the test. Particularly if your test is a long one, drink water during the breaks. And if possible, take an energy-boosting snack to eat between sections.

Along with sleep and diet, a third important part of physical health is exercise. Maintaining a steady workout schedule is helpful, but even taking 5-minute study breaks to walk can help get your blood pumping faster and clear your head. Exercise also releases endorphins, which contribute to a positive feeling and can help combat test anxiety.

When you nurture your physical health, you are also contributing to your mental health. If your body is healthy, your mind is much more likely to be healthy as well. So take time to rest, nourish your body with healthy food and water, and get moving as much as possible. Taking these physical steps will make you stronger and more able to take the mental steps necessary to overcome test anxiety.

Mental Steps for Beating Test Anxiety

Working on the mental side of test anxiety can be more challenging, but as with the physical side, there are clear steps you can take to overcome it. As mentioned earlier, test anxiety often stems from lack of preparation, so the obvious solution is to prepare for the test. Effective studying may be the most important weapon you have for beating test anxiety, but you can and should employ several other mental tools to combat fear.

First, boost your confidence by reminding yourself of past success—tests or projects that you aced. If you're putting as much effort into preparing for this test as you did for those, there's no reason you should expect to fail here. Work hard to prepare; then trust your preparation.

Second, surround yourself with encouraging people. It can be helpful to find a study group, but be sure that the people you're around will encourage a positive attitude. If you spend time with others who are anxious or cynical, this will only contribute to your own anxiety. Look for others who are motivated to study hard from a desire to succeed, not from a fear of failure.

Third, reward yourself. A test is physically and mentally tiring, even without anxiety, and it can be helpful to have something to look forward to. Plan an activity following the test, regardless of the outcome, such as going to a movie or getting ice cream.

When you are taking the test, if you find yourself beginning to feel anxious, remind yourself that you know the material. Visualize successfully completing the test. Then take a few deep, relaxing breaths and return to it. Work through the questions carefully but with confidence, knowing that you are capable of succeeding.

Developing a healthy mental approach to test taking will also aid in other areas of life. Test anxiety affects more than just the actual test—it can be damaging to your mental health and even contribute to depression. It's important to beat test anxiety before it becomes a problem for more than testing.

Study Strategy

Being prepared for the test is necessary to combat anxiety, but what does being prepared look like? You may study for hours on end and still not feel prepared. What you need is a strategy for test prep. The next few pages outline our recommended steps to help you plan out and conquer the challenge of preparation.

Step 1: Scope Out the Test

Learn everything you can about the format (multiple choice, essay, etc.) and what will be on the test. Gather any study materials, course outlines, or sample exams that may be available. Not only will this help you to prepare, but knowing what to expect can help to alleviate test anxiety.

Step 2: Map Out the Material

Look through the textbook or study guide and make note of how many chapters or sections it has. Then divide these over the time you have. For example, if a book has 15 chapters and you have five days to study, you need to cover three chapters each day. Even better, if you have the time, leave an extra day at the end for overall review after you have gone through the material in depth.

If time is limited, you may need to prioritize the material. Look through it and make note of which sections you think you already have a good grasp on, and which need review. While you are studying, skim quickly through the familiar sections and take more time on the challenging parts.

Write out your plan so you don't get lost as you go. Having a written plan also helps you feel more in control of the study, so anxiety is less likely to arise from feeling overwhelmed at the amount to cover.

Step 3: Gather Your Tools

Decide what study method works best for you. Do you prefer to highlight in the book as you study and then go back over the highlighted portions? Or do you type out notes of the important information? Or is it helpful to make flashcards that you can carry with you? Assemble the pens, index cards, highlighters, post-it notes, and any other materials you may need so you won't be distracted by getting up to find things while you study.

If you're having a hard time retaining the information or organizing your notes, experiment with different methods. For example, try color-coding by subject with colored pens, highlighters, or post-it notes. If you learn better by hearing, try recording yourself reading your notes so you can listen while in the car, working out, or simply sitting at your desk. Ask a friend to quiz you from your flashcards, or try teaching someone the material to solidify it in your mind.

Step 4: Create Your Environment

It's important to avoid distractions while you study. This includes both the obvious distractions like visitors and the subtle distractions like an uncomfortable chair (or a too-comfortable couch that makes you want to fall asleep). Set up the best study environment possible: good lighting and a comfortable work area. If background music helps you focus, you may want to turn it on, but otherwise keep the room quiet. If you are using a computer to take notes, be sure you don't have any other windows open, especially applications like social media, games, or anything else that could distract you. Silence your phone and turn off notifications. Be sure to keep water close by so you stay hydrated while you study (but avoid unhealthy drinks and snacks).

Also, take into account the best time of day to study. Are you freshest first thing in the morning? Try to set aside some time then to work through the material. Is your mind clearer in the afternoon or evening? Schedule your study session then. Another method is to study at the same time of day that you will take the test, so that your brain gets used to working on the material at that time and will be ready to focus at test time.

Step 5: Study!

Once you have done all the study preparation, it's time to settle into the actual studying. Sit down, take a few moments to settle your mind so you can focus, and begin to follow your study plan. Don't give in to distractions or let yourself procrastinate. This is your time to prepare so you'll be ready to fearlessly approach the test. Make the most of the time and stay focused.

Of course, you don't want to burn out. If you study too long you may find that you're not retaining the information very well. Take regular study breaks. For example, taking five minutes out of every hour to walk briskly, breathing deeply and swinging your arms, can help your mind stay fresh.

As you get to the end of each chapter or section, it's a good idea to do a quick review. Remind yourself of what you learned and work on any difficult parts. When you feel that you've mastered the material, move on to the next part. At the end of your study session, briefly skim through your notes again.

But while review is helpful, cramming last minute is NOT. If at all possible, work ahead so that you won't need to fit all your study into the last day. Cramming overloads your brain with more information than it can process and retain, and your tired mind may struggle to recall even previously learned information when it is overwhelmed with last-minute study. Also, the urgent nature of cramming and the stress placed on your brain contribute to anxiety. You'll be more likely to go to the test feeling unprepared and having trouble thinking clearly.

So don't cram, and don't stay up late before the test, even just to review your notes at a leisurely pace. Your brain needs rest more than it needs to go over the information again. In fact, plan to finish your studies by noon or early afternoon the day before the test. Give your brain the rest of the day to relax or focus on other things, and get a good night's sleep. Then you will be fresh for the test and better able to recall what you've studied.

Step 6: Take a Practice Test

Many courses offer sample tests, either online or in the study materials. This is an excellent resource to check whether you have mastered the material, as well as to prepare for the test format and environment.

Check the test format ahead of time: the number of questions, the type (multiple choice, free response, etc.), and the time limit. Then create a plan for working through them. For example, if you have 30 minutes to take a 60-question test, your limit is 30 seconds per question. Spend less time on the questions you know well so that you can take more time on the difficult ones.

If you have time to take several practice tests, take the first one open book, with no time limit. Work through the questions at your own pace and make sure you fully understand them. Gradually work up to taking a test under test conditions: sit at a desk with all study materials put away and set a timer. Pace yourself to make sure you finish the test with time to spare and go back to check your answers if you have time.

After each test, check your answers. On the questions you missed, be sure you understand why you missed them. Did you misread the question (tests can use tricky wording)? Did you forget the information? Or was it something you hadn't learned? Go back and study any shaky areas that the practice tests reveal.

Taking these tests not only helps with your grade, but also aids in combating test anxiety. If you're already used to the test conditions, you're less likely to worry about it, and working through tests until you're scoring well gives you a confidence boost. Go through the practice tests until you feel comfortable, and then you can go into the test knowing that you're ready for it.

Test Tips

On test day, you should be confident, knowing that you've prepared well and are ready to answer the questions. But aside from preparation, there are several test day strategies you can employ to maximize your performance.

First, as stated before, get a good night's sleep the night before the test (and for several nights before that, if possible). Go into the test with a fresh, alert mind rather than staying up late to study.

Try not to change too much about your normal routine on the day of the test. It's important to eat a nutritious breakfast, but if you normally don't eat breakfast at all, consider eating just a protein bar. If you're a coffee drinker, go ahead and have your normal coffee. Just make sure you time it so that the caffeine doesn't wear off right in the middle of your test. Avoid sugary beverages, and drink enough water to stay hydrated but not so much that you need a restroom break 10 minutes into the test. If your test isn't first thing in the morning, consider going for a walk or doing a light workout before the test to get your blood flowing.

Allow yourself enough time to get ready, and leave for the test with plenty of time to spare so you won't have the anxiety of scrambling to arrive in time. Another reason to be early is to select a good seat. It's helpful to sit away from doors and windows, which can be distracting. Find a good seat, get out your supplies, and settle your mind before the test begins.

When the test begins, start by going over the instructions carefully, even if you already know what to expect. Make sure you avoid any careless mistakes by following the directions.

Then begin working through the questions, pacing yourself as you've practiced. If you're not sure on an answer, don't spend too much time on it, and don't let it shake your confidence. Either skip it and come back later, or eliminate as many wrong answers as possible and guess among the remaining ones. Don't dwell on these questions as you continue—put them out of your mind and focus on what lies ahead.

Be sure to read all of the answer choices, even if you're sure the first one is the right answer. Sometimes you'll find a better one if you keep reading. But don't second-guess yourself if you do immediately know the answer. Your gut instinct is usually right. Don't let test anxiety rob you of the information you know.

If you have time at the end of the test (and if the test format allows), go back and review your answers. Be cautious about changing any, since your first instinct tends to be correct, but make sure you didn't misread any of the questions or accidentally mark the wrong answer choice. Look over any you skipped and make an educated guess.

At the end, leave the test feeling confident. You've done your best, so don't waste time worrying about your performance or wishing you could change anything. Instead, celebrate the successful completion of this test. And finally, use this test to learn how to deal with anxiety even better next time.

Review Video: Test Anxiety
Visit mometrix.com/academy and enter code: 100340

Important Qualification

Not all anxiety is created equal. If your test anxiety is causing major issues in your life beyond the classroom or testing center, or if you are experiencing troubling physical symptoms related to your anxiety, it may be a sign of a serious physiological or psychological condition. If this sounds like your situation, we strongly encourage you to seek professional help.

Online Resources

Due to our efforts to try to keep this book to a manageable length, we've created a link that will give you access to all of your online resources:

mometrix.com/resources719/clepwescivii

It's Your Moment, Let's Celebrate It!

Share your story @mometrixtestpreparation